Named Entities Workshop 2011

(NEWS 2011)

Held at IJCNLP 2011

Chiang Mai, Thailand
12 November 2011

ISBN: 978-1-62276-453-2

Printed from e-media with permission by:

Curran Associates, Inc.
57 Morehouse Lane
Red Hook, NY 12571

Some format issues inherent in the e-media version may also appear in this print version.

Printed by Curran Associates, Inc. (2012)

Association for Computational Linguistics
209 N. Eighth Street
Stroudsburg, Pennsylvania 18360

Phone: 1-570-476-8006
Fax: 1-570-476-0860

acl@aclweb.org

Additional copies of this publication are available from:

Curran Associates, Inc.
57 Morehouse Lane
Red Hook, NY 12571 USA
Phone: 845-758-0400
Fax: 845-758-2634
Email: curran@proceedings.com
Web: www.proceedings.com

Table of Contents

Preface

The workshop series, Named Entities WorkShop (NEWS), focuses on research on all aspects of the Named Entities, such as, identifying and analyzing named entities, mining, translating and transliterating named entities, etc. The first of the NEWS workshops (NEWS 2009) was held as a part of ACL-IJCNLP 2009 conference in Singapore, and the second one, NEWS 2010, was held as an ACL 2010 workshop in Uppsala, Sweden. The current edition, NEWS 2011, was held as an IJCNLP 2011 workshop, in Chiang Mai, Thailand.

The purpose of the NEWS workshop is to bring together researchers across the world interested in identification, analysis, extraction, mining and transformation of named entities in monolingual or multilingual natural language text corpora. The workshop scope includes many interesting specific research areas pertaining to the named entities, such as, orthographic and phonetic characteristics, corpus analysis, unsupervised and supervised named entities extraction in monolingual or multilingual corpus, transliteration modeling, and evaluation methodologies, to name a few. For this year edition, 8 research papers were submitted, each of which was reviewed by at least 3 reviewers from the program committee. 5 papers were chosen for publication, covering main research areas, from named entities identification, classification, to machine transliteration and transliteration mining from comparable corpus and wiki. All accepted research papers are published in the workshop proceedings.

Following the tradition of the NEWS workshop series, NEWS 2011 continued the machine transliteration shared task this year as well. The shared task was first introduced in NEWS 2009 and continued in NEWS 2010. In NEWS 2011, by leveraging on the previous success of NEWS 2009 and NEWS 2011, we significantly increased the hand-crafted parallel named entities corpora to include 14 different language pairs from 11 language families, and made them available as the common dataset for the shared task. We published the details of the shared task and the training and development data several months ahead of the conference that attracted an overwhelming response from the research community. In total, 10 international teams participated from around the globe. The approaches ranged from traditional unsupervised learning methods (such as, Phrasal SMT-based, Conditional Random Fields, etc.) to somewhat new approaches (such as, Non-Parametric Bayesian Co-segmentation, Multi-to-Multi Joint Source Channel Model and Leveraging Transliterations from Multiple Languages), in addition to several teams resorting to model/system combinations for results re-ranking. A report of the shared task that summarizes all submissions and the original whitepaper are also included in the proceedings, and will be presented in the workshop. The participants in the shared task were asked to submit short system papers (4 content pages each) describing their approaches, and each of such papers was reviewed by at least three members of the program committee to help improve the quality. All the 10 system papers were finally accepted to be published in the workshop proceedings.

It is heartening for us to report that the previous year's NEWS datasets are being regularly requested by research groups throughout the year outside the NEWS shared tasks, for calibration of new approaches by groups that had not previously participated in the shared tasks. We expect such trend to continue, establishing the NEWS parallel names corpora as a standard dataset, and NEWS metrics as a standard measure for future machine transliteration research.

We hope that NEWS 2011 would provide an exciting and productive forum for researchers working in this research area. We wish to thank all the researchers for their research submission and the enthusiastic participation in the transliteration shared tasks. We wish to express our gratitude to CJK Institute, Institute for Infocomm Research, Microsoft Research India, Thailand National Electronics and Computer Technology Centre and The Royal Melbourne Institute of Technology (RMIT)/Sarvnaz Karimi for preparing the data released as a part of the shared tasks. Finally, we thank all the program committee members for reviewing the submissions in spite of the tight schedule.

Workshop Chairs
Haizhou Li, Institute for Infocomm Research, Singapore
A Kumaran, Microsoft Research, India
Min Zhang, Institute for Infocomm Research, Singapore

12 November 2011,
Chiang Mai, Thailand

Organizers:

Workshop Co-Chair: Haizhou Li, Institute for Infocomm Research, Singapore
Workshop Co-Chair: A Kumaran, Microsoft Research, India
Workshop Co-Chair: Min Zhang, Institute for Infocomm Research, Singapore

Program Committee:

Kalika Bali, Microsoft Research, India
Rafael Banchs, Institute for Infocomm Research, Singapore
Sivaji Bandyopadhyay, University of Jadavpur, India
Pushpak Bhattacharyya, IIT-Bombay, India
Monojit Choudhury, Microsoft Research, India
Marta Ruiz Costa-jussa, UPC, Spain
Gregory Grefenstette, Exalead, France
Guohong Fu, Heilongjiang University, China
Sarvnaz Karimi, NICTA and the University of Melbourne, Australia
Mitesh Khapra, IIT-Bombay, India
Greg Kondrak, University of Alberta, Canada
Olivia Kwong, City University, Hong Kong
Ming Liu, Institute for Infocomm Research, Singapore
Jong-Hoon Oh, NICT, Japan
Yan Qu, Advertising.com, USA
Sudeshna Sarkar, IIT-Kharagpur, India
Keh-Yih Su, Behavior Design Corporation, Taiwan
Raghavendra Udupa, Microsoft Research, India
Vasudeva Varma, IIIT-Hyderabad, India
Haifeng Wang, Baidu.com, China
Chai Wutiwiwatchai, NECTEC, Thailand
Chengqing Zong, Institute of Automation, CAS, China

We wish to thank our sponsors

Gold Sponsors

www.google.com

www.baidu.com

The Office of Naval Research (ONR)

The Asian Office of Aerospace Research and Development (AOARD)

Department of Systems Engineering and Engineering Managment, The Chinese University of Hong Kong

Silver Sponsors

Microsoft Corporation

Bronze Sponsors

Chinese and Oriental Languages Information Processing Society (COLIPS)

Supporter

Thailand Convention and Exhibition Bureau (TCEB)

We wish to thank our sponsors

Organizers

Asian Federation of Natural Language Processing (AFNLP)

National Electronics and Computer Technology Center (NECTEC), Thailand

Sirindhorn International Institute of Technology (SIIT), Thailand

Rajamangala University of Technology Lanna (RMUTL), Thailand

Maejo University, Thailand

Chiang Mai University (CMU), Thailand

Conference Program

November 12, 2011

8:30-10:00 Session 1

8:30–8:40 Opening Remarks by Haizhou Li, A Kumaran, Min Zhang and Ming Liu

8:40–9:00 *Integrating Models Derived from non-Parametric Bayesian Co-segmentation into a Statistical Machine Transliteration System*
Andrew Finch, Paul Dixon and Eiichiro Sumita

9:00–9:20 *Simple Discriminative Training for Machine Transliteration*
Canasai Kruengkrai, Thatsanee Charoenporn and Virach Sornlertlamvanich

9:20–9:40 *English-Korean Named Entity Transliteration Using Statistical Substring-based and Rule-based Approaches*
Yu-Chun Wang and Richard Tzong-Han Tsai

9:40–10:00 *Leveraging Transliterations from Multiple Languages*
Aditya Bhargava, Bradley Hauer and Grzegorz Kondrak

10:00-10:30 Morning Break

November 12, 2011 (continued)

10:00-12:00 Session 2

10:00–10:30 *Comparative Evaluation of Spanish Segmentation Strategies for Spanish-Chinese Transliteration*
Rafael E. Banchs

10:30–11:00 *Using Features from a Bilingual Alignment Model in Transliteration Mining*
Takaaki Fukunishi, Andrew Finch, Seiichi Yamamoto and Eiichiro Sumita

11:00–11:30 *Product Name Identification and Classification in Thai Economic News*
Nattadaporn Lertcheva and Wirote Aroonmanakun

11:30–12:00 *Mining Multi-word Named Entity Equivalents from Comparable Corpora*
Abhijit Bhole, Goutham Tholpadi and Raghavendra Udupa

12:00–14:00 Lunch Break

14:00-15:30 Session 3

14:00–14:30 *An Unsupervised Alignment Model for Sequence Labeling: Application to Name Transliteration*
Najmeh Mousavi Nejad and Shahram Khadivi

14:30–14:50 *Forward-backward Machine Transliteration between English and Chinese Based on Combined CRFs*
Ying Qin and GuoHua Chen

14:50–15:10 *English-to-Chinese Machine Transliteration using Accessor Variety Features of Source Graphemes*
Mike Tian-Jian Jiang, Chan-Hung Kuo and Wen-Lian Hsu

15:10–15:30 *The Amirkabir Machine Transliteration System for NEWS 2011: Farsi-to-English Task*
Najmeh Mousavi Nejad, Shahram Khadivi and Kaveh Taghipour

15:30–16:00 Afternoon Break

November 12, 2011 (continued)

16:00-17:00 Session 4

16:00–16:20 *English-Chinese Personal Name Transliteration by Syllable-Based Maximum Matching*
Oi Yee Kwong

16:20–16:40 *Statistical Machine Transliteration with Multi-to-Multi Joint Source Channel Model*
Yu Chen, Rui Wang and Yi Zhang

16:40–17:00 *Named Entity Transliteration Generation Leveraging Statistical Machine Translation Technology*
Pradeep Dasigi and Mona Diab

17:00-17:10 Closing

Report of NEWS 2011 Machine Transliteration Shared Task

Min Zhang[†], **Haizhou Li**[†], **A Kumaran**[‡] **and Ming Liu**[†]

[†]Institute for Infocomm Research, A*STAR, Singapore 138632
{mzhang,hli,mliu}@i2r.a-star.edu.sg

[‡]Multilingual Systems Research, Microsoft Research India
A.Kumaran@microsoft.com

Abstract

This report documents the Machine Transliteration Shared Task conducted as a part of the Named Entities Workshop (NEWS 2011), an IJCNLP 2011 workshop. The shared task features machine transliteration of proper names from English to 11 languages and from 3 languages to English. In total, 14 tasks are provided. 10 teams from 7 different countries participated in the evaluations. Finally, 73 standard and 4 non-standard runs are submitted, where diverse transliteration methodologies are explored and reported on the evaluation data. We report the results with 4 performance metrics. We believe that the shared task has successfully achieved its objective by providing a common benchmarking platform for the research community to evaluate the state-of-the-art technologies that benefit the future research and development.

1 Introduction

Names play a significant role in many Natural Language Processing (NLP) and Information Retrieval (IR) systems. They are important in Cross Lingual Information Retrieval (CLIR) and Machine Translation (MT) as the system performance has been shown to positively correlate with the correct conversion of names between the languages in several studies (Demner-Fushman and Oard, 2002; Mandl and Womser-Hacker, 2005; Hermjakob et al., 2008; Udupa et al., 2009). The traditional source for name equivalence, the bilingual dictionaries — whether handcrafted or statistical — offer only limited support because new names always emerge.

All of the above point to the critical need for robust Machine Transliteration technology and systems. Much research effort has been made to address the transliteration issue in the research community (Knight and Graehl, 1998; Meng et al., 2001; Li et al., 2004; Zelenko and Aone, 2006; Sproat et al., 2006; Sherif and Kondrak, 2007; Hermjakob et al., 2008; Al-Onaizan and Knight, 2002; Goldwasser and Roth, 2008; Goldberg and Elhadad, 2008; Klementiev and Roth, 2006; Oh and Choi, 2002; Virga and Khudanpur, 2003; Wan and Verspoor, 1998; Kang and Choi, 2000; Gao et al., 2004; Zelenko and Aone, 2006; Li et al., 2009b; Li et al., 2009a). These previous work fall into three categories, i.e., grapheme-based, phoneme-based and hybrid methods. Grapheme-based method (Li et al., 2004) treats transliteration as a direct orthographic mapping and only uses orthography-related features while phoneme-based method (Knight and Graehl, 1998) makes use of phonetic correspondence to generate the transliteration. Hybrid method refers to the combination of several different models or knowledge sources to support the transliteration generation.

The first machine transliteration shared task (Li et al., 2009b; Li et al., 2009a) was held in NEWS 2009 at ACL-IJCNLP 2009. It was the first time to provide common benchmarking data in diverse language pairs for evaluation of state-of-the-art techniques. While the focus of the 2009 shared task was on establishing the quality metrics and on baselining the transliteration quality based on those metrics, the 2010 shared task (Li et al., 2010a; Li et al., 2010b) expanded the scope of the transliteration generation task to about a dozen languages, and explored the quality depending on the direction of transliteration, between the languages. NEWS 2011 was a continued effort of NEWS 2010 and NEWS 2009.

The rest of the report is organised as follows. Section 2 outlines the machine transliteration task and the corpora used and Section 3 discusses the metrics chosen for evaluation, along with the ratio-

Proceedings of the 2011 Named Entities Workshop, IJCNLP 2011, pages 1–13,
Chiang Mai, Thailand, November 12, 2011.

nale for choosing them. Sections 4 and 5 present the participation in the shared task and the results with their analysis, respectively. Section 6 concludes the report.

2 Transliteration Shared Task

In this section, we outline the definition and the description of the shared task.

2.1 "Transliteration": A definition

There exists several terms that are used interchangeably in the contemporary research literature for the conversion of names between two languages, such as, transliteration, transcription, and sometimes Romanisation, especially if Latin scripts are used for target strings (Halpern, 2007).

Our aim is not only at capturing the name conversion process from a source to a target language, but also at its practical utility for downstream applications, such as CLIR and MT. Therefore, we adopted the same definition of transliteration as during the NEWS 2009 workshop (Li et al., 2009a) to narrow down "transliteration" to three specific requirements for the task, as follows: *"Transliteration is the conversion of a given name in the source language (a text string in the source writing system or orthography) to a name in the target language (another text string in the target writing system or orthography), such that the target language name is: (i) phonemically equivalent to the source name (ii) conforms to the phonology of the target language and (iii) matches the user intuition of the equivalent of the source language name in the target language, considering the culture and orthographic character usage in the target language."*

In NEWS 2011, we introduce three back-transliteration tasks. We define back-transliteration as a process of restoring transliterated words to their original languages. For example, NEWS 2011 offers the tasks to convert western names written in Chinese and Thai into their original English spellings, and romanized Japanese names into their original Kanji writings.

2.2 Shared Task Description

Following the tradition in NEWS 2010, the shared task at NEWS 2011 is specified as development of machine transliteration systems in one or more of the specified language pairs. Each language pair of the shared task consists of a source and a target language, implicitly specifying the transliteration direction. Training and development data in each of the language pairs have been made available to all registered participants for developing a transliteration system for that specific language pair using any approach that they find appropriate.

At the evaluation time, a standard hand-crafted test set consisting of between 500 and 3,000 source names (approximately 5-10% of the training data size) have been released, on which the participants are required to produce a ranked list of transliteration candidates in the target language for each source name. The system output is tested against a reference set (which may include multiple correct transliterations for some source names), and the performance of a system is captured in multiple metrics (defined in Section 3), each designed to capture a specific performance dimension.

For every language pair each participant is required to submit at least one run (designated as a "standard" run) that uses only the data provided by the NEWS workshop organisers in that language pair, and no other data or linguistic resources. This standard run ensures parity between systems and enables meaningful comparison of performance of various algorithmic approaches in a given language pair. Participants are allowed to submit more "standard" runs, up to 4 in total. If more than one "standard" runs is submitted, it is required to name one of them as a "primary" run, which is used to compare results across different systems. In addition, up to 4 "non-standard" runs could be submitted for every language pair using either data beyond that provided by the shared task organisers or linguistic resources in a specific language, or both. This essentially may enable any participant to demonstrate the limits of performance of their system in a given language pair.

The shared task timelines provide adequate time for development, testing (approximately 1 month after the release of the training data) and the final result submission (7 days after the release of the test data).

2.3 Shared Task Corpora

We considered two specific constraints in selecting languages for the shared task: language diversity and data availability. To make the shared task interesting and to attract wider participation, it is important to ensure a reasonable variety among the languages in terms of linguistic diversity, orthography and geography. Clearly, the ability of procuring and distributing a reasonably large (approximately 10K paired names for training and testing together) hand-crafted corpora consisting primarily of paired names is critical for this process. At the end of the planning stage and after discussion with the data providers, we have chosen the set of 14 tasks shown in Table 1 (Li et al., 2004; Kumaran and Kellner, 2007; MSRI, 2009; CJKI, 2010).

NEWS 2011 leverages on the success of NEWS 2010 by utilizing the training and dev data of NEWS 2010 as the training data of NEWS 2011 and the test data of NEWS 2010 as the dev data of NEWS 2011. NEWS 2011 provides entirely new test data across all 14 tasks for evaluation. In addition to the 12 tasks inherited from NEWS 2010, NEWS 2011 is augmented with 2 new tasks with two new languages (Persian, Hebrew).

The names given in the training sets for Chinese, Japanese, Korean, Thai, Persian and Hebrew languages are Western names and their respective transliterations; the Japanese Name (in English) $\rightarrow$ Japanese Kanji data set consists only of native Japanese names; the Arabic data set consists only of native Arabic names. The Indic data set (Hindi, Tamil, Kannada, Bangla) consists of a mix of Indian and Western names.

For all of the tasks chosen, we have been able to procure paired names data between the source and the target scripts and were able to make them available to the participants. For some language pairs, such as English-Chinese and English-Thai, there are both transliteration and back-transliteration tasks. Most of the task are just one-way transliteration, although Indian data sets contained mixture of names of both Indian and Western origins. The language of origin of the names for each task is indicated in the first column of Table 1.

Finally, it should be noted here that the corpora procured and released for NEWS 2011 represent perhaps the most diverse and largest corpora to be used for any common transliteration tasks today.

3 Evaluation Metrics and Rationale

The participants have been asked to submit results of up to four standard and four non-standard runs. One standard run must be named as the primary submission and is used for the performance summary. Each run contains a ranked list of up to 10 candidate transliterations for each source name. The submitted results are compared to the ground truth (reference transliterations) using 4 evaluation metrics capturing different aspects of transliteration performance. The same as the NEWS 2010, we have dropped two MAP metrics used in NEWS 2009 because they don't offer additional information to MAP_{ref}. Since a name may have multiple correct transliterations, all these alternatives are treated equally in the evaluation, that is, any of these alternatives is considered as a correct transliteration, and all candidates matching any of the reference transliterations are accepted as correct ones.

The following notation is further assumed:

N	:	Total number of names (source words) in the test set
n_i	:	Number of reference transliterations for i-th name in the test set ($n_i \geq 1$)
$r_{i,j}$	:	j-th reference transliteration for i-th name in the test set
$c_{i,k}$	:	k-th candidate transliteration (system output) for i-th name in the test set ($1 \leq k \leq 10$)
K_i	:	Number of candidate transliterations produced by a transliteration system

3.1 Word Accuracy in Top-1 (ACC)

Also known as Word Error Rate, it measures correctness of the first transliteration candidate in the candidate list produced by a transliteration system. $ACC = 1$ means that all top candidates are correct transliterations i.e. they match one of the references, and $ACC = 0$ means that none of the top candidates are correct.

$$ACC = \frac{1}{N} \sum_{i=1}^{N} \left\{ \begin{array}{l} 1 \text{ if } \exists r_{i,j} : r_{i,j} = c_{i,1}; \\ 0 \text{ otherwise} \end{array} \right\} \quad (1)$$

3.2 Fuzziness in Top-1 (Mean F-score)

The mean F-score measures how different, on average, the top transliteration candidate is from its closest reference. F-score for each source word is a function of Precision and Recall and equals 1 when the top candidate matches one of the references, and 0 when there are no common characters between the candidate and any of the references.

Precision and Recall are calculated based on the length of the Longest Common Subsequence

Name origin	Source script	Target script	Data Owner	Data Size Train	Dev	Test	Task ID
Western	English	Chinese	Institute for Infocomm Research	37K	2.8K	2K	EnCh
Western	Chinese	English	Institute for Infocomm Research	28K	2.7K	2K	ChEn
Western	English	Korean Hangul	CJK Institute	7K	1K	1K	EnKo
Western	English	Japanese Katakana	CJK Institute	26K	2K	3K	EnJa
Japanese	English	Japanese Kanji	CJK Institute	10K	2K	3K	JnJk
Arabic	Arabic	English	CJK Institute	27K	2.5K	2.5K	ArEn
Mixed	English	Hindi	Microsoft Research India	12K	1K	2K	EnHi
Mixed	English	Tamil	Microsoft Research India	10K	1K	2K	EnTa
Mixed	English	Kannada	Microsoft Research India	10K	1K	2K	EnKa
Mixed	English	Bangla	Microsoft Research India	13K	1K	2K	EnBa
Western	English	Thai	NECTEC	27K	2K	2K	EnTh
Western	Thai	English	NECTEC	25K	2K	2K	ThEn
Western	English	Persian	Sarvnaz Karimi/RMIT	10K	2K	1K	EnPe
Western	English	Hebrew	Microsoft Research India	9.5K	1K	2K	EnHe

Table 1: Source and target languages for the shared task on transliteration.

(LCS) between a candidate and a reference:

$$LCS(c,r) = \frac{1}{2}\left(|c| + |r| - ED(c,r)\right) \qquad (2)$$

where ED is the edit distance and $|x|$ is the length of x. For example, the longest common subsequence between "abcd" and "afcde" is "acd" and its length is 3. The best matching reference, that is, the reference for which the edit distance has the minimum, is taken for calculation. If the best matching reference is given by

$$r_{i,m} = \arg\min_j \left(ED(c_{i,1}, r_{i,j})\right) \qquad (3)$$

then Recall, Precision and F-score for i-th word are calculated as

$$R_i = \frac{LCS(c_{i,1}, r_{i,m})}{|r_{i,m}|} \qquad (4)$$

$$P_i = \frac{LCS(c_{i,1}, r_{i,m})}{|c_{i,1}|} \qquad (5)$$

$$F_i = 2\frac{R_i \times P_i}{R_i + P_i} \qquad (6)$$

- The length is computed in distinct Unicode characters.
- No distinction is made on different character types of a language (e.g., vowel vs. consonants vs. combining diereses etc.)

3.3 Mean Reciprocal Rank (MRR)

Measures traditional MRR *for any right answer* produced by the system, from among the candidates. $1/MRR$ tells approximately the average rank of the correct transliteration. MRR closer to 1 implies that the correct answer is mostly produced close to the top of the n-best lists.

$$RR_i = \begin{cases} \min_j \frac{1}{j} \text{ if } \exists r_{i,j}, c_{i,k} : r_{i,j} = c_{i,k}; \\ 0 \text{ otherwise} \end{cases} \qquad (7)$$

$$MRR = \frac{1}{N}\sum_{i=1}^{N} RR_i \qquad (8)$$

3.4 MAP$_{ref}$

Measures tightly the precision in the n-best candidates for i-th source name, for which reference transliterations are available. If all of the references are produced, then the MAP is 1. Let's denote the number of correct candidates for the i-th source word in k-best list as $num(i,k)$. MAP$_{ref}$ is then given by

$$MAP_{ref} = \frac{1}{N}\sum_{i}^{N} \frac{1}{n_i}\left(\sum_{k=1}^{n_i} num(i,k)\right) \qquad (9)$$

4 Participation in Shared Task

10 teams from 7 countries and regions (Canada, Hong Kong/Mainland China, Iran, Germany, USA, Japan, Thailand) submitted their transliteration results.

Two teams have participated in all or almost all tasks while others participated in 1 to 4 tasks. Each language pair has attracted on average around 4 teams. The details are shown in Table 3.

Teams are required to submit at least one standard run for every task they participated in. In total, we receive 73 standard and 4 non-standard runs. Table 2 shows the number of standard and non-standard runs submitted for each task. It is clear that the most "popular" task is the transliteration from English to Chinese being attempted by 7 participants. The next most popular is back-transliteration from Chinese to English being attempted by 6 participants. This is somewhat different from NEWS 2010, where the two most popular tasks were English to Hindi and English to other Indic scripts (Tamil,Kannada,Bangla) and Thai transliteration.

5 Task Results and Analysis

5.1 Standard runs

All the results are presented numerically in Tables 4–17, for all evaluation metrics. These are the official evaluation results published for this edition of the transliteration shared task.

The methodologies used in the ten submitted system papers are summarized as follows. Finch et al. (2011) employ non-Parametric Bayesian method to co-segment bilingual named entities for model training and report very good performance. This system is based on phrase-based statistical machine transliteration (SMT) (Finch and Sumita, 2008), an approach initially developed for machine translation (Koehn et al., 2003), where the SMT system's log-linear model is augmented with a set of features specifically suited to the task of transliteration. In particular, the model utilizes a feature based on a joint source-channel model, and a feature based on a maximum entropy model that predicts target grapheme sequences using the local context of graphemes and grapheme sequences in both source and target languages.

Jiang et al. (2011) extensively explore the use of accessor variety (a similarity measure) of the source graphemes as a feature under CRF framework for machine transliteration and report promising results. Kruengkrai et al. (2011) study discriminative training based on the Margin Infused Relaxed Algorithm with simple character alignments under SMT framework for machine transliteration. They report very impressive results. Bhargava et al. (2011) attemp to improve transliteration performance by leveraging transliterations from multiple languages. Dasigi and Diab (2011) adopt the approach of phrase-based statistical machine transliteration (Finch and Sumita, 2008). Chen et al. (2011) extend the joint source-channel model (Li et al., 2004) on the transliteration task into a multi-to-multi joint source-channel model, which allows alignments between substrings of arbitrary lengths in both source and target strings. Qin and Chen (2011) adopt the approach of Conditional Random Fields (CRF) (Lafferty et al., 2001).

Kwong (2011) present their transliteration system with a syllable-based Backward Maximum Matching method. The system uses the Onset First Principle to syllabify English names and align them with Chinese names. The bilingual lexicon containing aligned segments of various syllable lengths subsequently allows direct transliteration by chunks. Wang and Tsai (2011) adopt the substring-based transliteration approach which groups the characters of named entity in both source and target languages into substrings and then formulate the transliteration as a sequential tagging problem to tag the substrings in the source language with the substrings in the target language. The CRF algorithm is then used to deal with this tagging problem. They also construct a rule-based transliteration method for comparison. Nejad et al. (2011) report three systems for transliteration: the first system is a maximum entropy model with a newly proposed alignment algorithm. The second system is Sequitur g2p tool, an open source grapheme to phoneme convertor. The third system is Moses, a phrased based statistical machine translation system. In addition, several new features are introduced to enhance the overall accuracy in the maximum entropy model. Their results show that the combination of maximum entropy system with Sequitur g2p tool and Moses lead to a considerable improvement over individual systems.

5.2 Non-standard runs

For the non-standard runs, we pose no restrictions on the use of data or other linguistic resources. The purpose of non-standard runs is to see how best personal name transliteration can be, for a given language pair. In NEWS 2011, the approaches used in non-standard runs are typical and may be summarised as follows:

- with supplemental transliteration data from other languages of NEWS 2011 data. (Bhargava et al., 2011). Significant performance improvement is reported with this additional knowledge.

- with English phonemic information from CMU Pronouncing Dictionary v0.7a1

	English to Chinese	Chinese to English	English to Thai	Thai to English	English to Hindi	English to Tamil	English to Kannada
Language pair code	EnCh	ChEn	EnTh	ThEn	EnHi	EnTa	EnKa
Standard runs	15	13	4	4	9	4	4
Non-standard runs	0	0	0	0	1	0	0
	English to Japanese Katakana	English to Korean Hangul	English to Japanese Kanji	Arabic to English	English to Bengali (Bangla)	English to Persian	English to Hebrew
Language pair code	EnJa	EnKo	JnJk	ArEn	EnBa	EnPe	EnHe
Standard runs	2	2	1	3	3	6	3
Non-standard runs	0	3	0	0	0	0	0

Table 2: Number of runs submitted for each task. Number of participants coincides with the number of standard runs submitted.

Team ID	Organisation	EnCh	ChEn	EnTh	ThEn	EnHi	EnTa	EnKa	EnJa	EnKo	JnJk	ArEn	EnBa	EnPe	EnHe
1	Amirkabir University of Technology													x	
2	NICT	x	x	x	x	x	x	x	x	x	x	x	x	x	x
3	Beijing Foreign Studies University	x	x												
4	DFKI GmbH	x	x												
5	City University of Hong Kong	x	x												
6	NECTEC	x	x	x	x	x	x	x					x	x	x
7	University of Alberta	x				x			x						
8	Yuan Ze University and National Taiwan University									x					
9	National Tsing Hua University	x	x												
10	Columbia University					x						x		x	

Table 3: Participation of teams in different tasks.

(http://www.speech.cs.cmu.edu/cgi-bin/cmudict) (Das et al., 2010). However, performance drops very much when using the English phonemic information.

6 Conclusions and Future Plans

The Machine Transliteration Shared Task in NEWS 2011 shows that the community has a continued interest in this area. This report summarizes the results of the shared task. Again, we are pleased to report a comprehensive calibration and baselining of machine transliteration approaches as most state-of-the-art machine transliteration techniques are represented in the shared task. In addition to the most popular techniques such as Phrase-Based Machine Transliteration (Koehn et al., 2003), system combination and re-ranking in the NEWS 2010, we are delighted to see that several new techniques have been proposed and explored with promising results reported, including Non-Parametric Bayesian Co-segmentation (Finch et al., 2011), Multi-to-Multi Joint Source Channel Model (Chen et al., 2011), Leveraging Transliterations from Multiple Languages (Bhargava et al., 2011) and discriminative training based on the Margin Infused Relaxed Algorithm (Kruengkrai et al., 2011) . As the standard runs are limited by the use of corpus, most of the systems are implemented under the direct orthographic mapping (DOM) framework (Li et al., 2004). While the standard runs allow us to conduct meaningful comparison across different algorithms, we recognise that the non-standard runs open up more opportunities for exploiting a variety of additional linguistic corpora.

Encouraged by the success of the NEWS workshop series, we would like to continue this event in the future conference to promote the machine transliteration research and development.

Acknowledgements

The organisers of the NEWS 2011 Shared Task would like to thank the Institute for Infocomm Research (Singapore), Microsoft Research India, CJK Institute (Japan), National Electronics and Computer Technology Center (Thailand) and Sarvnaz Karim / RMIT for providing the corpora and technical support. Without those, the Shared Task would not be possible. We thank those participants who identified errors in the data and sent us the errata. We also want to thank the members of programme committee for their invaluable comments that improve the quality of the shared task papers. Finally, we wish to thank all the participants for their active participation that have made this first machine transliteration shared task a comprehensive one.

References

Yaser Al-Onaizan and Kevin Knight. 2002. Machine transliteration of names in arabic text. In *Proc. ACL-2002 Workshop: Computational Apporaches to Semitic Languages*, Philadelphia, PA, USA.

Aditya Bhargava, Bradley Hauer, and Grzegorz Kondrak. 2011. Leveraging transliterations from multiple languages. In *Proc. Named Entities Workshop at IJCNLP 2011.*

Yu Chen, Rui Wang, and Yi Zhang. 2011. Statistical machine transliteration with multi-to-multi joint source channel model. In *Proc. Named Entities Workshop at IJCNLP 2011.*

CJKI. 2010. CJK Institute. http://www.cjk.org/.

Amitava Das, Tanik Saikh, Tapabrata Mondal, Asif Ekbal, and Sivaji Bandyopadhyay. 2010. English to Indian languages machine transliteration system at NEWS 2010. In *Proc. Named Entities Workshop at ACL 2010.*

Pradeep Dasigi and Mona Diab. 2011. Named entity transliteration using a statistical machine translation framework. In *Proc. Named Entities Workshop at IJCNLP 2011.*

D. Demner-Fushman and D. W. Oard. 2002. The effect of bilingual term list size on dictionary-based cross-language information retrieval. In *Proc. 36-th Hawaii Int'l. Conf. System Sciences*, volume 4, page 108.2.

Andrew Finch and Eiichiro Sumita. 2008. Phrase-based machine transliteration. In *Proc. 3rd Int'l. Joint Conf NLP*, volume 1, Hyderabad, India, January.

Andrew Finch, Paul Dixon, and Eiichiro Sumita. 2011. Integrating models derived from non-parametric bayesian co-segmentation into a statistical machine transliteration system. In *Proc. Named Entities Workshop at IJCNLP 2011.*

Wei Gao, Kam-Fai Wong, and Wai Lam. 2004. Phoneme-based transliteration of foreign names for OOV problem. In *Proc. IJCNLP*, pages 374–381, Sanya, Hainan, China.

Yoav Goldberg and Michael Elhadad. 2008. Identification of transliterated foreign words in Hebrew script. In *Proc. CICLing*, volume LNCS 4919, pages 466–477.

Dan Goldwasser and Dan Roth. 2008. Transliteration as constrained optimization. In *Proc. EMNLP*, pages 353–362.

Jack Halpern. 2007. The challenges and pitfalls of Arabic romanization and arabization. In *Proc. Workshop on Comp. Approaches to Arabic Script-based Lang.*

Ulf Hermjakob, Kevin Knight, and Hal Daumé. 2008. Name translation in statistical machine translation: Learning when to transliterate. In *Proc. ACL*, Columbus, OH, USA, June.

Mike Tian-Jian Jiang, Chan-Hung Kuo, and Wen-Lian Hsu. 2011. English-to-chinese machine transliteration using accessor variety features of source graphemes. In *Proc. Named Entities Workshop at IJCNLP 2011*.

Byung-Ju Kang and Key-Sun Choi. 2000. English-Korean automatic transliteration/back-transliteration system and character alignment. In *Proc. ACL*, pages 17–18, Hong Kong.

Alexandre Klementiev and Dan Roth. 2006. Weakly supervised named entity transliteration and discovery from multilingual comparable corpora. In *Proc. 21st Int'l Conf Computational Linguistics and 44th Annual Meeting of ACL*, pages 817–824, Sydney, Australia, July.

Kevin Knight and Jonathan Graehl. 1998. Machine transliteration. *Computational Linguistics*, 24(4).

P. Koehn, F. J. Och, and D. Marcu. 2003. Statistical phrase-based translation. In *Proc. HLT-NAACL*.

Canasai Kruengkrai, Thatsanee Charoenporn, and Virach Sornlertlamvanich. 2011. Simple discriminative training for machine transliteration. In *Proc. Named Entities Workshop at IJCNLP 2011*.

A Kumaran and T. Kellner. 2007. A generic framework for machine transliteration. In *Proc. SIGIR*, pages 721–722.

Oi Yee Kwong. 2011. English-chinese personal name transliteration by syllable-based maximum matching. In *Proc. Named Entities Workshop at IJCNLP 2011*.

J. Lafferty, A. McCallum, and F. Pereira. 2001. Conditional random fields: Probabilistic models for segmenting and labeling sequence data. In *Proc. Int'l. Conf. Machine Learning*, pages 282–289.

Haizhou Li, Min Zhang, and Jian Su. 2004. A joint source-channel model for machine transliteration. In *Proc. 42nd ACL Annual Meeting*, pages 159–166, Barcelona, Spain.

Haizhou Li, A Kumaran, Vladimir Pervouchine, and Min Zhang. 2009a. Report of NEWS 2009 machine transliteration shared task. In *Proc. Named Entities Workshop at ACL 2009*.

Haizhou Li, A Kumaran, Min Zhang, and Vladimir Pervouchine. 2009b. ACL-IJCNLP 2009 Named Entities Workshop — Shared Task on Transliteration. In *Proc. Named Entities Workshop at ACL 2009*.

Haizhou Li, A Kumaran, Min Zhang, and Vladimir Pervouchine. 2010a. Report of news 2010 transliteration generation shared task. In *Proc. Named Entities Workshop at ACL 2010*.

Haizhou Li, A Kumaran, Min Zhang, and Vladimir Pervouchine. 2010b. Whitepaper of news 2010 shared task on transliteration generation. In *Proc. Named Entities Workshop at ACL 2010*.

T. Mandl and C. Womser-Hacker. 2005. The effect of named entities on effectiveness in cross-language information retrieval evaluation. In *Proc. ACM Symp. Applied Comp.*, pages 1059–1064.

Helen M. Meng, Wai-Kit Lo, Berlin Chen, and Karen Tang. 2001. Generate phonetic cognates to handle name entities in English-Chinese cross-language spoken document retrieval. In *Proc. ASRU*.

MSRI. 2009. Microsoft Research India. http://research.microsoft.com/india.

Najmeh Mousavi Nejad, Shahram Khadivi, and Kaveh Taghipour. 2011. The machine transliteration system description for news 2011. In *Proc. Named Entities Workshop at IJCNLP 2011*.

Jong-Hoon Oh and Key-Sun Choi. 2002. An English-Korean transliteration model using pronunciation and contextual rules. In *Proc. COLING 2002*, Taipei, Taiwan.

Ying Qin and GuoHua Chen. 2011. Forward-backward machine transliteration between english and chinese based on combined crfs. In *Proc. Named Entities Workshop at IJCNLP 2011*.

Tarek Sherif and Grzegorz Kondrak. 2007. Substring-based transliteration. In *Proc. 45th Annual Meeting of the ACL*, pages 944–951, Prague, Czech Republic, June.

Richard Sproat, Tao Tao, and ChengXiang Zhai. 2006. Named entity transliteration with comparable corpora. In *Proc. 21st Int'l Conf Computational Linguistics and 44th Annual Meeting of ACL*, pages 73–80, Sydney, Australia.

Raghavendra Udupa, K. Saravanan, Anton Bakalov, and Abhijit Bhole. 2009. "They are out there, if you know where to look": Mining transliterations of OOV query terms for cross-language information retrieval. In *LNCS: Advances in Information Retrieval*, volume 5478, pages 437–448. Springer Berlin / Heidelberg.

Paola Virga and Sanjeev Khudanpur. 2003. Transliteration of proper names in cross-lingual information retrieval. In *Proc. ACL MLNER*, Sapporo, Japan.

Stephen Wan and Cornelia Maria Verspoor. 1998. Automatic English-Chinese name transliteration for development of multilingual resources. In *Proc. COLING*, pages 1352–1356.

Yu-Chun Wang and Richard Tzong-Han Tsai. 2011. English-korean named entity transliteration using statistical substring-based and rule-based approaches. In *Proc. Named Entities Workshop at IJC-NLP 2011*.

Dmitry Zelenko and Chinatsu Aone. 2006. Discriminative methods for transliteration. In *Proc. EMNLP*, pages 612–617, Sydney, Australia, July.

Team ID	ACC	F-score	MRR	MAP_{ref}	Organisation
			Primary runs		
2	0.3485	0.700095	0.462495	0.341924	NICT
6	0.342	0.701729	0.40574	0.331184	NECTEC
7	0.3405	0.691719	0.4203	0.331469	University of Alberta
9	0.3265	0.688231	0.423711	0.318296	National Tsing Hua University
4	0.3195	0.673834	0.396812	0.308382	DFKI GmbH
3	0.308	0.666474	0.337148	0.305857	Beijing Foreign Studies University
5	0.3055	0.672302	0.377732	0.296502	City University of Hong Kong
			Non-primary standard runs		
6	0.328	0.695756	0.392008	0.318354	NECTEC
3	0.308	0.666474	0.337148	0.305857	Beijing Foreign Studies University
9	0.3035	0.675249	0.383354	0.293095	National Tsing Hua University
7	0.2875	0.661642	0.2875	0.27303	University of Alberta
5	0.2855	0.659605	0.349497	0.276169	City University of Hong Kong
4	0.26	0.638255	0.340081	0.250505	DFKI GmbH
9	0.2025	0.610451	0.282637	0.195431	National Tsing Hua University
9	0	0.124144	0.000063	0	National Tsing Hua University

Table 4: Runs submitted for English to Chinese task.

Team ID	ACC	F-score	MRR	MAP_{ref}	Organisation
			Primary runs		
3	0.166814	0.764739	0.201932	0.166703	Beijing Foreign Studies University
5	0.154898	0.765737	0.215209	0.155119	City University of Hong Kong
2	0.144748	0.764534	0.242493	0.144417	NICT
4	0.132833	0.745695	0.210143	0.132723	DFKI GmbH
6	0.131068	0.729656	0.19266	0.131178	NECTEC
9	0.000883	0.014535	0.00248	0.000883	National Tsing Hua University
			Non-primary standard runs		
5	0.153575	0.756761	0.205823	0.153685	City University of Hong Kong
6	0.121359	0.726054	0.176186	0.121139	NECTEC
6	0.120035	0.713803	0.184312	0.119925	NECTEC
4	0.117387	0.730918	0.176915	0.117277	DFKI GmbH
6	0.113416	0.713676	0.169103	0.113305	NECTEC
3	0.097087	0.692511	0.127462	0.096867	Beijing Foreign Studies University
9	0	0.010269	0.000412	0	National Tsing Hua University

Table 5: Runs submitted for Chinese to English back-transliteration task.

Team ID	ACC	F-score	MRR	MAP_{ref}	Organisation
			Primary runs		
6	0.3545	0.85371	0.450846	0.350021	NECTEC
2	0.338	0.85323	0.443537	0.335972	NICT
			Non-primary standard runs		
6	0.3545	0.857262	0.457232	0.350625	NECTEC
6	0.354	0.855659	0.456143	0.349931	NECTEC

Table 6: Runs submitted for English to Thai task.

Team ID	ACC	F-score	MRR	MAP_{ref}	Organisation
			Primary runs		
2	0.29641	0.845061	0.427258	0.296617	NICT
6	0.28359	0.840587	0.401574	0.282973	NECTEC
			Non-primary standard runs		
6	0.282564	0.841174	0.400137	0.280754	NECTEC
6	0.280513	0.839531	0.397005	0.278251	NECTEC

Table 7: Runs submitted for Thai to English back-transliteration task.

Team ID	ACC	F-score	MRR	MAP_{ref}	Organisation
			Primary runs		
2	0.478	0.879438	0.591206	0.4765	NICT
7	0.471	0.878619	0.571162	0.46975	University of Alberta
6	0.436	0.870378	0.53784	0.435	NECTEC
10	0.387	0.859914	0.51587	0.38675	Columbia University
			Non-primary standard runs		
7	0.493	0.883611	0.581677	0.492	University of Alberta
7	0.457	0.877803	0.551577	0.45475	University of Alberta
6	0.42	0.866161	0.518392	0.41875	NECTEC
6	0.417	0.867697	0.522927	0.41575	NECTEC
10	0.386	0.859778	0.515204	0.38575	Columbia University
			Non-standard runs		
7	0.521	0.896287	0.606057	0.5205	University of Alberta

Table 8: Runs submitted for English to Hindi task.

Team ID	ACC	F-score	MRR	MAP_{ref}	Organisation
			Primary runs		
2	0.441	0.900489	0.577195	0.44	NICT
6	0.432	0.895693	0.55284	0.4305	NECTEC
			Non-primary standard runs		
6	0.42	0.890297	0.521162	0.4185	NECTEC
6	0.409	0.890383	0.511919	0.4075	NECTEC

Table 9: Runs submitted for English to Tamil task.

Team ID	ACC	F-score	MRR	MAP_{ref}	Organisation
			Primary runs		
2	0.419	0.885498	0.539931	0.41725	NICT
6	0.398	0.877997	0.501557	0.396722	NECTEC
			Non-primary standard runs		
6	0.378	0.871573	0.469133	0.375861	NECTEC
6	0.371	0.869731	0.46439	0.368333	NECTEC

Table 10: Runs submitted for English to Kannada task.

Team ID	ACC	F-score	MRR	MAP_{ref}	Organisation
			Primary runs		
7	0.434711	0.815425	0.434711	0.434435	University of Alberta
2	0.393939	0.802719	0.535614	0.393939	NICT

Table 11: Runs submitted for English to Japanese Katakana task.

Team ID	ACC	F-score	MRR	MAP_{ref}	Organisation
			Primary runs		
8	0.430213	0.711027	0.430213	0.422824	Yuan Ze University and National Taiwan University
2	0.356322	0.68032	0.461892	0.352627	NICT
			Non-standard runs		
8	0.331691	0.653147	0.331691	0.325123	Yuan Ze University and National Taiwan University
8	0.331691	0.653147	0.466886	0.331691	Yuan Ze University and National Taiwan University
8	0.215107	0.474405	0.215107	0.208949	Yuan Ze University and National Taiwan University

Table 12: Runs submitted for English to Korean task.

Team ID	ACC	F-score	MRR	MAP_{ref}	Organisation
			Primary runs		
2	0.45359	0.640551	0.568179	0.45359	NICT

Table 13: Runs submitted for English to Japanese Kanji back-transliteration task.

Team ID	ACC	F-score	MRR	MAP_{ref}	Organisation
			Primary runs		
10	0.525502	0.928104	0.628327	0.386179	Columbia University
2	0.447063	0.910865	0.550146	0.351398	NICT
			Non-primary standard runs		
10	0.518547	0.926968	0.61153	0.382576	Columbia University

Table 14: Runs submitted for Arabic to English task.

Team ID	ACC	F-score	MRR	MAP$_{ref}$	Organisation
			Primary runs		
2	0.478	0.89183	0.596738	0.4765	NICT
6	0.455	0.886901	0.556766	0.453	NECTEC
			Non-primary standard runs		
6	0.456	0.884593	0.554751	0.4545	NECTEC

Table 15: Runs submitted for English to Bengali (Bangla) task.

Team ID	ACC	F-score	MRR	MAP$_{ref}$	Organisation
			Primary runs		
1	0.872	0.979153	0.912697	0.869435	Amirkabir University of Technology
6	0.6435	0.942838	0.744343	0.629047	NECTEC
2	0.6145	0.93794	0.741716	0.603994	NICT
10	0.6055	0.933434	0.696681	0.589026	Columbia University
			Non-primary standard runs		
6	0.642	0.943011	0.747032	0.626604	NECTEC
10	0.6045	0.933263	0.696521	0.588117	Columbia University

Table 16: Runs submitted for English to Persian task.

Team ID	ACC	F-score	MRR	MAP$_{ref}$	Organisation
			Primary runs		
6	0.602	0.931385	0.701797	0.602	NECTEC
2	0.6	0.928666	0.715443	0.6	NICT
			Non-primary standard runs		
6	0.601	0.929689	0.697298	0.601	NECTEC

Table 17: Runs submitted for English to Hebrew task.

Whitepaper of NEWS 2011 Shared Task on Machine Transliteration*

Min Zhang[†]**, A Kumaran**[‡]**, Haizhou Li**[†]

[†]Institute for Infocomm Research, A*STAR, Singapore 138632
{mzhang, hli}@i2r.a-star.edu.sg

[‡]Multilingual Systems Research, Microsoft Research India
A.Kumaran@microsoft.com

Abstract

Transliteration is defined as phonetic translation of names across languages. Transliteration of Named Entities (NEs) is necessary in many applications, such as machine translation, corpus alignment, cross-language IR, information extraction and automatic lexicon acquisition. All such systems call for high-performance transliteration, which is the focus of shared task in the NEWS 2011 workshop. The objective of the shared task is to promote machine transliteration research by providing a common benchmarking platform for the community to evaluate the state-of-the-art technologies.

1 Task Description

The task is to develop machine transliteration system in one or more of the specified language pairs being considered for the task. Each language pair consists of a source and a target language. The training and development data sets released for each language pair are to be used for developing a transliteration system in whatever way that the participants find appropriate. At the evaluation time, a test set of source names only would be released, on which the participants are expected to produce a ranked list of transliteration candidates in another language (i.e. n-best transliterations), and this will be evaluated using common metrics. For every language pair the participants must submit at least one run that uses only the data provided by the NEWS workshop organisers in a given language pair (designated as "standard" run, primary submission). Users may submit more "stanrard" runs. They may also submit several "non-standard" runs for each language pair that use other data than those provided by the NEWS 2011 workshop; such runs would be evaluated and reported separately.

*http://translit.i2r.a-star.edu.sg/news2011/

2 Important Dates

Research paper submission deadline	6 July 2011
Shared task	
Registration opens	1 April 2011
Registration closes	31 May 2011
Training/Development data release	20 April 2011
Test data release	13 June 2011
Results Submission Due	20 June 2011
Results Announcement	30 June 2011
Task (short) Papers Due	6 July 2011
For all submissions	
Acceptance Notification	6 Aug 2011
Camera-Ready Copy Deadline	19 Aug 2011
Workshop Date	12 Nov 2011

3 Participation

1. Registration (1 April 2011)
   (a) NEWS Shared Task opens for registration.
   (b) Prospective participants are to register to the NEWS Workshop homepage.
2. Training & Development Data (20 April 2011)
   (a) Registered participants are to obtain training and development data from the Shared Task organiser and/or the designated copyright owners of databases.
   (b) All registered participants are required to participate in the evaluation of at least one language pair, submit the results and a short paper and attend the workshop at IJCNLP 2011.
3. Evaluation Script (20 April 2011)

Proceedings of the 2011 Named Entities Workshop, IJCNLP 2011, pages 14–22,
Chiang Mai, Thailand, November 12, 2011.

(a) A sample test set and expected user output format are to be released.
(b) An evaluation script, which runs on the above two, is to be released.
(c) The participants must make sure that their output is produced in a way that the evaluation script may run and produce the expected output.
(d) The same script (with held out test data and the user outputs) would be used for final evaluation.

4. Test data (13 June 2011)

(a) The test data would be released on 13 June 2011, and the participants have a maximum of 7 days to submit their results in the expected format.
(b) One "standard" run must be submitted from every group on a given language pair. Additional "standard" runs may be submitted, up to 4 "standard" runs in total. However, the participants must indicate one of the submitted "standard" runs as the "primary submission". The primary submission will be used for the performance summary. In addition to the "standard" runs, more "non-standard" runs may be submitted. In total, maximum 8 runs (up to 4 "standard" runs plus up to 4 "non-standard" runs) can be submitted from each group on a registered language pair. The definition of "standard" and "non-standard" runs is in Section 5.
(c) Any runs that are "non-standard" must be tagged as such.
(d) The test set is a list of names in source language only. Every group will produce and submit a ranked list of transliteration candidates in another language for each given name in the test set. Please note that this shared task is a "transliteration generation" task, i.e., given a name in a source language one is supposed to generate one or more transliterations in a target language. It is not the task of "transliteration discovery", i.e., given a name in the source language and a set of names in the target language evaluate how to find the appropriate names from the target set that are transliterations of the given source name.

5. Results (30 June 2011)

(a) On 30 June 2011, the evaluation results would be announced and will be made available on the Workshop website.
(b) Note that only the scores (in respective metrics) of the participating systems on each language pairs would be published, and no explicit ranking of the participating systems would be published.
(c) Note that this is a shared evaluation task and not a competition; the results are meant to be used to evaluate systems on common data set with common metrics, and not to rank the participating systems. While the participants can cite the performance of their systems (scores on metrics) from the workshop report, they should not use any ranking information in their publications.
(d) Furthermore, all participants should agree not to reveal identities of other participants in any of their publications unless you get permission from the other respective participants. By default, all participants remain anonymous in published results, unless they indicate otherwise at the time of uploading their results. Note that the results of all systems will be published, but the identities of those participants that choose not to disclose their identity to other participants will be masked. As a result, in this case, your organisation name will still appear in the web site as one of participants, but it will not be linked explicitly to your results.

6. Short Papers on Task (6 July 2011)

(a) Each submitting site is required to submit a 4-page system paper (short paper) for its submissions, including their approach, data used and the results on either test set or development set or by n-fold cross validation on training set.
(b) The review of the system papers will be done to improve paper quality and readability and make sure the authors' ideas and methods can be understood by the

workshop participants. We are aiming at accepting all system papers, and selected ones will be presented orally in the NEWS 2011 workshop.

(c) All registered participants are required to register and attend the workshop to introduce your work.

(d) All paper submission and review will be managed electronically through https://www.softconf.com/ijcnlp2011/NEWS.

4 Language Pairs

The tasks are to transliterate personal names or place names from a source to a target language as summarised in Table 1. NEWS 2011 Shared Task offers 14 evaluation subtasks, among them ChEn and ThEn are the back-transliteration of EnCh and EnTh tasks respectively. NEWS 2011 releases training, development and testing data for each of the language pairs. NEWS 2011 continues some language pairs that were evaluated in NEWS 2010. In such cases, the training and development data in the release of NEWS 2011 may overlap with those in NEWS 2010. However, the test data in NEWS 2011 are entirely new.

The names given in the training sets for Chinese, Japanese, Korean, Thai and Persian languages are Western names and their respective transliterations; the Japanese Name (in English) → Japanese Kanji data set consists only of native Japanese names; the Arabic data set consists only of native Arabic names. The Indic data set (Hindi, Tamil, Kannada, Bangla) consists of a mix of Indian and Western names.

Examples of transliteration:

English → Chinese
Timothy → 蒂莫西

English → Japanese Katakana
Harrington → ハリントン

English → Korean Hangul
Bennett → 베넷

Japanese name in English → Japanese Kanji
Akihiro → 秋宏

English → Hindi
San Francisco → सैन फ्रान्सिस्को

English → Tamil
London → லண்டன்

English → Kannada
Tokyo → ಟೋಕ್ಯೋ

Arabic → Arabic name in English
خالد → Khalid

5 Standard Databases

Training Data (Parallel)
Paired names between source and target languages; size 5K – 32K.
Training Data is used for training a basic transliteration system.

Development Data (Parallel)
Paired names between source and target languages; size 2K – 6K.
Development Data is in addition to the Training data, which is used for system fine-tuning of parameters in case of need. Participants are allowed to use it as part of training data.

Testing Data
Source names only; size 2K – 3K.
This is a held-out set, which would be used for evaluating the quality of the transliterations.

1. Participants will need to obtain licenses from the respective copyright owners and/or agree to the terms and conditions of use that are given on the downloading website (Li et al., 2004; MSRI, 2010; CJKI, 2010). NEWS 2011 will provide the contact details of each individual database. The data would be provided in Unicode UTF-8 encoding, in XML format; the results are expected to be submitted in UTF-8 encoding in XML format. The XML formats details are available in Appendix A.

2. The data are provided in 3 sets as described above.

3. Name pairs are distributed as-is, as provided by the respective creators.

   (a) While the databases are mostly manually checked, there may be still inconsistency (that is, non-standard usage, region-specific usage, errors, etc.) or incompleteness (that is, not all right variations may be covered).

   (b) The participants may use any method to further clean up the data provided.

Name origin	Source script	Target script	Data Owner	Data Size			Task ID
				Train	Dev	Test	
Western	English	Chinese	Institute for Infocomm Research	37K	2.8K	2K	EnCh
Western	Chinese	English	Institute for Infocomm Research	28K	2.7K	2.2K	ChEn
Western	English	Korean Hangul	CJK Institute	7K	1K	609	EnKo
Western	English	Japanese Katakana	CJK Institute	26K	2K	1.8K	EnJa
Japanese	English	Japanese Kanji	CJK Institute	10K	2K	571	JnJk
Arabic	Arabic	English	CJK Institute	27K	2.5K	2.6K	ArEn
Mixed	English	Hindi	Microsoft Research India	12K	1K	1K	EnHi
Mixed	English	Tamil	Microsoft Research India	10K	1K	1K	EnTa
Mixed	English	Kannada	Microsoft Research India	10K	1K	1K	EnKa
Mixed	English	Bangla	Microsoft Research India	13K	1K	1K	EnBa
Western	English	Thai	NECTEC	27K	2K	2K	EnTh
Western	Thai	English	NECTEC	25K	2K	1.9K	ThEn
Western	English	Persian	Sarvnaz Karimi / RMIT	10K	2K	2K	EnPe
Western	English	Hebrew	Microsoft Research India	9.5K	1K	1K	EnHe

Table 1: Source and target languages for the shared task on transliteration.

i. If they are cleaned up manually, we appeal that such data be provided back to the organisers for redistribution to all the participating groups in that language pair; such sharing benefits all participants, and further ensures that the evaluation provides normalisation with respect to data quality.

ii. If automatic cleanup were used, such cleanup would be considered a part of the system fielded, and hence not required to be shared with all participants.

4. *Standard Runs* We expect that the participants to use only the data (parallel names) provided by the Shared Task for transliteration task for a "standard" run to ensure a fair evaluation. One such run (using only the data provided by the shared task) is mandatory for all participants for a given language pair that they participate in.

5. *Non-standard Runs* If more data (either parallel names data or monolingual data) were used, then all such runs using extra data must be marked as "non-standard". For such "non-standard" runs, it is required to disclose the size and characteristics of the data used in the system paper.

6. A participant may submit a maximum of 8 runs for a given language pair (including the mandatory 1 "standard" run marked as "primary submission").

6 Paper Format

Paper submissions to NEWS 2011 should follow the IJCNLP 2011 paper submission policy, including paper format, blind review policy and title and author format convention. Full papers (research paper) are in two-column format without exceeding eight (8) pages of content plus two (2) extra page for references and short papers (task paper) are also in two-column format without exceeding four (4) pages content plus two (2) extra page for references. Submission must conform to the official IJCNLP 2011 style guidelines. For details, please refer to the IJCNLP 2011 website[2].

7 Evaluation Metrics

We plan to measure the quality of the transliteration task using the following 4 metrics. We accept up to 10 output candidates in a ranked list for each input entry.

Since a given source name may have multiple correct target transliterations, all these alternatives are treated equally in the evaluation. That is, any of these alternatives are considered as a correct transliteration, and the first correct transliteration in the ranked list is accepted as a correct hit.

The following notation is further assumed:

[2]http://www.ijcnlp2011.org/

N	:	Total number of names (source words) in the test set
n_i	:	Number of reference transliterations for i-th name in the test set ($n_i \geq 1$)
$r_{i,j}$	:	j-th reference transliteration for i-th name in the test set
$c_{i,k}$	:	k-th candidate transliteration (system output) for i-th name in the test set ($1 \leq k \leq 10$)
K_i	:	Number of candidate transliterations produced by a transliteration system

1. Word Accuracy in Top-1 (ACC) Also known as Word Error Rate, it measures correctness of the first transliteration candidate in the candidate list produced by a transliteration system. $ACC = 1$ means that all top candidates are correct transliterations i.e. they match one of the references, and $ACC = 0$ means that none of the top candidates are correct.

$$ACC = \frac{1}{N}\sum_{i=1}^{N}\left\{\begin{array}{l} 1 \text{ if } \exists\, r_{i,j} : r_{i,j} = c_{i,1}; \\ 0 \text{ otherwise} \end{array}\right\} \tag{1}$$

2. Fuzziness in Top-1 (Mean F-score) The mean F-score measures how different, on average, the top transliteration candidate is from its closest reference. F-score for each source word is a function of Precision and Recall and equals 1 when the top candidate matches one of the references, and 0 when there are no common characters between the candidate and any of the references.

Precision and Recall are calculated based on the length of the Longest Common Subsequence between a candidate and a reference:

$$LCS(c,r) = \frac{1}{2}\left(|c| + |r| - ED(c,r)\right) \tag{2}$$

where ED is the edit distance and $|x|$ is the length of x. For example, the longest common subsequence between "abcd" and "afcde" is "acd" and its length is 3. The best matching reference, that is, the reference for which the edit distance has the minimum, is taken for calculation. If the best matching reference is given by

$$r_{i,m} = \arg\min_{j}\left(ED(c_{i,1}, r_{i,j})\right) \tag{3}$$

then Recall, Precision and F-score for i-th word are calculated as

$$R_i = \frac{LCS(c_{i,1}, r_{i,m})}{|r_{i,m}|} \tag{4}$$

$$P_i = \frac{LCS(c_{i,1}, r_{i,m})}{|c_{i,1}|} \tag{5}$$

$$F_i = 2\frac{R_i \times P_i}{R_i + P_i} \tag{6}$$

- The length is computed in distinct Unicode characters.

- No distinction is made on different character types of a language (e.g., vowel vs. consonants vs. combining diereses' etc.)

3. Mean Reciprocal Rank (MRR) Measures traditional MRR *for any right answer* produced by the system, from among the candidates. $1/MRR$ tells approximately the average rank of the correct transliteration. MRR closer to 1 implies that the correct answer is mostly produced close to the top of the n-best lists.

$$RR_i = \left\{\begin{array}{l} \min_j \frac{1}{j} \text{ if } \exists r_{i,j}, c_{i,k} : r_{i,j} = c_{i,k}; \\ 0 \text{ otherwise} \end{array}\right\} \tag{7}$$

$$MRR = \frac{1}{N}\sum_{i=1}^{N} RR_i \tag{8}$$

4. MAP$_{ref}$ Measures tightly the precision in the n-best candidates for i-th source name, for which reference transliterations are available. If all of the references are produced, then the MAP is 1. Let's denote the number of correct candidates for the i-th source word in k-best list as $num(i,k)$. MAP$_{ref}$ is then given by

$$MAP_{ref} = \frac{1}{N}\sum_{i}^{N}\frac{1}{n_i}\left(\sum_{k=1}^{n_i} num(i,k)\right) \tag{9}$$

8 Contact Us

If you have any questions about this share task and the database, please email to

Mr. Ming Liu
Institute for Infocomm Research (I^{2}R), A*STAR
1 Fusionopolis Way
#08-05 South Tower, Connexis
Singapore 138632
mliu@i2r.a-star.edu.sg

Dr. Min Zhang
Institute for Infocomm Research (I^2R), A*STAR
1 Fusionopolis Way
#08-05 South Tower, Connexis
Singapore 138632
mzhang@i2r.a-star.edu.sg

References

[CJKI2010] CJKI. 2010. CJK Institute. http://www.cjk.org/.

[Li et al.2004] Haizhou Li, Min Zhang, and Jian Su. 2004. A joint source-channel model for machine transliteration. In *Proc. 42nd ACL Annual Meeting*, pages 159–166, Barcelona, Spain.

[MSRI2010] MSRI. 2010. Microsoft Research India. http://research.microsoft.com/india.

A Training/Development Data

- File Naming Conventions:
  `NEWS11_train_XXYY_nnnn.xml`
  `NEWS11_dev_XXYY_nnnn.xml`
  `NEWS11_test_XXYY_nnnn.xml`
  - `XX`: Source Language
  - `YY`: Target Language
  - `nnnn`: size of parallel/monolingual names ("25K", "10000", etc)
- File formats:
  All data will be made available in XML formats (Figure 1).
- Data Encoding Formats:
  The data will be in Unicode UTF-8 encoding files without byte-order mark, and in the XML format specified.

B Submission of Results

- File Naming Conventions:
  You can give your files any name you like. During submission online you will need to indicate whether this submission belongs to a "standard" or "non-standard" run, and if it is a "standard" run, whether it is the primary submission.
- File formats:
  All data will be made available in XML formats (Figure 2).
- Data Encoding Formats:
  The results are expected to be submitted in UTF-8 encoded files without byte-order mark only, and in the XML format specified.

```
<?xml version="1.0" encoding="UTF-8"?>

<TransliterationCorpus
    CorpusID = "NEWS2011-Train-EnHi-25K"
    SourceLang = "English"
    TargetLang = "Hindi"
    CorpusType = "Train|Dev"
    CorpusSize = "25000"
    CorpusFormat = "UTF8">

    <Name ID=" 1" >
        <SourceName>eeeeee1</SourceName>
        <TargetName ID="1">hhhhhh1_1</TargetName>
            <TargetName ID="2">hhhhhh1_2</TargetName>
        ...
        <TargetName ID="n">hhhhhh1_n</TargetName>
    </Name>
    <Name ID=" 2" >
        <SourceName>eeeeee2</SourceName>
        <TargetName ID="1">hhhhhh2_1</TargetName>
        <TargetName ID="2">hhhhhh2_2</TargetName>
        ...
        <TargetName ID="m">hhhhhh2_m</TargetName>
    </Name>
    ...
    <!-- rest of the names to follow -->
    ...
</TransliterationCorpus>
```

Figure 1: File: NEWS2011_Train_EnHi_25K.xml

```xml
<?xml version="1.0" encoding="UTF-8"?>

<TransliterationTaskResults
    SourceLang = "English"
    TargetLang = "Hindi"
    GroupID = "Trans University"
    RunID = "1"
    RunType = "Standard"
    Comments = "HMM Run with params: alpha=0.8 beta=1.25">

    <Name ID="1">
        <SourceName>eeeeee1</SourceName>
        <TargetName ID="1">hhhhhh11</TargetName>
        <TargetName ID="2">hhhhhh12</TargetName>
        <TargetName ID="3">hhhhhh13</TargetName>
        ...
        <TargetName ID="10">hhhhhh110</TargetName>

        <!-- Participants to provide their
        top 10 candidate transliterations -->
    </Name>
    <Name ID="2">
        <SourceName>eeeeee2</SourceName>
        <TargetName ID="1">hhhhhh21</TargetName>
        <TargetName ID="2">hhhhhh22</TargetName>
        <TargetName ID="3">hhhhhh23</TargetName>
        ...
        <TargetName ID="10">hhhhhh110</TargetName>
        <!-- Participants to provide their
        top 10 candidate transliterations -->
    </Name>
    ...
    <!-- All names in test corpus to follow -->
    ...
</TransliterationTaskResults>
```

Figure 2: Example file: NEWS2011_EnHi_TUniv_01_StdRunHMMBased.xml

Integrating Models Derived from non-Parametric Bayesian Co-segmentation into a Statistical Machine Transliteration System

Andrew Finch
NICT
3-5 Hikaridai
Keihanna Science City
619-0289 JAPAN
andrew.finch@nict.go.jp

Paul Dixon
NICT
3-5 Hikaridai
Keihanna Science City
619-0289 JAPAN
paul.dixon@nict.go.jp

Eiichiro Sumita
NICT
3-5 Hikaridai
Keihanna Science City
619-0289 JAPAN
eiichiro.sumita@nict.go.jp

Abstract

The system presented in this paper is based upon a phrase-based statistical machine transliteration (SMT) framework. The SMT system's log-linear model is augmented with a set of features specifically suited to the task of transliteration. In particular our model utilizes a feature based on a joint source-channel model, and a feature based on a maximum entropy model that predicts target grapheme sequences using the local context of graphemes and grapheme sequences in both source and target languages. The segmentation for our approach was performed using a non-parametric Bayesian co-segmentation model, and in this paper we present experiments comparing the effectiveness of this segmentation relative to the publicly available state-of-the-art m2m alignment tool. In all our experiments we have taken a strictly language independent approach. Each of the language pairs were processed automatically with no special treatment.

1 Introduction

In the NEWS2010 workshop, (Finch and Sumita, 2010b) reported that the performance of a phrase-based statistical machine transliteration system (Finch and Sumita, 2008; Rama and Gali, 2009) could be improved significantly by combining it with a model based on the n-gram context of source-target grapheme sequence pairs: a joint source-channel model similar to that of (Li et al., 2004). Their system integrated the two approaches by using a re-scoring step at the end of the decoding process. Our system goes one step further and integrates a joint source-channel model directly into the SMT decoder to allow the probabilities from it to be taken into account within a single search process in the similar manner to (Banchs et al., 2005).

2 System Description

2.1 Bayesian Co-segmentation

The typical method of deriving a translation-model for a machine translation is to use GIZA++ (Och and Ney, 2003) to perform word alignment and a set of heuristics for phrase-pair extraction. A commonly used set of heuristics is known as grow-diag-final-and. This type of approach was taken by (Finch and Sumita, 2010b; Rama and Gali, 2009) to train their models.

An alternative approach is to use a non-parametric Bayesian technique to co-segment both source and target in a single step (Finch and Sumita, 2010a; Huang et al., 2011). This approach has the advantage of being symmetric with respect to source and target languages, and furthermore Bayesian techniques tend to give rise to models with few parameters that do not overfit the data in the same way as traditional maximum likelihood training. In experiments on an English-Japanese transliteration task, (Finch and Sumita, 2010a) showed that that a Bayesian approach offered higher performance than using GIZA++ together with heuristic phrase-pair extraction. Their approach unfortunately required a simple set of agglomeration heuristics in order get good performance from the system. Similarly, (Huang et al., 2011) show that their Bayesian system is able to outperform a baseline based on EM alignment, by removing the need to align to a single grapheme in one language to avoid over-fitting.

In our approach, we adopt the same Bayesian co-segmentation (bilingual alignment) framework as (Finch and Sumita, 2010a), and replace the agglomeration heuristics by incorporating a joint source-channel model directly into the decoder as an additional feature. Our motivation for this was simply that the phrase-based translation model lacks contextual information, and in the experiments of (Finch and Sumita, 2010a), the model gained this contextual information implicitly by the use of agglomerated phrases. In other words,

Proceedings of the 2011 Named Entities Workshop, IJCNLP 2011, pages 23–27,
Chiang Mai, Thailand, November 12, 2011.

the longer phrases carried with them their own built-in context. In our model these contextual dependencies are made explicit and modeled directly by the joint source-channel model.

The termination condition for our Bayesian co-segmentation algorithm was set based on pilot experiments that showed very little gain in system performance after iteration 10, and no loss in performance by continuing the training. We arbitrarily chose iteration 30 in all our experiments as the final iteration.

2.2 Phrase-based SMT Models

The decoding was performed using a specially modified version of the CLEOPATRA decoder (Finch et al., 2007), an in-house multi-stack phrase-based decoder that operates on the same principles as the MOSES decoder (Koehn et al., 2007). The system we used in this shared task is a log-linear combination of 5 different models, the following sections describe each of these models in detail. Due to the small size of many of the data sets in the shared tasks, we used all of the data to build models for the final systems.

2.2.1 Joint source-channel model

The joint source-channel model was trained from the Viterbi co-segmentation arising from the final iteration of the Bayesian segmentation process on the training data (for model used in parameter tuning), and the training data added to the development data (for the model used to decode the test data). We used the MIT language modeling toolkit (Bo-june et al., 2008) with modified Knesser-Ney smoothing to build this model. In all experiments we used a language model of order 5.

2.2.2 Target Language model

The target model was trained from target side of the training data (for model used in parameter tuning), and the training data added to the development data (for the model used to decode the test data). We used the MIT language modeling toolkit with Knesser-Ney smoothing to build this model. In all experiments we used a language model of order 5.

2.2.3 Insertion penalty models

Both grapheme based and grapheme-sequence-based insertion penalty models are simple models that add a constant value to their score each time a grapheme (or grapheme sequence) is added to the target hypotheses. These models control the tendency both of the joint source-channel model and the target language model to generate derivations that are too short.

2.2.4 Maximum-entropy model

In a typical phrase-based SMT system, the translation model contains a context-independent probability of the target grapheme sequence (phrase) given the source. Our system replaces this with a more sophisticated maximum entropy model that takes the local context of source and target graphemes and grapheme sequences into account. The features can be partitioned into two classes: grapheme-based features and grapheme sequence-based features. In both cases we use a context of 2 to the left and right for the source, and 2 to the left for the target. Sequence begin and end markers are added to both source and target and are used in the context. The features used in the ME model consist of all possible bigrams of contiguous elements in the context. We do not mix features at the grapheme level and grapheme sequence level, so for example, a grapheme sequence bigram can only consist of grapheme sequences (including sequences of length 1).

2.3 Parameter Tuning

The exponential log-linear model weights of our system are set by tuning the system on development data using the MERT procedure (Och, 2003) by means of the publicly available ZMERT toolkit [1] (Zaidan, 2009). The systems reported in this paper used a metric based on the word-level F-score, an official evaluation metric for the shared tasks, which measures the relationship of the longest common subsequence of the transliteration pair to the lengths of both source and target sequences.

2.4 Official Results

The official scores for our system are given in Table 1. Some of the data tracks will benefit from a language-dependent treatment (for example in Korean it is advantageous to decompose the characters), and in these tracks our language-independent approach was not competitive. Our system typically gave a strong relative performance on those tracks with larger amounts of training data.

3 Segmentation Experiments

A novel feature of our system is the Bayesian co-segmentation approach used to bilingually segment the data in order to yield training data from which to train the models in our system. It has been

[1] http://www.cs.jhu.edu/~ozaidan/zmert/

	En-Ch	Ch-En	En-Th	Th-En	En-Hi	En-Ta	En-Ka
Acc.	0.348	0.145	0.338	0.296	0.478	0.441	0.419
F-score	0.700	0.765	0.853	0.854	0.879	0.900	0.885

	En-Ja	En-Ko	Jn-Jk	Ar-En	En-Ba	En-Pe	En-He
Acc.	0.394	0.356	0.454	0.447	0.478	0.615	0.600
F-score	0.803	0.680	0.641	0.911	0.892	0.938	0.929

Table 1: The Evaluation Results on the 2011 Shared Task for our System in terms of the official F-score and Top-1 accuracy metrics.

shown (Finch and Sumita, 2010a) that in transliteration, this Bayesian approach can give rise to a smaller and more useful phrase-table than that derived by using GIZA++ for alignment and the grow-diag-final-and heuristics which have been shown to be effective for transliteration (Rama and Gali, 2009). In these experiments we compare the Bayesian segmenter to a similar state-of-the-art segmentation tool that is capable of many-to-many alignments: the publicly available m2m alignment tool [2] (Jiampojamarn et al., 2007) that is trained using the EM algorithm and is based on the principles set out in (Ristad and Yianilos, 1998).

We used a similar system to that in the shared task, but without the maximum entropy model. The experiments were run in the same way using the same script, the only difference being the choice of aligner used. We used data from the 2009 NEWS workshop for our experiments, and evaluated using the F-score metric used for the shared task evaluation. The aligners were run with their default settings, and with the same limits for source and target segment size. It may have been possible to obtain better performance from the aligners by adjusting specific parameters, but no attempt was made to do this. The results are shown in Table 2. In all experiments, the Bayesian segmenter gave the best performance, and the largest improvement was on language pairs that have large grapheme set sizes on the target side. The grapheme set size is shown in Table 2 in the 'Target Types' column. The source grapheme set sizes were very similar and small (around 27) for all experiments, as the source language was either English or in the case of Jn-Jk, a romanized form of Japanese. Looking at the n-gram statistics in Table 2, for languages with large grapheme sets the number of unigrams in the Bayesian model is less than half that used by the m2m model. Learning a compact model is one of the signature characteristics of the Bayesian model we use; adding a new parameter to the model is extremely costly, and the algorithm will therefore strongly prefer to learn a model in which the parameters are re-used.

[2]http://code.google.com/p/m2m-aligner/

Initially we considered the hypotheses that the difference in performance between these two approaches came from differences in the sparseness of the language models. Surprisingly however, the numbers of bi-grams and tri-grams in the joint language models are quite similar.

Another explanation is that the smaller number of unigrams indicates that the segmentation is more self-consistent and therefore makes the generation task less ambiguous. This is supported by looking at the development set perplexity. On the Jn-Jk task where the differences between the systems are the largest, we found that a joint language model trained on the Bayesian segmentation had 1-, 2-, and 3-gram perplexities of 218.3, 88.4 and 87.5 respectively, whereas the corresponding m2m model's perplexities were 321.8, 120.5 and 119.3. The number of segments used to segment the corpus was the same for both systems in this experiment.

Table 3 gives an example from the data of the differences in segmentation consistency. The Bayesian segmentation is strongly self-consistent. The source sequence 'ara' has been segmented identically as a single unit in all cases. The m2m system also shows self-consistency, but uses a few different strategies to segment the start of the sequence. Interestingly the Bayesian method in this example has segmented according to the correct linguistic readings of the kanji. We investigate this further in the next section.

3.1 Linguistic Agreement

In this experiment, we attempt to assess the ability of each segmentation scheme to discover the underlying linguistic segmentation of the data. We took a random sample of 100 word-pairs from the Japanese romaji to Japanese Kanji training corpus. The segmentation of this sample using both systems was then labeled as either 'correct' or 'incorrect' by a human judge using a Japanese

Language Pairs	Target Types	m2m F-score	Bayesian F-score	m2m			Bayesian		
				1-grams	2-grams	3-grams	1-grams	2-grams	3-grams
En-Ch	372	0.858	0.880	9379	44003	75513	4706	38647	72905
En-Hi	84	0.874	0.884	3114	15209	30195	1867	20218	34657
En-Ko	687	0.623	0.651	4337	11891	14112	2968	11233	14729
En-Ru	66	0.919	0.922	1638	6351	14869	1105	12607	23250
En-Ta	64	0.885	0.892	2852	14696	27869	1561	17195	30244
Jn-Jk	1514	0.669	0.767	7942	27286	38365	3532	22717	37560

Table 2: System performance in terms of F-score, by using alternative segmentation schemes together with statistics relating to be number of parameters in the models derived from the segmentations.

m2m			Bayesian		
arad↦荒	a↦田		ara↦荒	da↦田	
ar↦新	ae↦江		ara↦新	e↦江	
ar↦荒	ahori↦堀		ara↦荒	hori↦堀	
ar↦新	ai↦井		ara↦新	i↦井	
ar↦新	ai↦居		ara↦新	i↦居	
ar↦荒	ai↦井		ara↦荒	i↦井	
ar↦荒	ai↦居		ara↦荒	i↦居	
araj↦荒	ima↦島		ara↦荒	jima↦島	
arak↦新	i↦木		ara↦新	ki↦木	
arak↦荒	i↦木		ara↦荒	ki↦木	
ar↦荒	akid↦木	a↦田	ara↦荒	ki↦木	da↦田
ar↦荒	ao↦尾		ara↦荒	o↦尾	
ar↦荒	ao↦生		ara↦荒	o↦生	
ar↦荒	aoka↦岡		ara↦荒	oka↦岡	
arasa↦荒	wa↦沢		ara↦荒	sawa↦沢	
ar↦荒	aseki↦関		ara↦荒	seki↦関	

Table 3: Example segmentations from the m2m segmenter and the Bayesian segmenter, taken from a long contiguous section of the training set where both techniques disagree on the segmentation.

name reading dictionary as a reference. We found that Bayesian segmentation agreed with the human segmentation in 96% of the test cases, and whereas the m2m system agreed in 42% of cases.

4 Conclusion

The system entered in the year's shared task is built within a statistical machine translation framework, but has been augmented by adding features specifically suited to transliteration. In particular, a joint source-channel model and a maximum entropy model were integrated into the decoder to enhance the translation model of the SMT system by contributing local contextual information. Our system uses a novel Bayesian co-segmentation technique to perform a many-to-many source-target sequence alignment of the corpus. The models of our system are trained directly from this co-segmentation. We have shown that this technique is very effective for producing training data for a joint source-channel model, and is able to accurately induce the linguistic segmentation of Japanese names, building a compact model based on a self-consistent segmentation of the data. In the future we would like to develop more sophisticated Bayesian models, and investigate methods for identifying and dealing with different source languages. We would also like to measure the utility of training the language model component of our system independently on large amounts of monolingual data, which is often much more readily available than aligned bilingual corpora.

Acknowledgements

For the English-Japanese, English-Korean and Arabic-English datasets, the reader is referred to the CJK website: http://www.cjk.org. For English-Hindi, English-Tamil, and English-Kannada, and English-Bangla the data sets originated from the work of (Kumaran and Kellner, 2007).

References

Rafael E. Banchs, Josep Maria Crego, Adria Degispert, Patrik Lambert, Marta Ruiz, and Jose A. R. Fonollosa. 2005. Bilingual n-gram statistical machine translation. In *Proc. of Machine Translation Summit X*, pages 275–282.

Bo-june, Paul Hsu, and James Glass. 2008. Iterative language model estimation: Efficient data structure and algorithms. In *Proc. Interspeech*.

Andrew Finch and Eiichiro Sumita. 2008. Phrase-based machine transliteration. In *Proc. 3rd International Joint Conference on NLP*, volume 1, Hyderabad, India.

Andrew Finch and Eiichiro Sumita. 2010a. A Bayesian Model of Bilingual Segmentation for Transliteration. In Marcello Federico, Ian Lane, Michael Paul, and François Yvon, editors, *Proceedings of the seventh International Workshop on Spoken Language Translation (IWSLT)*, pages 259–266.

Andrew Finch and Eiichiro Sumita. 2010b. Transliteration using a phrase-based statistical machine translation system to re-score the output of a joint multigram model. In *Proceedings of the 2010 Named Entities Workshop*, NEWS '10, pages 48–52, Stroudsburg, PA, USA. Association for Computational Linguistics.

Andrew Finch, Etienne Denoual, Hideo Okuma, Michael Paul, Hirofumi Yamamoto, Keiji Yasuda, Ruiqiang Zhang, and Eiichiro Sumita. 2007. The NICT/ATR speech translation system for IWSLT 2007. In *Proceedings of the IWSLT*, Trento, Italy.

Yun Huang, Min Zhang, and Chew Lim Tan. 2011. Nonparametric Bayesian Machine Transliteration with Synchronous Adaptor Grammars. In *ACL (Short Papers)*, pages 534–539.

Sittichai Jiampojamarn, Grzegorz Kondrak, and Tarek Sherif. 2007. Applying many-to-many alignments and hidden markov models to letter-to-phoneme conversion. In *Human Language Technologies 2007: The Conference of the North American Chapter of the Association for Computational Linguistics; Proceedings of the Main Conference*, pages 372–379, Rochester, New York, April. Association for Computational Linguistics.

Philipp Koehn, Hieu Hoang, Alexandra Birch, Chris Callison-Burch, Marcello Federico, Nicola Bertoldi, Brooke Cowa, Wade Shen, Christine Moran, Richard Zens, Chris Dyer, Ondrej Bojar, Alexandra Constantin, and Evan Herbst. 2007. Moses: open source toolkit for statistical machine translation. In *ACL 2007: proceedings of demo and poster sessions*, pages 177–180, Prague, Czeck Republic, June.

A. Kumaran and Tobias Kellner. 2007. A generic framework for machine transliteration. In *SIGIR '07*, pages 721–722.

Haizhou Li, Min Zhang, and Jian Su. 2004. A joint source-channel model for machine transliteration. In *ACL '04: Proceedings of the 42nd Annual Meeting on Association for Computational Linguistics*, page 159, Morristown, NJ, USA. Association for Computational Linguistics.

Franz Josef Och and Hermann Ney. 2003. A systematic comparison of various statistical alignment models. *Computational Linguistics*, 29(1):19–51.

Franz J. Och. 2003. Minimum error rate training for statistical machine translation. In *Proceedings of the ACL*.

Taraka Rama and Karthik Gali. 2009. Modeling machine transliteration as a phrase based statistical machine translation problem. In *NEWS '09: Proceedings of the 2009 Named Entities Workshop: Shared Task on Transliteration*, pages 124–127, Morristown, NJ, USA. Association for Computational Linguistics.

Eric Sven Ristad and Peter N. Yianilos. 1998. Learning string edit distance. *IEEE Transactions on Pattern Recognition and Machine Intelligence*, 20(5):522–532, May.

Omar F. Zaidan. 2009. Z-MERT: A fully configurable open source tool for minimum error rate training of machine translation systems. *The Prague Bulletin of Mathematical Linguistics*, 91:79–88.

Simple Discriminative Training for Machine Transliteration

Canasai Kruengkrai, Thatsanee Charoenporn, Virach Sornlertlamvanich
National Electronics and Computer Technology Center
Thailand Science Park, Klong Luang, Pathumthani 12120, Thailand
{canasai.kruengkrai,thatsanee.charoenporn,virach.sornlertlamvanich}@nectec.or.th

Abstract

In this paper, we describe our system used in the NEWS 2011 machine transliteration shared task. Our system consists of two main components: simple strategies for generating training examples based on character alignment, and discriminative training based on the Margin Infused Relaxed Algorithm. We submitted results for 10 language pairs on standard runs. Our system achieves the best performance for English-to-Thai and English-to-Hebrew.

1 Introduction

We aim to develop a machine transliteration system that performs well in any given language pair without much effort in pre- and post-processing, and parameter tuning. To compare the performance of our system against state-of-the-art approaches, we participated in the machine transliteration shared task conducted as a part of the Named Entities Workshop (NEWS 2011), an IJCNLP 2011 workshop. Specifically, we focus on standard runs where only the corpus (containing parallel names) provided by the shared task is used for training. We submitted results for 10 language pairs.

2 Background

2.1 Motivation

As discussed in (Li et al., 2004), machine transliteration can be viewed as two levels of decoding: (1) segmenting the source language character string into transliteration units, and (2) relating the source language transliteration units with units in the target language by resolving different combinations of alignments and unit mappings. A transliteration unit could be one or more characters. Typically, the source and target language transliteration units are not given in the training corpus.

The process of machine transliteration is very similar to that of phrase-based statistical machine translation (SMT) (Koehn et al., 2003). As a result, a number of previous studies directly applied phrase-based SMT techniques to machine transliteration (Finch and Sumita, 2009; Rama and Gali, 2009; Finch and Sumita, 2010; Avinesh and Parikh, 2010). However, unlike word alignment in phrase-based SMT, character alignment in machine transliteration seems to be monotonic in which reordering of target language characters rarely occurs but is still possible in some language pairs.

After alignment, the target language transliteration units can be considered as tags (or labels) of the source language transliteration units. As a result, some previous studies viewed machine transliteration as simply as a sequence labeling problem (Aramaki and Abekawwa, 2009; Shishtla et al., 2009). With this problem setting, the system can apply any powerful discriminative training algorithm (e.g., Conditional Random Fields (CRFs) (Lafferty, 2001)) incorporated with rich features. Our system follows this research direction, but we pay more attention on how to extract appropriate transliteration units and train our model using the Margin Infused Relaxed Algorithm (MIRA) (Crammer et al., 2005; McDonald, 2006).

2.2 Problem Setting

Here, we formulate the process of machine transliteration based on discriminative learning. Given a character string $\boldsymbol{x}$ in the source language, we need to find the most likely character string $\hat{\boldsymbol{y}}$ out of all possible character strings in the target language. We express this process by:

$$\hat{\boldsymbol{y}} = \operatorname*{argmax}_{\boldsymbol{y} \in \mathcal{Y}} s(\boldsymbol{x}, \boldsymbol{y}; \mathbf{w}) , \tag{1}$$

Proceedings of the 2011 Named Entities Workshop, IJCNLP 2011, pages 28–31,
Chiang Mai, Thailand, November 12, 2011.

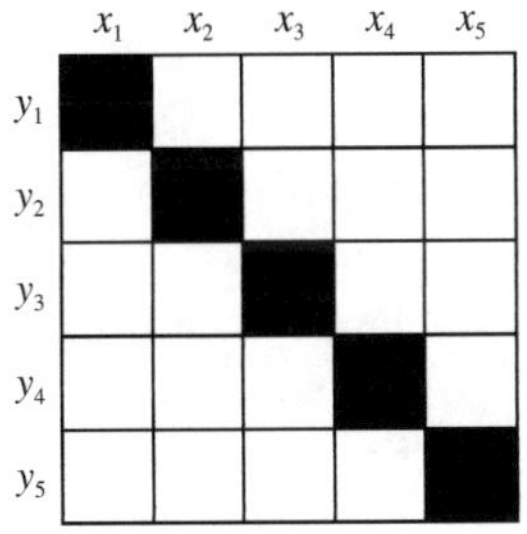

Figure 1: Ideal alignment.

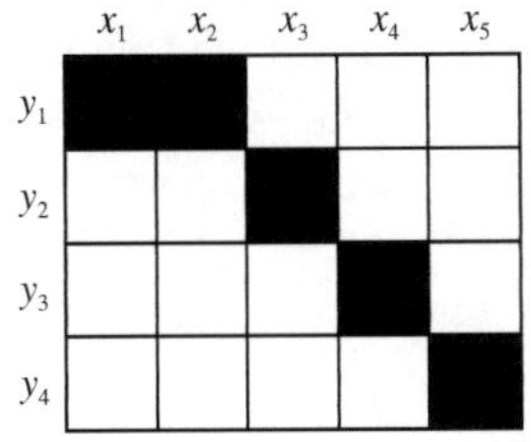

Figure 2: The source language character string $\boldsymbol{x}$ is longer than the target language character string $\boldsymbol{y}$. The aligner maps two source language characters to a single target language character.

where s denotes a discriminant function over a pair of a source language character string $\boldsymbol{x}$ and a hypothesized target language character string $\boldsymbol{y}$ given a parameter $\mathbf{w}$.

3 Strategies for Generating Training Examples

In this section, we describe how to generate training examples from a parallel name corpus. Our training example construction is based on character alignment.

At the first step, we can apply any word alignment tool commonly used in SMT. Given a training corpus containing parallel name pairs, we use the aligner to obtain initial character alignments. Figure 1 shows an ideal alignment example between the source language character string $\boldsymbol{x}$ and the target language character string $\boldsymbol{y}$. Now, assume that we have only one parallel name pair. Thus, our training example can be directly written as $(\langle x_1, y_1\rangle, \langle x_2, y_2\rangle, \ldots, \langle x_5, y_5\rangle)$.

Unfortunately, the lengths of parallel name pairs in the training corpus are typically unequal. The source language character string $\boldsymbol{x}$ could be shorter or longer than the target language character string $\boldsymbol{y}$. Figure 2 shows an example when $\boldsymbol{x}$ is longer than $\boldsymbol{y}$, and the aligner maps two

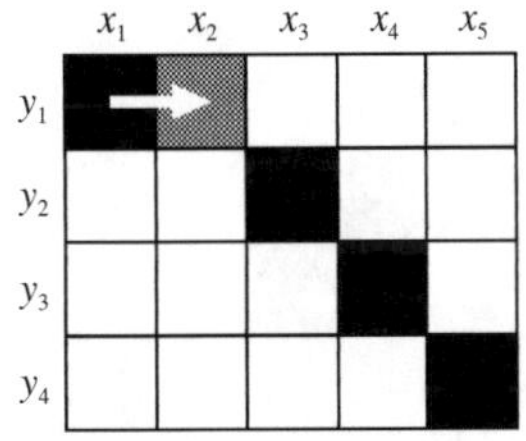

Figure 3: The aligner cannot map x_2 to any target language character. Based on the information from the previous alignment, we align x_2 to y_1.

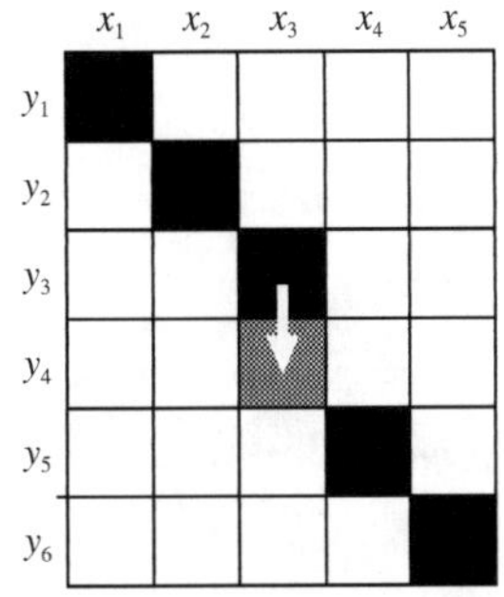

Figure 4: The aligner cannot map y_4 to any source language character. Based on the information from the previous alignment, we align y_4 to x_3.

source language characters to a single target language character, i.e., $\{x_1, x_2\} \rightarrow y_1$. To handle this case, we associate the position-of-character (POC) tags with the target language character. Our POC tags includes $\{\mathrm{B}, \mathrm{I}\}$, indicating the beginning and the intermediate positions, respectively. Our training example becomes $(\langle x_1, \text{B-}y_1\rangle, \langle x_2, \text{I-}y_1\rangle, \langle x_3, \text{B-}y_2\rangle, \langle x_4, \text{B-}y_3\rangle, \langle x_5, \text{B-}y_4\rangle)$.

In practice, the aligner often yields incomplete alignments. Some target language characters could not be aligned to source language characters, and vice versa. To handle this case, we use simple heuristics by looking at neighboring alignments. We find unaligned characters in both the source and target character strings. If the previous alignment is already established, we expand it to the empty alignment. If the previous alignment is not available (e.g., the unaligned character occurs at the beginning position), we instead use the information from the next alignment.

Figure 3 shows an example when the aligner cannot map x_2 to any target language character. Based on our heuristics, we align x_2 to y_1. As a result, our training example is identical to that

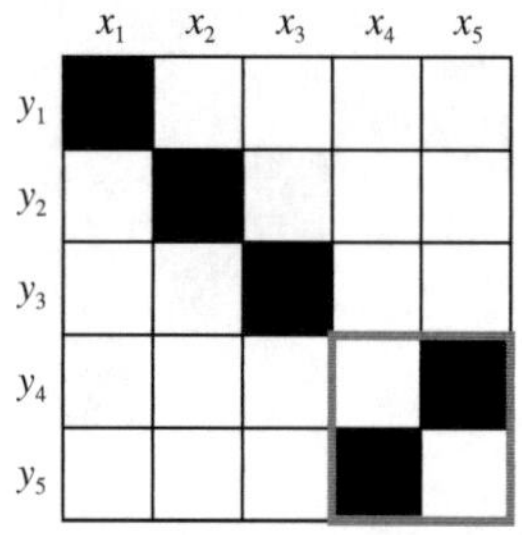

Figure 5: Reordering occurs in the target language characters. y_4 and y_5 are first merged into a single transliteration unit y_4y_5, and x_4 and x_5 are then aligned to B-y_4y_5 and I-y_4y_5, respectively.

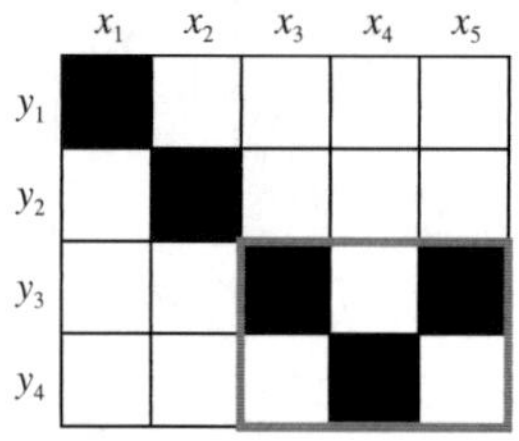

Figure 6: Another possible character reordering.

of Figure 2. Figure 4 shows another example when the aligner cannot map y_4 to any source language character. In this case, we align y_4 to x_3. Now, a single source language character is associated with two target language characters, i.e., $x_3 \rightarrow \{y_3, y_4\}$. As a result, we merge y_3 and y_4 into a single transliteration unit y_3y_4. Our training example becomes $(\langle x_1, \text{B-}y_1\rangle, \langle x_2, \text{B-}y_2\rangle, \langle x_3, \text{B-}y_3y_4\rangle, \langle x_4, \text{B-}y_5\rangle, \langle x_5, \text{B-}y_6\rangle)$.

Note that character reordering can be found in the alignments. Figure 5 shows an example when reordering occurs in the target language characters. To be able to perform the monotone search in decoding, we merge y_4 and y_5 into a single transliteration unit y_4y_5. Our training example becomes $(\langle x_1, \text{B-}y_1\rangle, \langle x_2, \text{B-}y_2\rangle, \langle x_3, \text{B-}y_3\rangle, \langle x_4, \text{B-}y_4y_5\rangle, \langle x_5, \text{I-}y_4y_5\rangle)$.

Figure 6 shows another possible character reordering. We use the same scheme as the previous example. Thus, our training example becomes $(\langle x_1, \text{B-}y_1\rangle, \langle x_2, \text{B-}y_2\rangle, \langle x_3, \text{B-}y_4y_5\rangle, \langle x_4, \text{I-}y_4y_5\rangle, \langle x_5, \text{I-}y_4y_5\rangle)$. To summarize, we examine whether reordering occurs in the target language characters. If so, we merge those target language characters until the alignments become monotonic.

4 Learning and Decoding

The goal of our model is to learn a mapping from source language character strings $\boldsymbol{x} \in \mathcal{X}$ to target language character strings $\boldsymbol{y} \in \mathcal{Y}$ based on training examples of source-target language name pairs $\mathcal{D} = \{(\boldsymbol{x}_t, \boldsymbol{y}_t)\}_{t=1}^{T}$.

In our model, we apply a generalized version of MIRA (Crammer et al., 2005; McDonald, 2006) that can incorporate k-best decoding in the update procedure. From Equation (1), the linear discriminant function s becomes the dot product between a feature function $\mathbf{f}$ of the source language character string $\boldsymbol{x}$ and the target language character string $\boldsymbol{y}$ and a corresponding weight vector $\mathbf{w}$:

$$s(\boldsymbol{x}, \boldsymbol{y}; \mathbf{w}) = \langle \mathbf{w}, \mathbf{f}(\boldsymbol{x}, \boldsymbol{y}) \rangle \; . \tag{2}$$

In each iteration, MIRA updates the weight vector $\mathbf{w}$ by keeping the norm of the change in the weight vector as small as possible. With this framework, we can formulate the optimization problem as follows (McDonald, 2006):

$$\begin{aligned} &\mathbf{w}^{(i+1)} = \text{argmin}_{\mathbf{w}} \|\mathbf{w} - \mathbf{w}^{(i)}\| \\ &\text{s.t. } \forall \hat{\boldsymbol{y}} \in \text{best}_k(\boldsymbol{x}_t; \mathbf{w}^{(i)}) : \\ &s(\boldsymbol{x}_t, \boldsymbol{y}_t; \mathbf{w}) - s(\boldsymbol{x}_t, \hat{\boldsymbol{y}}; \mathbf{w}) \geq L(\boldsymbol{y}_t, \hat{\boldsymbol{y}}) \, , \end{aligned} \tag{3}$$

where $\text{best}_k(\boldsymbol{x}_t; \mathbf{w}^{(i)})$ represents a set of top k-best outputs given the weight vector $\mathbf{w}^{(i)}$. We generate $\text{best}_k(\boldsymbol{x}_t; \mathbf{w}^{(i)})$ using a dynamic programming search (Nagata, 1994). We measure $L(\boldsymbol{y}_t, \hat{\boldsymbol{y}})$ using the zero-one loss function. Our basic features operate over the window of ± 4 source language characters and the target language character bigrams.

5 Development and Final Results

In development, we were interested in how the quality of alignment affects the performance of transliteration because errors in alignment inevitably propagate to the learning phase. We used two popular alignment tools, including GIZA++[1] (Och and Ney, 2003) and BerkeleyAligner[2] (Liang et al., 2006). With their default parameter settings, GIZA++ yields better performance than BerkeleyAligner on all development data sets. As a result, our submitted primary runs on the test data sets are based on the resulting alignments from GIZA++. Our learning algorithm

[1] http://code.google.com/p/giza-pp
[2] http://code.google.com/p/berkeleyaligner

Language Pair	ACC	F-score	MRR	MAP_{ref}	Rank (# of all primary runs)
En→Ch	0.342	0.702	0.406	0.331	2 (7)
Ch→En	0.131	0.730	0.193	0.131	5 (6)
En→Th	**0.354**	**0.854**	**0.451**	**0.350**	**1** (2)
Th→En	0.284	0.841	0.402	0.283	2 (2)
En→Hi	0.436	0.870	0.538	0.435	3 (4)
En→Ta	0.432	0.896	0.553	0.430	2 (2)
En→Ka	0.398	0.878	0.502	0.397	2 (2)
En→Ba	0.455	0.887	0.557	0.453	2 (2)
En→Pe	0.643	0.943	0.744	0.629	2 (4)
En→He	**0.602**	**0.931**	**0.702**	**0.602**	**1** (2)

Table 1: Final results showing the "standard run" performance of our system on the test data sets. Language acronyms include En = English, Ch = Chinese, Th = Thai, Hi = Hindi, Ta = Tamil, Ka = Kannada, Ba = Bengali (Bangla), Pe = Persian, and He = Hebrew.

has two tunable parameters: the number of training iterations N and the number of top k-best outputs. We heuristically set $N = 10$ and $k = 5$ for all experiments.

Final results showing the "standard run" performance of our system on the test data sets are given in Table 1. Evaluation metrics include word accuracy in top-1 (ACC), fuzziness in top-1 (F-score), mean reciprocal rank (MRR), and MAP_{ref} described in more detail in (Zhang et al., 2011). The table shows the scores of our primary runs, and the last column indicates our ranks in which we compare our scores with those of other participants.

Our system performs reasonably well across language pairs, except for Chinese-to-English back-transliteration. We achieve the best performance for English-to-Thai and English-to-Hebrew, and the second-best performance (in the cases that more than two primary runs were submitted) for English-to-Chinese and English-to-Persian.

References

Eiji Aramaki and Takeshi Abekawwa. 2009. Fast decoding and easy implementation: transliteration as sequential labeling. In *Proceedings of the 2009 Named Entities Workshop*, pages 65–68.

P. V. S. Avinesh and Ankur Parikh. 2010. Phrase-based transliteration system with simple heuristics. In *Proceedings of the 2010 Named Entities Workshop*, pages 81–84.

Koby Crammer, Ryan McDonald, and Fernando Pereira. 2005. Scalable large-margin online learning for structured classification. In *NIPS Workshop on Learning With Structured Outputs*.

Andrew Finch and Eiichiro Sumita. 2009. Transliteration by bidirectional statistical machine translation. In *Proceedings of the 2009 Named Entities Workshop*, pages 52–56.

Andrew Finch and Eiichiro Sumita. 2010. Transliteration using a phrase-based statistical machine translation system to re-score the output of a joint multigram model. In *Proceedings of the 2010 Named Entities Workshop*, pages 48–52.

Philipp Koehn, Franz Josef Och, and Daniel Marcu. 2003. Statistical phrase-based translation. In *Proceedings of HLT-NAACL*, pages 48–54.

John Lafferty. 2001. Conditional random fields: Probabilistic models for segmenting and labeling sequence data. In *Proceedings of ICML*, pages 282–289.

Haizhou Li, Min Zhang, and Su Jian. 2004. A joint source-channel model for machine transliteration. In *Proceedings of ACL*, pages 159–166.

Percy Liang, Ben Taskar, and Dan Klein. 2006. Alignment by agreement. In *Proceedings of HLT-NAACL*, pages 104–111.

Ryan McDonald. 2006. *Discriminative Training and Spanning Tree Algorithms for Dependency Parsing*. University of Pennsylvania, PhD Thesis.

Masaki Nagata. 1994. A stochastic japanese morphological analyzer using a forward-DP backward-A* n-best search algorithm. In *Proceedings of COLING*, pages 201–207.

Franz Josef Och and Hermann Ney. 2003. A systematic comparison of various statistical alignment models. *Comput. Linguist.*, 29:19–51.

Taraka Rama and Karthik Gali. 2009. Modeling machine transliteration as a phrase based statistical machine translation problem. In *Proceedings of the 2009 Named Entities Workshop*, pages 124–127.

Praneeth Shishtla, V. Surya Ganesh, Sethuramalingam Subramaniam, and Vasudeva Varma. 2009. A language-independent transliteration schema using character aligned models at news 2009. In *Proceedings of the 2009 Named Entities Workshop*, pages 40–43.

Min Zhang, A Kumaran, and Haizhou Li. 2011. Whitepaper of news 2011 shared task on machine transliteration. `http://translit.i2r.a-star.edu.sg/news2011`.

English-Korean Named Entity Transliteration Using Statistical Substring-based and Rule-based Approaches

Yu-Chun Wang
Department of Computer Science
and Information Engineering
National Taiwan University, Taiwan
d97023@csie.ntu.edu.tw

Richard Tzong-Han Tsai
Department of Computer Science
and Engineering
Yuan Ze University, Taiwan
thtsai@saturn.yzu.edu.tw

Abstract

This paper describes our approach to English-Korean transliteration in NEWS 2011 Shared Task on Machine Transliteration. We adopt the substring-based transliteration approach which group the characters of named entity in both source and target languages into substrings and then formulate the transliteration as a sequential tagging problem to tag the substrings in the source language with the substrings in the target language. The CRF algorithm are used to deal with this tagging problem. We also construct a rule-based transliteration method for comparison. Our standard and non-standard runs achieves 0.43 and 0.332 in top-1 accuracy which were ranked as the best for the English-Korean pair.

1 Introduction

Named entity translation plays an important role in machine translation, cross-language information retrieval, and question answering. However, named entities such as person names or organization names are generated everyday and do not often appear in dictionaries since bilingual dictionaries cannot update their contents frequently. Most name entity translation is based on transliteration, which is a method to map phonemes or graphemes from source language into target language. Therefore, it is necessary to construct a named entity transliteration system.

For English-Korean name entity transliteration, we adopt the substring-based transliteration proposed by Reddy and Waxmonsky (Reddy and Waxmonsky, 2009) with conditional random fields (CRF). The method treats the transliteration as a sequential labeling task where substring tokens in the source languages are tagged with the substring tokens in the target language with CRF. Since Korean writing system, Hangul, is alphabetic, we consider that the sequential labeling method is suitable for English-Korean transliteration. In addition, we also apply rule-based method with a pronouncing dictionary for comparison.

2 Our Approach

We comprises three different approaches for the transliteration: *grapheme substring-based*, *phoneme substring-based*, and *rule-based* methods. Grapheme and phoneme substring-based methods are both based on substring-based transliteration methods with CRF. The difference is that the substrings composed with English characters or English phonemes. The details of each methods are described in the following subsections.

2.1 Substring-based Approach

The substring-based approach comprise the following steps:

1. Pre-processing
2. Substring alignment
3. CRF training
4. Substring segmentation and transliteration

2.1.1 Pre-processing

Korean writing system, namely *Hangul*, is alphabetical. However, unlike western writing system with Latin alphabets, Korean alphabet is composed into syllabic blocks. For transliteration from other languages to Korean, one syllabic block contains two or three letters mainly, including 14 leading consonants, 10 vowels, and 7 tailing consonants. For instance, the syllabic block "한" (han) is composed with three letters: a leading consonant "ㅎ" (h), a vowel "ㅏ" (a), and a tailing consonant "ㄴ" (n).

Proceedings of the 2011 Named Entities Workshop, IJCNLP 2011, pages 32–35,
Chiang Mai, Thailand, November 12, 2011.

Thus, in order to deal with Korean training data, we have to decompose Korean syllabic blocks into letters before performing training. The Korean letters in syllabic blocks are almost perfectly corresponding to their phonological forms. However, the actual pronunciation of some consonant letters may vary in different positions in the syllabic block. For example, the letter "ㅅ" is pronounced as [s] in the leading consonant position, but as [t] in the tailing consonant position. We do not distinguish this pronunciation difference of these letters and treat them as the same tokens. For convenient processing, we convert the Korean letters into Roman symbols with the Revised Romanization of Korean proposed by the South Korea Government.

2.1.2 Substring alignment

Unlike Korean, English orthography might not reflect its actual phonological forms, which makes trivial one-to-one character alignment between English and Korean not practical. English may use several characters for one phoneme which is presented in one letter in Korean, such as "ch" to "ㅊ" and "oo" to "ㅜ". In contrast, English sometimes use a single character for a diphthong or consonant cluster, which are presented as several letters in Korean. For example, the letter "x' in the English name entity "Texas" corresponds to two letters "ㄱ" and "ㅅ" in Korean. Besides, some English letters in the word might not be pronounced, like "k" in the English word "knight".

Furthermore, due to Korean phonology, Korean may insert a specific vowel "ㅡ" [ɯ] between English consonant clusters or behind the last burst stop consonant of the syllable. For instance, the English name entity "Snell" is transliterated as "스넬" /s**ɯ** nel/ and "Albert" is transliterated as "앨버트" /æl bə t^{h}**ɯ**/.

In order to deal with these complex orthography problems, we adopt substring-based method to group characters into substrings. English words are segmented into several substrings and each substring maps to a substring in the target language, Korean.

To create training sets of substrings, we use the GIZA++ toolkit (Och and Ney, 2003) to align all the name entity pairs in the training data. The GIZA++ toolkit performs one-to-many alignments, which means that a single symbol in the source language may be aligned to at least one symbol in the target language. To obtain the many-to-many substring alignments, we run GIZA++ on the data in both directions from source language to target language and target language to source language. The final bidirectional alignment result is the union of the alignments in both directions. Inserted characters (aligned to NULL by GIZA++) in the alignment results are merged with the preceding character into the same substring. For example, the bidirectional alignment result of the English word "*KNOX*" to the Korean word "*nok sɯ*" (녹스) is [KN $\rightarrow$ n, O $\rightarrow$ o, X $\rightarrow$ k, *null* $\rightarrow$ s, *null* $\rightarrow$ ɯ]. The *null* $\rightarrow$ s and *null* $\rightarrow$ ɯ mappings are merged into the previous alignment to generate X $\rightarrow$ ksɯ. Finally, we get the one-to-one alignment as [KN $\rightarrow$ n, O $\rightarrow$ o, X $\rightarrow$ ksɯ].

After the processing of the bidirectional alignments, we transform the training data into one-to-one substring mapping pairs. These substrings pairs are used as token set fro the CRF training. A few pairs in the training data cannot be aligned one-to-one such as "THAILAND" to /t^{h}a i/ (타이) because they are not actual transliterations. We drop these pairs from the training data because CRF can handle one-to-one alignments only.

In addition, since Korean is a phonological writing system, for non-standard runs, we also adopt phonemic information for English name entities. The English word pronunciations are obtained from the CMU Pronouncing Dictionary v0.7a[1]. The CMU pronouncing dictionary provides the phonemic representations of English pronunciations with a sequence of phoneme symbols. For instance, the English word *KNOX* is segmented and tagged as the phonemic representation $<$ N AA K S $>$. Since the CMU pronouncing dictionary does not cover all the pronunciation information of the name entities in the training data, we also apply LOGIOS Lexicon Tool[2] to generate the phonemic representations of all other name entities not in the CMU pronouncing dictionary. After obtaining the phonemic representation of all the English named entities in the training data, we formulate the sequence of phoneme symbols of the English name entities as a string and apply the substring alignment method mentioned earlier to get the mappings from English phoneme symbols to Korean letters. For the previous example, the phoneme symbols $<$ N AA K S $>$ from the English name entity *KNOX* are aligned to the letters

[1] `http://www.speech.cs.cmu.edu./cgi-bin/cmudict`

[2] `http://www.speech.cs.cmu.edu/tools/lextool.html`

of its corresponding Korean word "*nok sɯ*" as [N → n, AA → o, K → k, S → sɯ]. We name this substring alignment based on the English phonemic representation as "phoneme substring-based" method for non-standard run, and the substring alignment based on the English orthography as "grapheme substring-based" for standard run.

2.1.3 CRF training

With the transformed substring training data, we now use CRF to train a sequential model with the substrings as the basic tokens. We adopt the CRF++ open-source toolkit (Kudo, 2005).

We train our CRF models with the unigram , bigram, and trigram features over the input substrings in the source language. The features are shown in the following.

- Unigram: s_{-1}, s_0, and s_1
- Bigram: $s_{-1}s_0$
- Trigram: $s_{-2}s_{-1}s_0$, $s_{-1}s_0s_1$, and $s_0s_1s_2$

where current substring is s_0 and s_i is other substrings relative to the position of the current substring.

2.1.4 Substring segmentation and transliteration

Because our method is based on the substrings from the transformed training data, we have to segment the unseen English named entities into the substrings before applying CRF testing of our model. For example, we have to segment the English named entity "SHASHI" into four substrings $<$ SH A SH I $>$. Since the substrings used to train the CRF model are generated by the bidirectional alignments from the training data, we also used CRF to train another model for substring segmentation of English named entities.

We adopt the segmentation approach motivated by the Chinese segmentation (Tsai et al., 2006) which treat Chinese segmentation as a tagging problem. The characters in a sentence are tagged in **B** class if it is the first character of a Chinese word or in **I** class if it is in a Chinese word but not the first character. Thus, we collect all the substring results from the bidirectional alignments and tag each character in the English named entity in the training data as **B** class (the first character of the substring) or **I** class (not the first character of the substring) to create a training data of substring segmentation for CRF. Since each character should belong to one substring, we need only **B** and **I** classes in the tag sets.

After the English named entities are segmented into substrings, it can be passed into the CRF model we trained in section 2.1.3 as input data to produce the transliteration results.

The transliteration results predicted by the CRF model is an romanized representation of Korean letters. Therefore, the romanized representation sequences should be converted back to Korean syllabic blocks. Because the position information of each Korean letters in the syllabic blocks (leading consonant, vowel and tailing consonant mentioned in section 2.1.1) does not remain while training, we have to organize the sequential letters into blocks based on the Korean orthography. Korean orthographic rules are applied to combine the letters into syllabic blocks. For example, the sequential Korean letters "ㅁ, ㅏ, ㄱ, ㅅ, ㅣ" (m, a, k, s, i) are combined into two syllabic blocks "막시" (mak-si) to make "k" in the tailing consonant position of the first syllable and "s" in the leading consonant position of the second syllable because consonant clusters are not allowed in a Korean syllabic block. Besides, between the successive vowel letters, the zero consonant letter " ㅇ " is inserted because of Korean orthography.

2.2 Rule-based Approach

We also construct a rule-based transliteration system. According to the "외래어 표기법" (Korean writing method of loanwords)[3] standardized by the National Institute of Korean Language, we build a transliteration mapping table from international phonetic alphabet (IPA) to Korean letters. The phonemic representations of English name entities in the test set are first extracted by the CMU Pronouncing Dictionary and LOGIOS Lexicon Tool. Then, each phoneme symbol is transliterated into corresponding Korean letter based on the transliteration mapping table. The results generated by the mapping table need to be composed into Korean syllabic blocks. We use the same technique described in section 2.1.4 to produce the final results of the rule-based method.

3 Results

Table 1 shows the final results of our transliteration approaches on the test data. We construct four

[3]http://www.korean.go.kr/09_new/dic/rule/rule_foreign_0101.jsp

Run	Accuracy	Mean F-score	MRR	MAP_{ref}
Grapheme substring-based	**0.430**	**0.711**	0.430	**0.423**
Phoneme substring-based	0.332	0.653	0.332	0.325
Rule-based	0.215	0.474	0.215	0.209
Mixed	0.332	0.653	**0.467**	0.332

Table 1: Final results on the test data

runs as following.

- **Grapheme substring-based**: CRF model with the substring training set based on English orthography.
- **Phoneme substring-based**: CRF model with the substring training set based on English phonemic representations.
- **Rule-based**: transliteration mapping table from English phonemes to Korean letters.
- **Mixed**: union of the results from the previous three runs in the order of Phoneme substring-based, Grapheme substring-based and Rule-based.

The results show that the grapheme-based approach achieves better than others in the four evaluation metrics. The rule-based one does not perform well due to the rules from the Korean writing method of loanwords may not be enough to cover most possible cases of the transliteration detailedly. However, the result of the phoneme substring-based approach is not as good as the grapheme substring-based one. It might be due to two reasons: one is that the Korean transliteration sometimes is based on the orthography not the actual pronunciation; the second reason is that the pronunciation from LOGIOS lexicon tool may not be accurate to get the correct phonemic forms. The phoneme substring-based and rule-based approaches suffer such problems. The performance of the mixed run which merged the results of above three runs shows that the joint result of different methods can help cover more possible transliterations.

4 Conclusion

In this paper, we adopt the substring-based transliteration approach with CRF model for English-Korean named entity transliteration. The characters in the source and target language are aligned in bi-direction and then group into substrings to generate the substring mappings from the source language to the target language. Then, the transliteration is formulated as a sequential tagging problem to tag the substrings in the source language with the substrings in the target language. The CRF algorithm is used to deal with this tagging problem. For English substring generation, we create two types of substrings. One is based on the English orthography, and the other is based on the phonemic symbols from the CMU pronouncing dictionary. In addition, we also construct a rule-based transliteration system based on the Korean writing method of loanwords from the National Institute of Korean language. From the evaluation results, the substring-based method based on the English orthography performs better than other runs.

For future work, we plan to add more phonetic features for the CRF training and try to integrate the CRF-based statistical based method and the rule-based methods to improve the transliteration performance. We also try to apply the re-ranking techniques from the web data to get better transliteration results.

References

Taku Kudo. 2005. CRF++: Yet another CRF toolkit. Available at http://chasen.org/ttaku/software/ctf++/.

Franz Josef Och and Hermann Ney. 2003. A systematic comparison of various statistical alignment models. *Computational Liguistics*, 29(4):417–449.

Sravana Reddy and Sonjia Waxmonsky. 2009. Substring-based transliteration with conditional random fields. *Proceedings of the 2009 Named Entities Workshop, ACL-IJCNLP*, pages 92–95.

Richard Tzong-Han Tsai, Hsieh-Chuan Hung, Cheng-Lung Sung, Hong-Jie Dai, , and Wen-Lian Hsu. 2006. On closed task of chinese word segmentation: An improved crf model coupled with character clustering and automatically generated template matching. *Proceedings of the Fifth SIGHAN Workshop on Chinese Language Processin*, pages 134–137.

Leveraging Transliterations from Multiple Languages

Aditya Bhargava, Bradley Hauer, and **Grzegorz Kondrak**
Department of Computing Science
University of Alberta
Edmonton, Alberta, Canada, T6G 2E8
{ab31,bmhauer,gkondrak}@ualberta.ca

Abstract

While past research on machine transliteration has focused on a single transliteration task, there exist a variety of supplemental transliterations available in other languages. Given an input for English-to-Hindi transliteration, for example, transliterations from other languages such as Japanese or Hebrew may be helpful in the transliteration process. In this paper, we propose the application of such supplemental transliterations to English-to-Hindi machine transliteration via an SVM re-ranking method with features based on n-gram alignments as well as system and alignment scores. This method achieves a relative improvement of over 10% over the base system used on its own. We further apply this method to system combination, demonstrating just under 5% relative improvement.

1 Introduction

The focus of significant previous work in machine transliteration, including that presented at past NEWS Shared Tasks (Li et al., 2009; Kumaran et al., 2010b), has been on single transliteration tasks in isolation of other other languages. This is despite the fact that the various languages provided represent a significant quantity of potentially useful data that is being ignored. In this NEWS 2011 Shared Task submission, we present a method which beneficially applies supplemental transliterations from other languages to English-to-Hindi transliteration.

In practice, this is a realistic situation in which transliterations from other languages can help. For example, Wikipedia contains articles on guitarist John Petrucci in English and Japanese, but not in Hindi. If we wanted to automatically generate a stub (skeleton) article in Hindi, we would need to transliterate his name into Hindi. Since a Japanese version already exists, we could extract from it additional information to help with the transliteration process. Importantly, since our article is about an American guitarist, we would explicitly want to start with the English (original) version of the name, and treat other languages as extra data, rather than vice versa.

In order to effectively incorporate the other-language data, we apply SVM re-ranking in a manner that has previously been shown to provide significant improvement for grapheme-to-phoneme conversion (Bhargava and Kondrak, 2011). This method is flexible enough to incorporate multiple languages; it employs features based on character alignments between potential outputs and existing transliterations from other languages, as well as scores of these alignments, which serve as a measure of similarity. We apply this approach on top of the same DIRECTL+ system as submitted last year (Jiampojamarn et al., 2010b) for English-to-Hindi machine transliteration. Compared to the base DIRECTL+ performance, we are able to achieve significantly better results, with a relative performance increase of over 10%. We also achieve improvements without supplemental transliterations by simply apply the same approach with another *system*'s output as extra data. We furthermore experiment with romanization for Hindi data as well as different alignment length settings for English-to-Chinese transliteration. This paper presents methods, methodology, and results for the above experiments.

2 Leveraging multiple transliterations

Bhargava and Kondrak (2011) present a method for applying transliterations to grapheme-to-phoneme conversion. Here, we apply this method verbatim to machine transliteration. The method is based on SVM re-ranking applied over n-best output lists generated by a base system. Intuitively, we have

Proceedings of the 2011 Named Entities Workshop, IJCNLP 2011, pages 36–40,
Chiang Mai, Thailand, November 12, 2011.

an existing base transliteration system that, for a given input, provides a set of n scored outputs, with the correct output not always appearing in the top position. In order to help bring the correct output to the top, we turn to existing transliterations of the input *from other languages*. In order to leverage a variety of features and transliterations from all available languages, SVM re-ranking is applied to this task.

For each output, a feature vector is constructed. Given alignments between the input and output, for example, binary indicator features based on grouping input and output n-grams in the style of DIRECTL+ (Jiampojamarn et al., 2010a) are constructed. The base system's score for the output would be included as well, along with differences between the given output's score and the scores for the other outputs in the list. This feature construction process is then repeated, replacing the input with an available transliteration, for each available transliteration language. The score in this latter case is used as a measure of how "similar" a candidate output is to a "reference" transliteration from another language. We refer to these other transliterations as *supplemental* transliterations. While the score features provide a global measure of similarity, the n-gram features allow weights to be learned for character combinations between the candidate output and supplemental transliterations; this provides very fine-grained features that can explicitly use certain characters in supplemental transliterations to help determine the quality of a candidate output.

There are, however, some practicalities that must be considered. Bhargava and Kondrak (2011) note the importance of applying multiple languages; they found it difficult to achieve significant improvements using transliterations from one language only. This is due in part to noise in the data (which has been observed in some of the NEWS Shared Task data (Jiampojamarn et al., 2009)) as well as differing conventions for various transliteration "schemes". These issues are handled implicitly in two ways: (1) the granularity of the n-gram features allows certain character combinations in the transliteration to be learned as being positive or negative indicators of a candidate output's quality, or that they should be ignored altogether; and (2) the use of multiple transliterations helps smooth out some of the noise. While we do not examine these methods here for brevity's sake, Bhargava and Kondrak (2011) show the effectiveness of the granular n-gram features vs. the score features as well as the importance of applying multiple transliteration languages.

3 Alignment of training data

Practically, we must consider how to generate the alignments between the candidate output transliterations and the supplemental transliterations for the n-gram features, as well as how to generate the similarity scores. M2M-ALIGNER (Jiampojamarn et al., 2007) addresses both of these. M2M-ALIGNER is an unsupervised character alignment system, meaning that it can learn to align data given sufficient training data consisting of unaligned input-output pairs. Once trained, M2M-ALIGNER will then produce an alignment for a new pair as well as an alignment score. Because the algorithm is a many-to-many extension of the unsupervised edit distance algorithm, we can see that the alignment score should represent some notion of script-agnostic similarity.

Since we will be applying M2M-ALIGNER between candidate output transliterations and supplemental transliterations for a variety of supplemental languages, we will need to build several alignment models, each being built from separate training data. The majority of the task data are English-source, so for any entry in one language corpus we can easily find corresponding transliterations in other language corpora. In other words, to generate training data for M2M-ALIGNER between the target transliteration language and a supplemental language, we need only intersect the two corpora on the basis of the common English input.

Table 1 shows the amount of overlap between the test data for the different English-source languages and the combined training and development data for the other English-source languages. Note that the Chinese- and Korean-target corpora show very high coverage; however, we focus on English-to-Hindi transliteration as it enables us to more closely examine the outputs based on our own linguistic familiarities. The use of other corpora here requires that these results be submitted as a non-standard run. Note that, because there is not complete coverage for the English-to-Hindi test data, we simply submit the base system's results as-is in cases where there is no transliteration available from other languages.

Language	Test set	Overlap
EnBa	1,000	498
EnCh	2,000	2,000
EnHe	1,000	525
EnHi	1,000	889
EnJa	1,815	734
EnKa	1,000	883
EnKo	609	608
EnPe	2,000	1,049
EnTa	1,000	884
EnTh	2,000	1,564

Table 1: The number of entries in the test data (per language) that have at least one supplemental transliteration available from another language corpus.

4 Base systems

Our principal base system that generates the n-best output lists is DIRECTL+, which has produced excellent results in the NEWS 2010 Shared Task on Transliteration (Jiampojamarn et al., 2010b). For re-ranking, note that training a re-ranker requires training data where the base system scores are representative of unseen data so that the re-ranker does not simply learn to follow the base system; we therefore split the training data into ten folds and perform a sort-of cross validation with DIRECTL+. This provides us with usable training data for re-ranking. We tune the SVM's hyperparameter based on performance on the provided development data, and use the best DIRECTL+ settings established in the NEWS 2010 Shared Task (Jiampojamarn et al., 2010b). Armed with optimal parameter settings, we combine the training and development data into a single set used to train our final DIRECTL+ system. We also repeat the cross-validation process for training the re-ranker.

We also apply the SVM re-ranking approach to system combination. In this case, we additionally train another system—here we use SEQUITUR (Bisani and Ney, 2008)—for English-to-Hindi transliteration. During test time, we feed the input into *both* DIRECTL+ and SEQUITUR, and use the top SEQUITUR output as supplemental data. We expect that sometimes SEQUITUR will provide a correct answer where DIRECTL+ does not; the hope is that the SVM re-ranking approach will be able to learn when this is the case based on the n-gram and score features.

Language	Type	System	Acc.
EnHi	Standard	DTL	47.1
EnHi	Standard	DTL+Rom.	45.7
EnHi	Standard	DTL+SEQ	49.3
EnHi	Non-Std.	DTL+Supp.	52.1
EnCh	Standard	DTL 3-1	34.1
	Standard	DTL 7-1	28.7
EnJa	Standard	DTL	43.5

Table 2: Word accuracy (%) for the various submitted runs. DTL is generic DIRECTL+; DTL+Rom. is DIRECTL+ trained on romanized data; DTL+SEQ is DIRECTL+ re-ranked with SEQUITUR outputs; and DTL+Supp. is DIRECTL+ re-ranked with supplemental transliteration data from other languages.

5 Hindi romanization

In addition to the above re-ranking approach, we experimented with a romanization method for the Hindi data. Since consonant characters in the Devanagari alphabet have vowels included by default, we romanize the text in order to provide DIRECTL+ with direct individual control over the consonant and vowel components of the Hindi characters. The default vowel is changed by means of diacritic-like characters, which in turn deletes the default vowel; this requires a context-sensitive (but still rule-based) romanization method, which we construct manually. We then train DIRECTL+ on the romanized data; during testing, we take the romanized output and convert it back into Devanagari Unicode characters, again using a manually-constructed context-sensitive rule-based converter.

6 Results

Table 2 shows that SVM re-ranking significantly improves the English-to-Hindi transliteration accuracy in comparison with the base system. Leveraging all of the English-source transliteration corpora as supplemental data yields an increase of over 10%. When applied using SEQUITUR's output as "supplemental" data, we see almost a 5% (relative) increase in word accuracy.

In contrast, our Hindi romanization approach decreases the accuracy. This differs from the results of the successful application of romanization to Japanese (Jiampojamarn et al., 2010b), demonstrating that it is not always possible to transfer an idea from one language to another.

The English-to-Chinese results, which use only the base DIRECTL+ system, demonstrate the importance of the alignment length parameter setting. DIRECTL+ requires aligned data for input, and the maximum length of the alignments will have an effect on what DIRECTL+ learns to produce. We submitted both 3-to-1 and 7-to-1 alignments because they gave similar results during development, and both were better than other tested possibilities. In the final results, we see a substantial difference between the two alignment settings. We hypothesize that the complexity of English-to-Chinese mappings is better captured by the alignments that map longer sequences of English letters to single Chinese characters. making it difficult to generalize to new data.

Finally, we observe very good overall accuracy in the English-to-Japanese results (which also only use base DIRECTL+), which further confirm the effectiveness of DIRECTL+ when applied to machine transliteration.

7 Previous work

There are three lines of research that are relevant to the work we have presented in this paper: (1) DIRECTL+ and SEQUITUR for machine transliteration; (2) applying multiple languages; and (3) system combination.

For the NEWS 2009 and 2010 Shared Tasks, the discriminative DIRECTL+ system that incorporates many-to-many alignments, online max-margin training and a phrasal decoder was shown to function well as a general string transduction tool; while originally designed for grapheme-to-phoneme conversion, it produced excellent results for machine transliteration (Jiampojamarn et al., 2009; Jiampojamarn et al., 2010b), leading us to re-use it here. Finch and Sumita (2010) also submitted a top-performing system that was based in part on SEQUITUR, which is a generative system based on joint n-gram modelling (Bisani and Ney, 2008).

In this paper, we applied multiple transliteration languages to a single transliteration task. While our method is based on SVM re-ranking with similar features as to those used in the base system (Bhargava and Kondrak, 2011), there have been other explorations into incorporating other language data, particularly when data are scarce. Zhang et al. (2010), for example, apply a pivoting approach to machine transliteration, and similarly Khapra et al. (2010) propose to transliterate through "bridge" languages. Along similar lines, Kumaran et al. (2010a) find increases in accuracy using a linear-combination-of-scores system that combined the outputs of a direct transliteration system with a system that transliterated through a third language. For statistical machine translation, Cohn and Lapata (2007) also explore the use of a third language.

Finally, we also touched briefly on system combination: we applied the SVM re-ranking method to combining the outputs of both DIRECTL+ and SEQUITUR, in particular treating DIRECTL+ as the base system and using SEQUITUR's best outputs to re-rank DIRECTL+'s output lists. Finch and Sumita (2010), in contrast, combine SEQUITUR's output with that of a phrase-based statistical machine translation system, achieving excellent results. Where our approach is based on SVM re-ranking, theirs merged the outputs of the two systems together and then used a linear combination of the system scores to re-rank the combined list.

8 Conclusion

In this paper, we described our submission to the NEWS 2011 Shared Task on machine transliteration. Our focus was on incorporating supplemental data, using a method based on SVM re-ranking, with features derived from n-gram alignments and alignment scores. We demonstrated improvements of over 10% when applying other transliteration data to English-to-Hindi machine transliteration, and just under 5% when applying another system's outputs in a similar manner. We also found that the romanization of Hindi characters brings about a decrease in performance, and that the alignment length parameter in the DIRECTL+ system has a critical effects on the results.

Acknowledgements

We are grateful to Ying Xu for examining our initial Chinese results. This research was supported by the Natural Sciences and Engineering Research Council of Canada.

References

Aditya Bhargava and Grzegorz Kondrak. 2011. How do you pronounce your name? Improving G2P with transliterations. In *Proceedings of the 49th Annual*

Meeting of the Association for Computational Linguistics: Human Language Technologies, Portland, Oregon, USA, June. Association for Computational Linguistics.

Maximilian Bisani and Hermann Ney. 2008. Joint-sequence models for grapheme-to-phoneme conversion. *Speech Communication*, 50(5):434–451, May.

Trevor Cohn and Mirella Lapata. 2007. Machine translation by triangulation: Making effective use of multi-parallel corpora. In *Proceedings of the 45th Annual Meeting of the Association of Computational Linguistics*, pages 728–735, Prague, Czech Republic, June. Association for Computational Linguistics.

Andrew Finch and Eiichiro Sumita. 2010. Transliteration using a phrase-based statistical machine translation system to re-score the output of a joint multigram model. In *Proceedings of the 2010 Named Entities Workshop*, pages 48–52, Uppsala, Sweden, July. Association for Computational Linguistics.

Sittichai Jiampojamarn, Grzegorz Kondrak, and Tarek Sherif. 2007. Applying many-to-many alignments and hidden Markov models to letter-to-phoneme conversion. In *Human Language Technologies 2007: The Conference of the North American Chapter of the Association for Computational Linguistics; Proceedings of the Main Conference*, pages 372–379, Rochester, New York, USA, April. Association for Computational Linguistics.

Sittichai Jiampojamarn, Aditya Bhargava, Qing Dou, Kenneth Dwyer, and Grzegorz Kondrak. 2009. DirecTL: a language independent approach to transliteration. In *Proceedings of the 2009 Named Entities Workshop: Shared Task on Transliteration (NEWS 2009)*, pages 28–31, Suntec, Singapore, August. Association for Computational Linguistics.

Sittichai Jiampojamarn, Colin Cherry, and Grzegorz Kondrak. 2010a. Integrating joint n-gram features into a discriminative training framework. In *Human Language Technologies: The 2010 Annual Conference of the North American Chapter of the Association for Computational Linguistics*, pages 697–700, Los Angeles, California, USA, June. Association for Computational Linguistics.

Sittichai Jiampojamarn, Kenneth Dwyer, Shane Bergsma, Aditya Bhargava, Qing Dou, Mi-Young Kim, and Grzegorz Kondrak. 2010b. Transliteration generation and mining with limited training resources. In *Proceedings of the 2010 Named Entities Workshop*, pages 39–47, Uppsala, Sweden, July. Association for Computational Linguistics.

Mitesh M. Khapra, A Kumaran, and Pushpak Bhattacharyya. 2010. Everybody loves a rich cousin: An empirical study of transliteration through bridge languages. In *Human Language Technologies: The 2010 Annual Conference of the North American Chapter of the Association for Computational Linguistics*, pages 420–428, Los Angeles, California, June. Association for Computational Linguistics.

A. Kumaran, Mitesh M. Khapra, and Pushpak Bhattacharyya. 2010a. Compositional machine transliteration. *ACM Transactions on Asian Language Information Processing (TALIP)*, 9(4):13:1–29, December.

A. Kumaran, Mitesh M. Khapra, and Haizhou Li. 2010b. Report of NEWS 2010 Transliteration Mining Shared Task. In *Proceedings of the 2010 Named Entities Workshop*, pages 21–28, Uppsala, Sweden, July. Association for Computational Linguistics.

Haizhou Li, A. Kumaran, Vladimir Pervouchine, and Min Zhang. 2009. Report of NEWS 2009 Machine Transliteration Shared Task. In *Proceedings of the 2009 Named Entities Workshop: Shared Task on Transliteration (NEWS 2009)*, pages 1–18, Suntec, Singapore, August. Association for Computational Linguistics.

Min Zhang, Xiangyu Duan, Vladimir Pervouchine, and Haizhou Li. 2010. Machine transliteration: Leveraging on third languages. In *Coling 2010: Posters*, pages 1444–1452, Beijing, China, August. Coling 2010 Organizing Committee.

Comparative Evaluation of Spanish Segmentation Strategies for Spanish-Chinese Transliteration

Rafael E. Banchs
Human Language Technology Department, Institute for Infocomm Research
1 Fusionopolis Way, #21-01 Connexis South, Singapore 138632
rembanchs@i2r.a-star.edu.sg

Abstract

This work presents a comparative evaluation among three different Spanish segmentation strategies for Spanish-Chinese transliteration. The transliteration task is implemented by means of Statistical Machine Translation, using Chinese characters and Spanish sub-word segments as the textual units to be translated. Three different Spanish segmentation strategies are evaluated: character-based, syllabic-based and a proposed sub-syllabic segmentation scheme. Experimental results show that syllabic-based segmentation is the most effective strategy for Spanish-to-Chinese transliteration, while the proposed sub-syllabic segmentation is the most effective scheme in the case of Chinese-to-Spanish transliteration.

1 Introduction

Transliteration can be defined as the process of transcribing a word from one language to another by using the characters of the latter's alphabet. This actually constitutes a "phonetic translation of names across languages" (Zhang *et al.*, 2011). Transliteration is typically used to construct appropriate translations for words that either do not have specific equivalents or are inexistent in the target language, such as, for instance, names of people, institutions or geographical locations.

Although they are conceptually similar tasks, technically speaking, translation and transliteration exhibit some important differences. For instance, while translation mainly operates at the word level, transliteration does it at the sub-word level. Perhaps, the most important difference is the fact that in the transliteration task, reordering of units is not required. As in the case of translation, transliteration results are not necessarily unique, i.e. one word might have different valid transliterations.

The transliteration task can be approached from either a rule-based or a statistical perspective, but in any case, the problem can be theoretically grounded on Finite-state Automata Theory (Knight, 2009). Several different approaches to transliteration have been proposed in the literature (Arbabi *et al.*, 1994; Divay and Vitale, 1997; Knight and Graehl, 1998; Al-Onaizan and Knight, 2002; Li *et al.*, 2004; Tao *et al.*, 2006; Yoon *et al.*, 2007; Jansche and Sproat, 2009) covering specific transliteration tasks between English and a large variety of languages such as Japanese (Knight and Graehl, 1998), French (Divay and Vitale, 1997), Arabic (Arbabi *et al.*, 1994; Al-Onaizan and Knight, 2002), Chinese (Ren et al., 2009; Kwong, 2009), Hindi (Chinnakotla and Damani, 2009; Das *et al.*, 2009; Haque *et al.*, 2009), Tamil (Vijayanand, 2009) and Korean (Hong *et al.*, 2009), among others.

Nevertheless, despite of the large body of research on automatic transliteration, and as far as we are concerned, there have not been research efforts reported on this area for the specific case of Spanish and Chinese. According to this, the main objective of this work is twofold: first, to create an experimental dataset for transliteration between Chinese and Spanish; and, second, to report some research results on transliteration tasks between these two languages.

The remaining of the paper is structured as follows. First, in section 2, the main technical issue evaluated in this work, which is the segmentation of Spanish words into sub-word units, is introduced and motivated. Then, in section 3, the selected SMT-based approach for Chinese-Spanish transliteration, is described. In section 4, the creation of an experimental dataset for Chinese-Spanish transliteration is described in detail. In section 5, experimental results are presented and discussed. Finally, in section 6, main conclusions and future research ideas are provided.

Proceedings of the 2011 Named Entities Workshop, IJCNLP 2011, pages 41–48,
Chiang Mai, Thailand, November 12, 2011.

2 Spanish Word Segmentation

The concept of isochronism in language was first introduced by Pike (1945). Three types of rhythmic patterns can be distinguished: stress-timed, syllable-timed and mora-timed. Although this theory has not been fully accepted, there is some accepted empirical evidence that both Spanish (Pamies Bertran, 1999) and Chinese (Lin and Wang, 2007) belong to the syllable-timed rhythmic group.

In the case of Chinese, syllabic segmentation is naturally induced by the basic association between the characters and their corresponding sounds. On the contrary, in the case of Spanish, as well as many other western languages, syllabic segmentation is a phonetic property that does not exhibit a direct or explicit association with orthographic properties of the language.

According to this, syllabic segmentation or syllabification constitutes a problem of interest in some natural language processing applications. This problem can be addressed by means of either rule-based or data-driven approaches (Adsett *et al.*, 2009). Syllabification algorithms based on finite-state transducers have been proposed for languages such as English and German (Kiraz and Mobius, 1998). For the effects of the present work, we implemented our own rule-based syllabic segmentation algorithm for Spanish by following the work of Cuayahuitl (2004).

Three different strategies for Spanish word segmentation are studied in this work with the objective of determining the most appropriate segmentation scheme for Chinese-Spanish transliteration. These three strategies are: character segmentation (the simple division of a word in characters), syllabic segmentation (the division of a word according to Spanish syllabic phonetic units) and an intermediate segmentation to be referred to as sub-syllabic segmentation. The rest of this section is devoted to motivate and explain this latter segmentation scheme.

The main motivation for the proposed sub-syllabic segmentation of Spanish words is the observed fact that, although they agree in most of the cases, syllabifications can often differ between Spanish and Chinese transliterated names. Consider, for instance, the examples presented in Figure 1. The first two examples illustrate cases in which the Chinese name contains less syllables than the corresponding Spanish name. On the other hand, the last three examples illustrate cases in which the Chinese name contains more syllables than the corresponding Spanish name.

Chinese	– Pinyin	Spanish
马其顿	– mǎ qí dùn	ma ce do nia
亚略巴古	– yà è ba gǔ	a re ó pa go
亚历山大	– yà lì shān dà	a le jan dro
塞缪尔	– sāi móu ěr	sa muel
亚伯拉罕	– yà bó lā hǎn	a bra ham
埃利亚斯	– āi lì yà sī	e lí as

Figure 1. Some examples of Chinese-Spanish name transliterations

A detailed analysis on the syllabic length ratios between Chinese and Spanish names on our experimental dataset (more details on the dataset are provided in section 4) reveals that the most common situation is that both Chinese and Spanish names have the same number of syllables. This occurs in about 75% of the cases. From the remaining 25% of cases, about 15% (and 10%) correspond to cases in which the Chinese versions of the names contain more (and less) syllables than their corresponding Spanish versions.

Further analysis show that some clear patterns for sub-syllabic segmentation can be observed in those cases of Chinese transliterations containing more syllables than their corresponding Spanish versions, which is not the case for the opposite situation. Some of these patterns include the segmentation of Spanish diphthongs such as *ue* into *u-e*, which will generate the more appropriate segmentation *sa-mu-el* for the fourth example in Figure 1; the separation of some multiple consonant constructions such as *br* into *b-r*, which will provide the more appropriate segmentation *a-b-ra-ham*; and the separation of some ending consonants such as *as* into *a-s*, which will generate *e-li-a-s*. This sub-syllabic segmentation strategy is expected to improve the performance of the transliteration task as it both reduces the vocabulary size of Spanish syllabic units and improves syllable correspondences between Chinese and Spanish. The complete set and sequence of rules implemented for sub-syllabic segmentation is presented in Figure 2.

Notice that the proposed sub-syllabic segmentation strategy is only addressing those cases in which the Chinese versions of the names contain more syllables than their corresponding Spanish versions. Addressing the opposite case, would require instead the definition of rules for merging consecutive Spanish syllables. We have not considered this case because of two reasons: first, according to our exploratory analysis of the data, it does not seem to be clear patterns for syllabic merging; and, second, a merging strategy would lead to an increment of the vocabulary of Spanish Syllabic units, which is not desirable in terms of the resulting transliteration model sparseness.

```
% Double consonant
([bcdfgpt])([lr]) → $1 $2

% Ending consonant
([aeiou])([bcdfghjklmnpqrstvwxz]) → $1 $2

% Diphthongs (first pass)
([aeiou])([aeiouy]) → $1 $2

% Diphthongs (second pass)
([aeiou])([aeiouy]) → $1 $2

% Diphthongs (exception correction)
([gq])u ([ei]) → $1u$2
```

Figure 2. Rules and their sequence of application for sub-syllabic segmentation

Notice that, those cases in which the Chinese versions of the names contain less syllables than their corresponding Spanish versions are basically unaddressed by our proposed segmentation strategy. This, however, should not constitute a problem in the case of Spanish-to-Chinese transliteration as the transliteration model just should be required to learn how to throw away some Spanish syllables. On the other hand, this certainly posses a problem for the case of Chinese-to-Spanish transliteration as the transliteration model must be able to generate Spanish syllables from no Chinese correspondents. However, we still expect an overall gain as the former case is more common that the latter one.

3 Transliteration Approach

For implementing the transliteration system, we have used the Phrase-Based Statistical Machine Translation approach, which has been proven to be a good strategy for transliteration (Noeman, 2009; Jia *et al.*, 2009). Within this approach, transliteration is performed as a machine translation task over substring units of both the source and the target languages. More specifically, we use the MOSES toolkit (Koehn *et al.*, 2007).

Although several parameters can be varied in order to study their effect over the overall transliteration performance, we will focus our study in three specific parameters, which we consider could have the largest incidence, as well as make an important difference, on quality for both transliterations directions under consideration: Spanish-to-Chinese and Chinese-to-Spanish.

The first parameter of interest is substring segmentation. Although we only consider Chinese characters as substring units for Chinese; in the case of Spanish, we consider three different types of substring units according to the three segmentation schemes described in the previous section. More specifically, characters, syllables and the proposed sub-syllabic units are considered for Spanish.

The other two parameters to be considered for evaluation purposes are the order of the target language model and the alignment strategy used for phrase extraction. In the case of the target language model, four different orders are compared, namely: *1*-gram, *2*-gram, *3*-gram and *4*-gram; and in the case of the alignment strategy, three different methods are compared, namely: source-to-target, target-to-source and grow-diag-final-and (Koehn *et al.*, 2007).

According to this, our experimental work involves the construction of 72 different transliteration systems, by considering 2 transliteration directions, 3 Spanish segmentation schemes, 4 target language model orders, and 3 alignment strategies. In each of these transliteration systems, the standard set of phrase-based features, which include the forward and backward relative frequencies and lexical models, as well as the target language and phrase-length penalty models, are used.

As evaluation metric for assessing transliteration quality we use the BLEU score (Papineni *et al.*, 2001). In the case of Spanish-to-Chinese transliterations, BLEU is computed at the Chinese character level. Similarly, and in order to make results among all three different Spanish segmentation schemes comparable, in the case of Chinese-to-Spanish transliterations, BLEU is computed at the character level too.

Finally, each of the implemented systems is tuned by means of the minimum error rate training procedure (Och, 2003), in which the BLEU score is minimized over a development dataset. Final system scores are computed over a test dataset, which is transliterated by using the tuned parameters. More details on the datasets are provided in the following section.

4 Dataset Construction

As no named entity dataset is available for transliteration purposes between Spanish and Chinese, the first objective of this work was the creation of such a dataset. Despite the fact that Chinese and Spanish are the most spoken native languages in the word, the amount of bilingual resources for this specific language pair happens to be very scarce (Costa-jussa *et al.* 2011).

According to this, we used one of the few bilingual resources that are available, the Holy Bible (Table 1 presents the basic statistics for this dataset), for constructing an experimental dataset for transliteration research purposes.

Language	Sentences	Words	Vocab.
Chinese	29,887	781,113	28,178
Spanish	29,887	848,776	13,126

Table 1. Basic statistics of the Bible dataset

In his section we present a description of the procedure followed for creating the dataset, as well as the basic statistics and characteristics of the constructed dataset.

The construction of the experimental dataset for transliteration can be summarized according to the following steps:

- A list of named entities was extracted from the Spanish side of the dataset. This extraction was conducted by using a standard labeling approach based on Conditional Random Fields (Lafferty *et al.*, 2001). From this step a list of 1,608 Spanish names were collected.

- A reduced list of named entities was generated by manually filtering the original list. In this process some errors derived from the first automatic step were removed, as well as any valid name entity not belonging to the two basic categories of persons and places. In this second step, the list was reduced to 948 names.

- The corresponding Chinese versions of the names were extracted from the Chinese side of the dataset. This was done automatically by aligning both corpus at the word level (Och and Ney, 2000), and using the alignment links to identify the corresponding transliteration candidates for each Spanish name in the list.

- The automatically extracted list of corresponding Chinese names was manually depurated. Because of the noisy nature of the alignment process, in several cases either more than one Chinese word was assigned to the same Spanish names or an erroneous Chinese word was selected. After this second filtering processing, the final bilingual list of 841 names was obtained.

For the preparation of the experimental dataset each side of the resulting corpus was segmented as follows: Chinese data was segmented at the character level, and Spanish data was segmented by following the three segmentation schemes described in section 2: character-based, syllable-based and sub-syllabic.

Two additional normalization processes were applied to the Spanish dataset: lowercasing and stress mark elimination. The total number of substring units and their vocabulary for each of the constructed versions of the dataset are presented in Table 2.

Dataset	Names	Substrings	Vocab.
Chinese	841	2,190	314
Spa (char)	841	4,766	24
Spa (sub)	841	3,005	108
Spa (syl)	841	2,165	491

Table 2. Names, substring units and vocabulary of substring units for each constructed dataset

As seen from the table, the tree Spanish word segmentations to be studied exhibit significantly different properties in terms of the total amount of running substrings and the vocabulary size of substring units. Indeed, the proposed sub-syllabic segmentation strategy represents an intermediate compromise in both, substrings and vocabulary, between the character-based segmentation and the syllabic-based segmentation.

In order to be able to use the generated dataset under the statistical machine translation framework described in section 3, the resulting bilingual dataset of 841 names was finally split into three subsets: train (with 691 names), development (with 50 names) and test (with 100 names).

Although a random sample strategy was used for splitting the original corpus into the three experimental subsets, special attention was paid to not include in the development and test subsets any name that would have produced out-of-vocabulary substrings.

5 Experimental Results

In this section we present and discuss the experimental results corresponding to all 72 implemented transliteration systems. All experiments were conducted over the experimental datasets described in section 4 by following the procedure described in section 3. Although we will focus our analysis on aggregated scores computed over different subsets of experiments, Tables 3a through 3f present individual system scores for all of the 72 implemented transliteration systems.

As seen from the tables, although individual results by themselves could exhibit some degree of noise due to the random variability derived from both, dataset selection and tuning processes, some clear and interesting trends can be observed form the results. For instance, notice how best scores tend to be always associated to language model of orders 3 and 4.

Similarly, it can be derived from the tables that the grow-diag-final-and alignment strategy tends to be the best alignment strategy only in those cases when the Spanish syllabic segmentation is used. Alternatively, it can be observed that in the other two cases, i.e. when Spanish character and sub-syllabic segmentations are used, the target-to-source alignment strategy is more beneficial for the Spanish-to-Chinese transliteration direction while the source-to-target alignment strategy happens to be more beneficial for the Chinese-to-Spanish direction.

In order to have a better grasp of the general trends in transliteration quality along the dimensions of each of the experimental parameters under consideration, let us now look at the aggregated results along each individual parameter variation. In this sense, Figures 3a, 3b and 3c summarize transliteration quality variations with respect to *n*-gram order, alignment strategy and Spanish segmentation, respectively.

Let us consider first Figure 3a. This figure shows the relative variations of transliteration quality with respect to *n*-gram order. These values have been computed by aggregating all system scores along the alignment strategy and Spanish segmentation dimensions for each of the two transliteration directions under consideration. Additionally, the resulting scores have been normalized with respect to the unigram case. As seen from the figure, there is a more critical incidence of the *n*-gram order on the case of Spanish-to-Chinese transliteration than in the opposite transliteration direction.

	src-2-trg	trg-2-src	g-d-f-a
1-gram	15.36	16.09	14.35
2-gram	18.98	21.87	19.43
3-gram	15.33	23.35	18.83
4-gram	18.19	24.05	19.85

Table 3a. BLEU scores for Spanish-to-Chinese systems with Spanish character segmentation

	src-2-trg	trg-2-src	g-d-f-a
1-gram	20.20	16.72	15.96
2-gram	15.58	22.85	15.37
3-gram	20.49	21.93	19.30
4-gram	21.80	21.72	19.17

Table 3b. BLEU scores for Spanish-to-Chinese systems with Spanish sub-syllabic segmentation

	src-2-trg	trg-2-src	g-d-f-a
1-gram	23.42	23.02	23.79
2-gram	25.27	24.28	31.98
3-gram	31.26	22.14	35.98
4-gram	30.83	24.41	35.48

Table 3c. BLEU scores for Spanish-to-Chinese systems with Spanish syllabic segmentation

	src-2-trg	trg-2-src	g-d-f-a
1-gram	38.38	33.96	35.58
2-gram	37.94	35.34	35.99
3-gram	35.41	39.34	37.21
4-gram	39.11	39.52	38.78

Table 3d. BLEU scores for Chinese-to-Spanish systems with Spanish character segmentation

	src-2-trg	trg-2-src	g-d-f-a
1-gram	40.17	36.53	39.94
2-gram	42.21	42.15	38.78
3-gram	39.67	43.03	40.89
4-gram	40.70	36.45	39.88

Table 3e. BLEU scores for Chinese-to-Spanish systems with Spanish sub-syllabic segmentation

	src-2-trg	trg-2-src	g-d-f-a
1-gram	37.50	30.74	37.77
2-gram	38.86	36.89	41.38
3-gram	38.66	37.20	40.83
4-gram	39.26	37.20	40.38

Table 3f. BLEU scores for Chinese-to-Spanish systems with Spanish syllabic segmentation

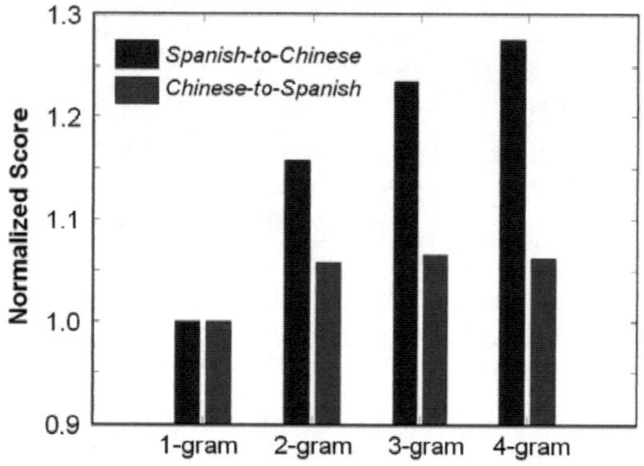

Figure 3a. Transliteration quality variations in terms of n-gram order

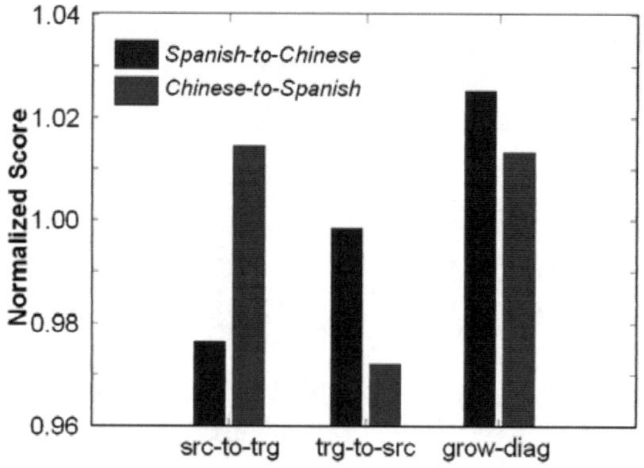

Figure 3b. Transliteration quality variations in terms of alignment strategy

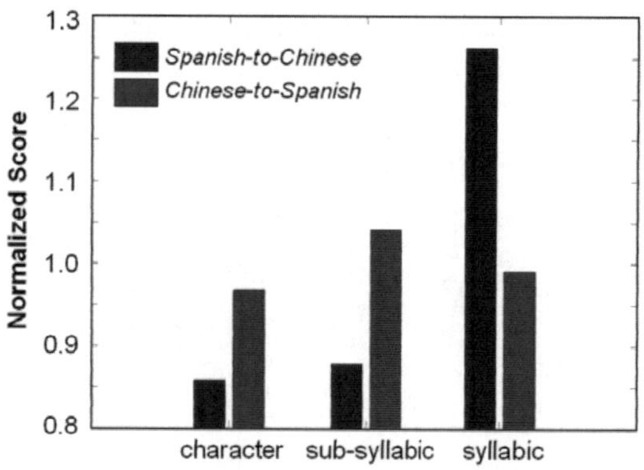

Figure 3c. Transliteration quality variations in terms of Spanish segmentation method

It is evident, from Figure 3a, that the transliteration tasks does not benefits from n-gram orders larger than 2 in the Chinese-to-Spanish direction, while it certainly does in the Spanish-to-Chinese case. This result can be explained by the larger character vocabulary size of Chinese when compared to Spanish segmentations.

In the case of Figure 3b, aggregation has been conducted along the n-gram orders and Spanish segmentations. In this case, the resulting scores have been normalized with respect to the average score value for each transliteration direction. While grow-diag-final-and is the best alignment strategy for the Spanish-to-Chinese case, source-to-target alignments also happen to be a good strategy in the Chinese-to-Spanish case. Notice, however, that relative variation of scores in Figure 3b is actually very low (about 2%), which suggests that the alignment strategy has a low incidence on transliteration quality for the tasks under consideration.

Finally, let us consider Figure 3c, where the relative variations of transliteration quality with respect to the selected Spanish segmentation method are depicted. In this cases system scores have been aggregated along both the n-gram order and the alignment strategy dimensions, and normalized with respect to average scores at each transliteration direction. Notice from the figure how syllabic segmentation is clearly the best option in the Spanish-to-Chinese transliteration direction, while the proposed sub-syllabic segmentation constitutes the best alternative in the Chinese-to-Spanish direction.

This latter interesting result can be explained in terms of the mapping functions required to map the corresponding substring units from one language into the other, as the larger the source vocabulary the better the mapping function is. So, in the case of the Spanish-to-Chinese task, the syllabic segmentation must provide a better mapping as it allows for a vocabulary reduction mapping, as can be verified from the vocabulary column in Table 2. On the other hand, in the Chinese-to-Spanish task the proposed method for sub-syllabic segmentation is the one providing a vocabulary reduction (as can be verified from the vocabulary column in Table 2) that allows for a better mapping function.

6 Conclusions and Future Research

In this work, we have presented a comparative evaluation among three different Spanish segmentation strategies for Spanish-Chinese transliteration, as well as two other important parameters of the transliteration system implementation: target language model order and alignment strategy for bilingual unit extraction. The transliteration task was implemented by means of Statistical Machine Translation, using Chinese characters and Spanish sub-word segments as the textual units to be translated. The three different Spanish segmentation strategies evaluated were: character-based, syllabic-based and a proposed sub-syllabic segmentation scheme. Experimental results shown that syllabic-based segmentation, along with a language model of order 4 and the grow-diag-final-and alignment method, constitutes the most effective strategy for Spanish-to-Chinese transliteration, while the proposed sub-syllabic segmentation, along with a language model of order 2 and the source-to-target alignment method, constitutes the most effective strategy for Chinese-to-Spanish transliteration.

As an additional contribution, and due to the lack of dataset for Chinese-Spanish transliteration research, we have constructed an experimental parallel corpus containing a total of 841 named entities in both Chinese and Spanish.

As future research work, we intend to expand the experimental dataset, as well as to continue evaluating the specific peculiarities of both Chinese-to-Spanish and Spanish-to-Chinese transliteration tasks. A comprehensive manual evaluation on the experimental results described here should be conducted in order to identify both, possible improvements to the proposed Spanish sub-syllabic segmentation method and some additional strategies for improving the performance of transliteration quality between Chinese and Spanish.

Acknowledgments

The author would like to thank the Institute for Infocomm Research (I^2R) and the Agency for Science, Technology And Research (A*STAR) for their support and permission to publish this work.

References

Connie R. Adsett, Yannick Marchand, and Vlado Keselj, 2009, Syllabification rules versus data-driven methods in a language with low syllabic complexity: The case of Italia*n, Computer Speech and Languages*, 23(4): 444-463.

Yaser Al-Onaizan and Kevin Knight, 2002, Machine Transliteration of names in Arabic text,In *Proceedings of the ACL Workshop on Computational Approaches to Semitic Languages*, Philadelphia, PA.

Mansur Arbabi, Scott M. Fischthal, Vincent C. Cheng, and Elizabeth Bart, 1994, Algorithms for Arabic name transliteration, *IBM Journal of Research and Development*, 38(2):183-193.

Manoj Kumar Chinnakotla, and Om P. Damani, 2009, Experiences with English-Hindi, English-Tamil and English-Kannada Transliteration Tasks at NEWS 2009, In *Proceedings of ACL-IJCNLP 2009 Named Entities Workshop* (NEWS 2009), pages 44-47, Singapore.

Marta R. Costa-jussa, Carlos A. Henriquez, and Rafael E. Banchs, 2011, Evaluating Indirect Strategies for Chinese-Spanish statistical machine translation with English as pivot language, In *Proceedings of the* 27th *Conference of the Spanish Society for Natural Language Processing*, Huelva, Spain.

Heriberto Cuayahuitl, 2004, A Syllabification Algorithm for Spanish, in A. Gelbukh (Ed.): CICLing 2004, LNCS 2945, pages 412-415, Springer.

Amitava Das, Asif Ekbal, Tapabrata Mondal, and Sivaji Bandyopadhyay, 2009, English to Hindi Machine Transliteration System at NEWS 2009, In *Proceedings of ACL-IJCNLP 2009 Named Entities Workshop* (NEWS 2009), pages 80-83, Singapore.

Michel Divay and Anthony J. Vitale, 1997, Algorithms for grapheme-phoneme translation for English and French: Applications, *Computational Linguistics*, 23(4):495-524.

Rejwanul Haque, Sandipan Dandapat, Ankit Kumar Srivastava, Sudip Kumar Naskar, and Andy Way, 2009, English-Hindi Transliteration Using Context-Informed PB-SMT: the DCU System for NEWS 2009, In *Proceedings of ACL-IJCNLP 2009 Named Entities Workshop* (NEWS 2009), pages 104-107, Singapore.

Gumwon Hong, Min-Jeong Kim, Do-Gil Lee, and Hae-Chang Rim, 2009, A Hybrid Approach to English-Korean Name Transliteration, In *Proceedings of ACL-IJCNLP 2009 Named Entities Workshop* (NEWS 2009), pages 108-111, Singapore.

Martin Jansche and Richard Sproat, 2009, Named Entity Transcription with Pair n-Gram Models, In *Proceedings of ACL-IJCNLP 2009 Named Entities Workshop* (NEWS 2009), pages 32-35, Singapore.

Yuxiang Jia, Danqing Zhu, Shiwen Yu, 2009, A Noisy Channel Model for Grapheme-based Machine Transliteration, In *Proceedings of ACL-IJCNLP 2009 Named Entities Workshop* (NEWS 2009), pages 88-91, Singapore.

G. A. Kiraz and B. Mobius, 1998, Multilingual syllabification using weighted finite-state transducers, In *Proceedings of the* 3rd *ESCA Workshop on Speech Synthesis*, Jenolan Caves, Australia.

Keving Knight and Jonathan Graehl, 1998, Machine Transliteration, *Computational Linguistics*, 24(4): 599-612.

Kevin Knight, 2009, Automata for Transliteration and Machine Translation, In *Proceedings of ACL-IJCNLP 2009 Named Entities Workshop* (NEWS 2009), page 27, Singapore.

P. Koehn, H. Hoang, A. Birch, C. Callison-Burch, M. Federico, N. Bertoldi, B. Cowan, W. Shen, C. Moran, R. Zens, C. Dyer, O. Bojar, A. Constantin, and E. Herbst, 2007, MOSES: Open source toolkit for statistical machine translation, In *Proceedings of the 45th ACL Annual Meeting*, pages 177-180, Prague, Czech Republic.

Oi Y. Kwong, 2009, Graphemic Approximation of Phonological Context for English-Chinese Transliteration, In *Proceedings of ACL-IJCNLP 2009 Named Entities Workshop* (NEWS 2009), pages 186-193, Singapore.

J. Lafferty, A. McCallum, and F. Pereira, 2001, Conditional Random Fields: Probabilistic models for segmenting and labeling sequence data, In *Proceedings of the International Conference on Machine Learning*, pages 282-289.

Haizhou Li, Min Zhang, and Jian Su, 2004, A joint source-channel model for machine transliteration, In *Proceedings of the 42nd ACL Annual Meeting*, pages 159-166, Barcelona, Spain.

Hua Lin and Qian Wang, 2007, Mandarin Rhythm: An Acoustic Study, *Journal of Chinese Language and Computing*, 17(3): 127-140.

Sara Noeman, 2009, Language Independent Transliteration system using phrase based SMT approach on substrings, In *Proceedings of ACL-IJCNLP 2009 Named Entities Workshop* (NEWS 2009), pages 112-115, Singapore.

Franz J. Och and Hermann Ney, 2000, A comparison of alignment models for statistical machine translation, In *Proceedings of the 18th Conference on Computational Linguistics*, pages 1086-1090, Morristown, NJ.

Franz J. Och, 2003, Minimum error rate training in statistical machine translation, *In Proceedings of the 41st ACL Annual Meeting*, pages 160-167, Sapporo, Japan.

Antonio Pamies Bertran, 1999, Prosodic Typology: On the Dichotomy between Stress-Timed and Syllable-Timed Languages, *Language Design*, 2: 103-130.

K. Papineni, S. Roukos, T. Ward, and W. J. Zhu, 2001, BLEU: a method for automatic evaluation of machine translation, *IBM Research Report RC-22176.*

Kenneth L. Pike, 1945, Step-by-step procedure for marking limited intonation with its related features of pause, stress and rhythm, in Charles C. Fries (Ed.), *Teaching and Learning English as a Foreign Language*, pages 62-74, Publication of the English Language Institute, University of Michigan, Ann Arbor.

Feiliang Ren, Muhua Zhu, Huizhen Wang, and Jingbo Zhu, 2009, Chinese-English Organization Name Translation Based on Correlative Expansion, In *Proceedings of ACL-IJCNLP 2009 Named Entities Workshop* (NEWS 2009), pages 143-151, Singapore.

Tao Tao, Su-Youn Yoon, Andrew Fister, Richard Sproat and Cheng-Xiang Zhai, 2006, Unsupervised Named Entity Transliteration Using Temporal and Phonetic Correlation, In *Proceedings of Empirical Methods in Natural Language Processing*, pages 22-23, Sydney, Australia.

Kommaluri Vijayanand, 2009, Testing and Performance Evaluation of Machine Transliteration System for Tamil Language, In *Proceedings of ACL-IJCNLP 2009 Named Entities Workshop* (NEWS 2009), pages 48-51, Singapore.

Su-Youn Yoon, Kyoung-Young Kim, and Richard Sproat, 2007, Multilingual Transliteration Using Feature based Phonetic Method, In *Proceedings of the 45th ACL Annual Meeting*, pages 112-119, Prague, Czech Republic.

Min Zhang, A. Kumaran, and Haizhou Li, 2011, Whitepaper of NEWS 2011 Shared Task on Machine Transliteration, In *Proceedings of IJCNLP 2011 Named Entities Workshop* (NEWS 2011), retrieved on June 15, 2011, from http://translit.i2r.a-star.edu.sg/news2011/news2011whitepaper.pdf

Using Features from a Bilingual Alignment Model in Transliteration Mining

Takaaki Fukunishi
Doshisha University
dtk0706@mail4.doshisha.ac.jp

Andrew Finch
NICT
andrew.finch@nict.go.jp

Seiichi Yamamoto
Doshisha University
seyamamo@mail.doshisha.ac.jp

Eiichiro Sumita
NICT
eiichiro.sumita@nict.go.jp

Abstract

In this paper we present a novel method for selecting transliteration word pairs from a set of candidate word pairs when mining for training data. Our method relies on a Bayesian technique that simultaneously co-segments and force-aligns the bilingual segments. The Bayesian model strongly rewards the re-use of features already present in its model, resulting in a very compact and efficient model. Our idea relies on the assumption that genuine transliteration pairs can be derived by using bilingual sequence pairs already present in the model, or at worst by introducing a very short unobserved pair into the derivation. We assume that incorrect pairs are likely to have larger contiguous segments that are costly to force-align with our model. We use features derived from the co-segmentation (alignment) of the candidate pair in combination with other heuristic features to train a classifier to label whether or not the candidate pair is a genuine transliteration pair. To evaluate our approach we used the all data-tracks from the 2010 Named-entity Workshop (NEWS2010). Our results show that the new features we propose are powerfully predictive, enabling our approach to achieve levels of performance on this task that are comparable to the state of the art.

1 Introduction

For some language pairs, especially those that use the same or very similar character sets, named entities are commonly unchanged in the process of translation between the languages. For example the term 'Michael Jackson' is used as is in the English, German and Italian languages. However, in languages that do not share the same writing system, such expressions are transcribed into the respective native writing system, usually in such a manner as to preserve the phonetics as far as possible. So for example, in Japanese the name would be transcribed into the katakana alphabet as マイケル・ジャクソン (MA-I-KE-RU・ JI-YA-KU-SO-N). The form in parentheses is a romanized (rōmaji) form of the preceding Japanese character sequence in Japanese script (katakana), where each roman character or character pair corresponds to a single character in the Japanese writing system, and furthermore corresponds very closely to the English phonetics of the character sequence. We will come back to this correspondence in the next section. This process of transcription from one language into another, usually based on phonetics, is known as transliteration.

Transliteration mining is the process of obtaining lists of bilingual word pairs (we will refer to these as *transliteration pairs*) automatically, that is pairs of words that are transliterations of each other in parallel or comparable corpora. The mined word pairs have many applications, for example as data for training a transliteration generation system, for the enhancement of the bilingual dictionary of a machine translation system to improve lexical coverage, and in query term translation for cross-language information retrieval.

2 Previous Work

The field of transliteration mining is currently being actively researched and there is a wealth of previous research (Brill et al., 2001; Lee and Chang, 2003a; Bilac and Tanaka, 2005; Tsuji and Kageura,

Proceedings of the 2011 Named Entities Workshop, IJCNLP 2011, pages 49–57,
Chiang Mai, Thailand, November 12, 2011.

2006; Oh and Isahara, 2006; Jiampojamarn et al., 2010; Darwish, 2010; Khapra et al., 2010; Nabende, 2010; Noeman and Madkour, 2010), and recently a shared task in the 2010 ACL Named Entities Workshop (NEWS2010) (Kumaran and Li, 2010).

One common strategy to determine cross-lingual phonetic similarity between words is to transcribe them into the roman alphabet and then use character level similarity measures to compare them, for example normalized edit distance (Jiampojamarn et al., 2010). In practice this seems to be an effective technique; in the previous example, it is easy to see that the romanized string 'maikeru jiyakuson' will be reasonably close in terms of edit distance to the English 'michael jackson', but very likely to be distanced from other English strings that it is not a transliteration of.

A large advantage of these approaches is that they can often be developed without the need to collect a training corpus. On the other hand, a potential drawback of these methods is that they are language dependent in nature, simply because they rely on a language specific romanization scheme. Furthermore, performance will depend on the particular romanization scheme chosen, and often there are several to choose from, in addition to bespoke romanization schemes that might be devised for this task (for example, deleting diacritics and performing character substitutions in European languages (Jiampojamarn et al., 2010)). In Japanese, for example, there are three main competing systems for romanizing Japanese kana characters: the Hepburn, Kunrei-shiki Rōmaji, and Nihon-shiki Rōmaji, romanization systems.

One way to eliminate this language dependency is to build a transliteration generation system to transduce a transliterated string into the other language, and then use a heuristic operating at the character level to measure the string-similarity between the two character sequences. This approach is taken by (Noeman and Madkour, 2010) who use an FST to generate a set of candidate transliterations and an FSA to accept those that can be used to form transliteration pairs. The approach is also used in the generation-based models of (Jiampojamarn et al., 2010), where forward and backward generated transliterations are compared by edit distance against the corresponding strings in the other languages; a score consisting of weighted edit distances of these comparisons in both directions was used to classify the candidate transliteration pair. Other examples of the use of this approach include: (Lee and Chang, 2003b; Tsuji and Kageura, 2006).

A second advantage of approaches that do not require a system for phonetically transcribing a language is that these approaches can handle non-phonetic transcriptions if necessary. For example, the words 'personal computer' would in Japanese be transcribed into 'PA-SO-KO-N', a contraction of the original word pair. The transcription of Japanese kanji into their rōmaji readings is another example commonly encountered in real-world Japanese named entity translation.

The approach we take in this paper is a direct approach that does not rely on an intermediate representation, but rather a direct grapheme-to-grapheme mapping between the languages. We use a generative model directly to assess whether two strings constitute a transliteration pair and avoid the necessity to explicitly generate strings in either language. This type of approach was taken by (Lee and Chang, 2003b), who use a noisy channel model to assess transliteration pair candidates. Our approach differs from theirs in the Bayesian model that we employ. Bayesian models such as the one we use have been successfully applied to transliteration generation (Finch and Sumita, 2010; Huang et al., 2011) and offer several benefits; primarily the technique has the ability to train models whilst avoiding over-fitting the data, and can typically construct compact models that have only a small number of well-chosen parameters. Our system further differs from theirs in that our underlying generative transliteration model is based on the joint source-channel model (Li et al., 2004), and is symmetric with respect to source and target language.

In the next section we will briefly describe the Dirichlet process model that drives the co-segmentation process that underpins our technique. We then present the methodology we use to exploit features from samples taken from this training process to determine whether two words constitute a transliteration pair. Next we describe the set of experiments we performed to investigate the effectiveness of our system on data from all the NEWS2010 shared tasks on transliteration mining, and also on a similar English-Japanese corpus that we constructed, and present our results in the following section. Finally, we conclude and offer some directions for future research.

Throughout the paper we use the following acronyms as shorthand for the various languages:

Ar=Arabic, En=English, Ch=Chinese, Hi=Hindi, Ja=Japanese, Ru=Russian, Ta=Tamil.

3 Using Features from Alignment

Our alignment model is based on a Dirichet process model: a stochastic process defined over a set S (in our case, the set of all possible bilingual sequence-pairs) whose sample path is a probability distribution on S. For brevity we provide only a brief description of the alignment model; for a full description, the reader is referred to (Finch and Sumita, 2010).

3.1 Dirichlet Process Model

Intuitively, the Dirichlet process model has two basic components: a model for generating an outcome that has already been generated at least once before, and a second model that assigns a probability to an outcome that has not yet been produced. To encourage the re-use of model parameters, the probability of generating a novel bilingual sequence-pair is considerably lower then the probability of generating a previously observed sequence pair. The probability distribution over these bilingual sequence-pairs (including an infinite number of unseen pairs) is learned directly from unlabeled data by Bayesian inference of the hidden co-segmentation of the corpus.

More formally, the underlying stochastic process for the generation of a corpus composed of bilingual phrase pairs γ is usually written in the following from:

$$G|_{\alpha,G_0} \sim DP(\alpha, G_0)$$
$$(\mathbf{s}_k, \mathbf{t}_k)|G \sim G \qquad (1)$$

G is a discrete probability distribution over the all bilingual sequence-pairs according to a *Dirichlet process prior* with *base measure* G_0 and concentration parameter α. The concentration parameter $\alpha > 0$ controls the variance of G; intuitively, the larger α is, the more similar G_0 will be to G. For the *base measure* G_0 that controls the generation of novel sequence-pairs, we use the joint spelling model described in (Finch and Sumita, 2010), that assigns exponentially smaller probabilities with increasing source/target sequence length.

3.1.1 The Generative Model

The generative model is given in Equation 2 below. The equation assignes a probability to the kth bilingual sequence-pair $(\mathbf{s}_k, \mathbf{t}_k)$ in a derivation of the corpus, given all of the other sequence-pairs observed so far $(\mathbf{s}_{-k}, \mathbf{t}_{-k})$. Here $-k$ is read as: "up to but not including k".

$$p((\mathbf{s}_k, \mathbf{t}_k))|(\mathbf{s}_{-k}, \mathbf{t}_{-k})) = \frac{N((\mathbf{s}_k, \mathbf{t}_k)) + \alpha G_0((\mathbf{s}_k, \mathbf{t}_k))}{N + \alpha} \qquad (2)$$

In this equation, N is the total number of bilingual sequence-pairs generated so far, $N((\mathbf{s}_k, \mathbf{t}_k))$ is the number of times the sequence-pair $(\mathbf{s}_k, \mathbf{t}_k)$ has occurred in the history.

3.2 Alignment

By repeatedly scoring bilingual sequence pairs with the probability from Equation 2, the algorithm is able to co-segment and align source and target grapheme sequences through an iterative process of Bayesian inference using Gibbs sampling. The training procedure is based on an extension of the forward filtering backward sampling algorithm (Mochihashi et al., 2009) which is too complex to describe in full here, but is covered in detail in (Finch and Sumita, 2010).

An example of an aligned grapheme sequence pair, the output of running this Dirichlet process model on the bilingual data, illustrated in Figure 1. Given such an alignment of source and target grapheme sequences, it is possible to perform generation by monotonic concatenation of grapheme sequence pairs to form words, as in the joint-source channel models of (Li et al., 2004). The probability of generating a bilingual word pair is given by the product of the probabilities of the bilingual grapheme sequence-pairs that generate it. Our idea is built on the assumption that the better able our model is to generate a bilingual word pair, the more likely it is that the word pair is a transliteration pair that we would like to mine. We use the Dirichlet process model to co-segment and align the data, extract features from this segmentation (explained in the next section) and use them to train a Support Vector Machine (SVM) (Cortes and Vapnik, 1995) to classify them as correct or incorrect transliteration pairs.

3.3 Feature Set

Figure 1 shows the bilingual segmentation and alignment together with the scores for each segment for the candidate pair ANDORIYUU (in Japanese) and 'andrew' in English. The scores in

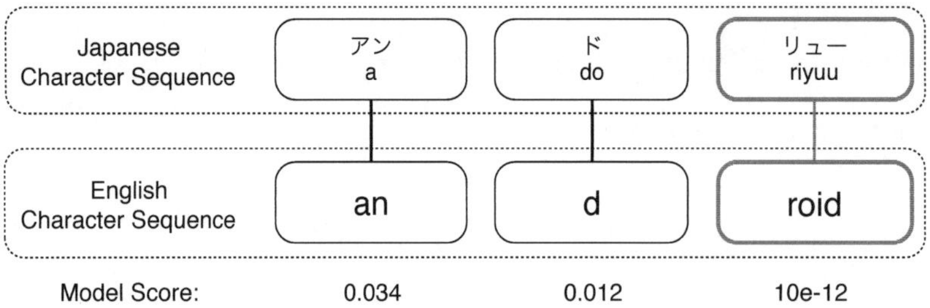

Figure 1: A co-segmentation of the transliteration word-pair candidate 'andoriyuu' (Japansese transliteration of the English 'andrew') and 'android' in English. The figure shows the co-segmentation together with the probabilities of each segment. It can be seen that the segments 'an' (Japanese), 'an' (English), and 'do' (Japanese) and 'd' (English) both receive high probabilities from the model, whereas the segment 'riyuu' (Japanese) and 'roid' in the English receives a very low probability from the model because source and target grapheme sequences are long, and this pairing has not been observed in the corpus.

$f1$	$f2$	$f3$	$f4$
$\frac{logprob}{numsegs}$	$\frac{\|t\|}{\|s\|}$	$\frac{\|s_{bad}\|+\|t_{bad}\|}{\|s\|+\|t\|}$	$minprob$

Table 1: The feature set used by the SVM to classify candidate transliteration pairs.

the figure for each of the bilingual character sequence pairs arise directly from applying Equation 2. In this example the candidate pair is not a transliteration pair, but nonetheless the pair comes quite close to being a transliteration pair because they share a common substring as a prefix. It would be possible to use any of a number of features derived from the alignment and the corresponding score. For example, using the log-probability itself would be possible, but it is strongly determined by sequence length, and therefore not directly comparable across lengths without modification.

The Bayesian model is able to align the corresponding parts of these two words using bilingual sequence pairs that have been observed a number of times in the training corpus. The non-corresponding subsequences of these two words will not have been observed in the data and the Bayesian model therefore must introduce a costly new feature into its model to generate them. In our model, the cost of introducing a new feature increases exponentially with the lengths of the source and target components (see (Finch and Sumita, 2010)). The features (described in detail below) we will use in our experiments are based on two basic hypotheses. The first is that the alignment scores for bad candidate pairs are likely to be lower than scores for good candidate pairs of the same length.

Our second hypothesis is based on the process of forced alignment which co-segments the candidate pair piece by piece. Unobserved pieces typically have extremely low probability and are therefore very costly to introduce into the segmentation hypotheses. As a consequence the model will be driven to generate as much as possible of the sequence pair by re-using the higher probability pieces that have already been observed. Our assumption is that the proportion of the sequence pair that cannot be generated using model features observed in the data will be a good indicator as to whether or not the pair is a correct transliteration pair.

We used a total of 4 features in our SVM classifier, these are shown in Table 1. Feature $f1$ is based on the first of the two assumptions above. Feature $f2$ is a simple length-based heuristic which was expected to be generally useful. Feature $f3$ is designed to capture the idea underpinning the second of the two hypotheses above, that is: what proportion of the candidate pair cannot modeled directly by the features learned by the Dirichlet process model. $f4$ focuses on the score of the weakest part of the derivation.

In Table 1, *logprob* is the log probability of the sampled derivation of the two grapheme sequences, according to our generative model. *numsegs* is the number of bilingual segments used in this derivation. *minprob* is the log probability of the segment with the lowest probability in the derivation. $|s|$ and $|t|$ are the lengths (in graphemes) of the source and target words respectively. $|s_{bad}| + |t_{bad}|$ is the total number of graphemes in both source and target, that are in *bad segments*. Here by *bad segment* we mean a bilingual segment that has not been observed in the training corpus and thus is only receiving a contribution from the base measure component of our Dirichlet process model (a *bad segment* is illustrated in Figure 1 as the rightmost segment in the sequence).

4 Experimental Evaluation

4.1 Corpora

For our experiments we used data from all tracks of the NEWS 2010 Named Entity Workshop (Kumaran et al., 2010b; Kumaran et al., 2010a; Kumaran and Li, 2010). A complete description of this shared task is given in (Kumaran et al., 2010b) and the results for all of the 15 systems evaluated is presented in (Kumaran et al., 2010a).

Our experiments were not part of the official NEWS2010 shared task, but used the same data sets. The training data for this track consisted of title-pairs of interlanguage links between wikipedia articles. These titles are noisy in the sense that they can be sequences of words, only some or even none of which may be transliterations of each other. The proportion of correct transliteration pairs to incorrect pairs in the training data was unknown. In addition, 1000 'seed' pairs of clean data were provided. The seed pairs contained only one word for each language and all were positive examples of transliteration pairs; no negative examples were included in the seed data.

For evaluation, the participants were expected to mine transliteration pairs from the full training set. A set of approximately 1000 interlanguage links (each giving rise to 0, 1 or more transliteration pairs) was randomly sampled from the training data, and not disclosed to the participants. In our experiments we used the same data and the same precision/recall/f-score evaluation metrics that were used in the official runs for the NEWS2010 workshop (refer to (Kumaran et al., 2010a) for full details).

4.2 The Mining Process

A flowchart illustrating the end-to-end process that was used in our experiments to mine transliteration pairs is shown in Figure 2. As can be seen from the figure, the process starts with the Bayesian alignment of the large corpus of noisy title-pairs.

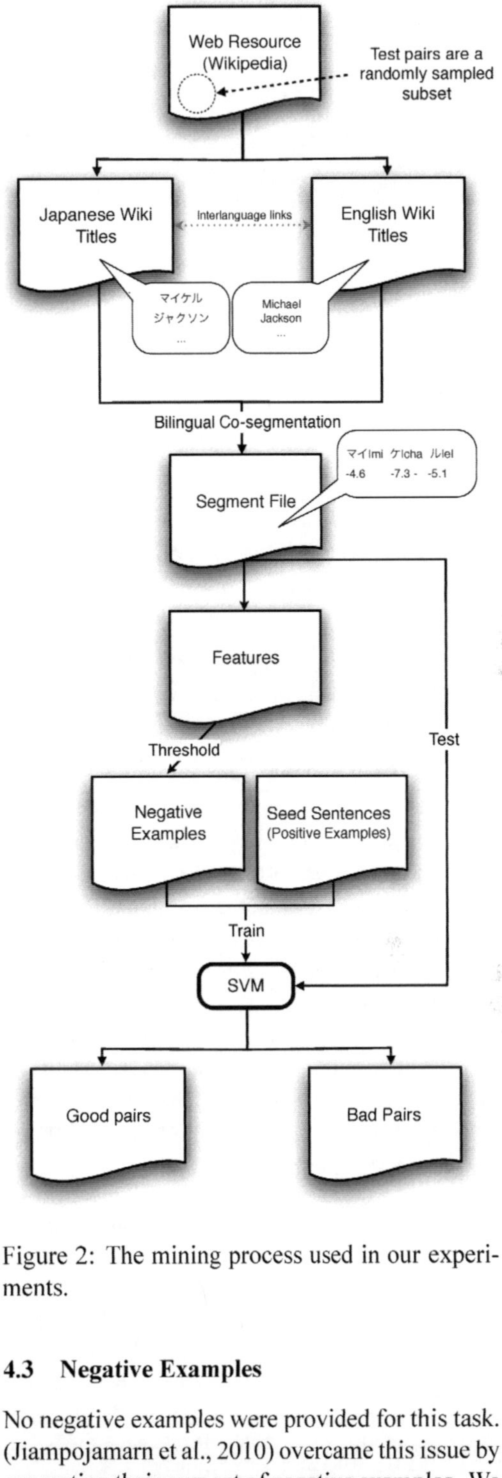

Figure 2: The mining process used in our experiments.

4.3 Negative Examples

No negative examples were provided for this task. (Jiampojamarn et al., 2010) overcame this issue by generating their own set of negative examples. We propose a novel approach that creates a set of negative examples by exploiting the natural clustering that is induced by the features derived from our Bayesian model (see Figure 3). This is described in the following section. We later compare this ap-

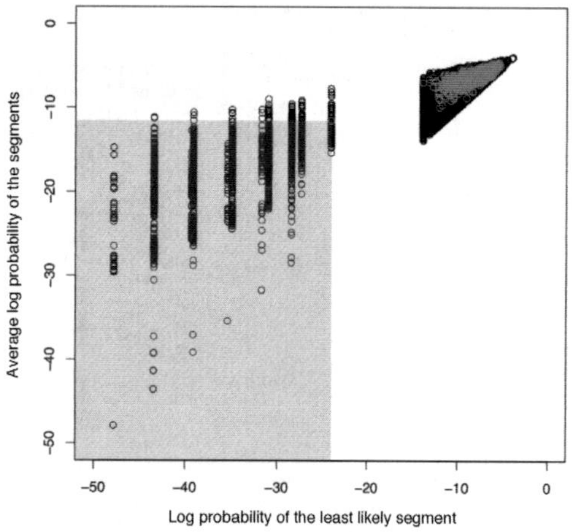

Figure 3: A scatter plot of two features derived from the model scores of the training data set for the English-Russian task. Negative examples were selected from the shaded area.

proach to two other strategies based on those employed in (Jiampojamarn et al., 2010) in the experimental section.

4.3.1 Model-based selection

Figure 3 shows a scatter plot of two plausible features over the En-Ru training data set. The first feature (vertical axis) is the arithmetic mean of the log-probabilities of each of the segments. This averaging allows sequences of differing lengths to be compared. The second feature (horizontal axis) is the log-probability of the least probable segment in the sequence. As can be seen from the plot, the second feature in particular partitions the data set quite cleanly into two clusters, 99.9% of the seed data (plotted on the graph in a lighter shade (red)) lie in the upper right-hand cluster.

We select negative examples, by means of thresholds on these features. The thresholds used to gather negative examples were set using the seed data by choosing the lowest values of any seed data points as the thresholds. This process is illustrated visually in Figure 3; the negative samples being extracted from the lower-left cluster (in the shaded area of the graph). The thresholds used for all language pairs are given in Table 2, together with the number of negative examples that were collected. We used these negative samples together with the provided seed sentences (known to be positive examples) to train an SVM classifier [1].

[1] In these experiments we used the publicly available SVM-lite classifier http://svmlight.joachims.org

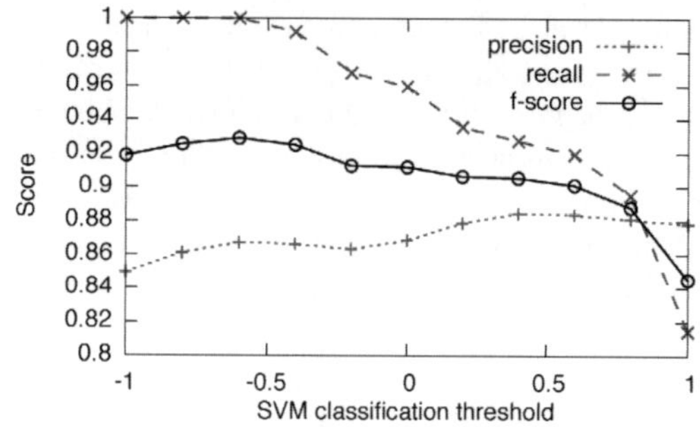

Figure 4: A graph showing the trade-off between precision and recall and its effect on the F-score for the English-Russian task.

4.3.2 Other approaches

Following (Jiampojamarn et al., 2010) we investigated two other methods of generating negative examples. These methods create a large set of incorrect candidates by pairing each source sequence in the seed data, with every target sequence except the correct target. In the first method of selecting negative examples, this large set of candidates is reduced to a smaller set by filtering out those candidates in which the source and target sequences are not phonetically similar. Phonetic similarity being measured as using the longest common subsequence ratio (LCSR) of the romanized forms. In our experiments we adjusted this threshold so that the same number of negative samples were generated in each case (10,000 samples). This approach generates negative examples that are similar to the positive examples, and it can be argued this is advantageous for training a discriminator.

The second approach simply takes a random sample from the large set of candidates. This approach generates samples that more closely approximate the similarity of examples in the real data. Results using each of these methods and also our model-based approach are shown in Figure 5.

4.4 Results

Figure 5 presents the results of our main experiment. Since the mixture of positive and negative examples in the test data is not known *a priori*, we provide results from our system for a range of values of the classification threshold on the output of the SVM. This gives precision/recall curves for each of the strategies for generating negative examples: our proposed approach, the approach based on LCSR, and the approach based on ran-

	En-Ar	En-Ch	En-Hi	En-Ja	En-Ru	En-Ta
Average	-11.35	-21.05	-7.55	-12.44	-7.9	-7.552
Minimum	-38.34	-42.11	-34.09	-38.28	-13.8	-34.09
Number	831	2061	890	160	9000	450

Table 2: Thresholds on each of the two features used (Average and Minimum segment probability) to obtain the negative examples for each language pair, together with the number of negative examples extracted at these thresholds.

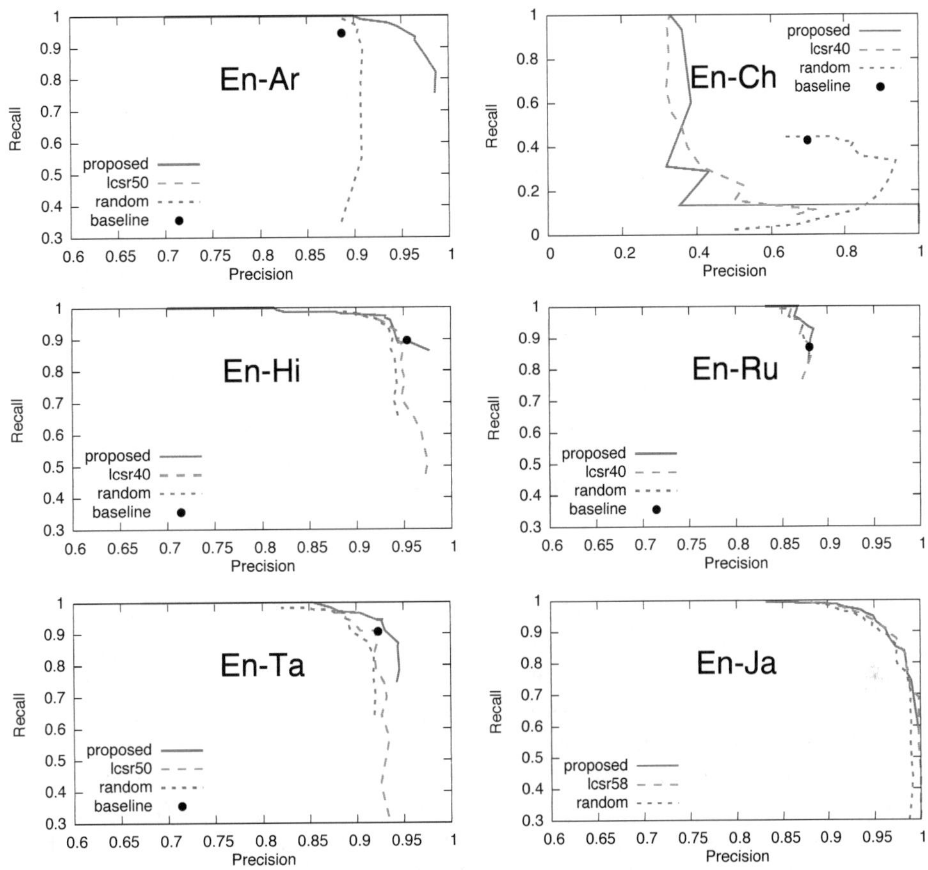

Figure 5: The precision and recall of our proposed method for all language pairs.

dom sampling. The precision/recall/f-score trade-off for En-Ru is shown in Figure 4. For the baseline we plot a point for the precision and recall of the top-ranked system in the NEWS2010 transliteration shared task to represent the current state of the art. The graph on the bottom right shows similar results on a new English-Japanese task that we constructed in a similar manner to the NEWS workshop tasks.

It is clear that the results on English to Chinese are anomalous. The results on this task were very dependent on the strategy for choosing negative examples and only the random sampling technique was effective. The English-Chinese task differs from the other language pairs in two important respects. Firstly, in the data as supplied for the task there is no segmentation information on the Chinese side, other languages contained word boundaries. We would not expect this to pose problems for our technique which performs unsupervised segmentation of both source and target during the alignment process. The second respect in which this language pair differs is that the grapheme vocabulary size is much larger for Chinese than for the other languages. We believe this is the cause of the anomalous result, and that the larger vocabulary size requires a larger amount of training data to build models that can function effectively. Choosing similar examples, by using the prosed technique or the technique based on LCSR, will reduce the variety of kanji seen in the negative examples, and this could handicap the models where the data size is too small.

On all the other language pairs, our proposed strategy for selecting negative examples performs as well as, or better than the other strategies. Of the other two strategies, the method based on LCSR is generally the the better approach. Moreover, our results show that our system is able to offer performance comparable to the state-of-the-art baseline systems on these language pairs. For the English-Arabic and English-Tamil tasks in particular, our strategy for selecting negative examples offers higher scores in terms of both precision and recall than the other strategies. Our approach typically makes errors on sequence pairs that are genuine but contain novel sub-sequences of graphemes for which our model has no corresponding sequence pair. Feature $f3$ in our model was designed to address this issue by balancing evidence from the lengths of the 'bad' segments in the pairs against evidence from the lengths of the 'good'. The idea being that an unobserved sequence pair within a much larger context of observed sequence pairs is likely to be a correct but novel alignment, rather than an incorrect alignment. Nonetheless some errors of this type remain, but the frequency of type of error can be expected to decrease with training set size.

We created a new task for our experiments based on English-Japanese data. Text from the titles of Wikipedia inter-language links was used as the data to be mined, and we used a set of English-Katakana pairs from the publicly available EDict dictionary [2] to create the seed data. 4000 pairs of interlanguage links were used, 1000 of which were hand-annotated as correct or incorrect transliteration pairs and used as test data. 1000 seed pairs were selected randomly from the bilingual dictionary. The precision and recall curves for the En-Ja task are shown in Figure 5. The results show that mining Japanese can be performed reasonably easily, relative to the language pairs used in the NEWS2010 tasks. All techniques for choosing negative examples were effective here; our proposed approach and the LCSR approach slightly outperforming random sampling. The English-Japanese precision/recall indicate that the automatic mining of English-Japanese transliteration pairs should be fruitful. We believe it would be possible to mine English-Japanese pairs at high-levels of precision and recall. In our experiments, for example, close to 100% precision can be achieved whilst still maintaining 70% recall.

5 Conclusion

In this paper we have presented a novel approach to identifying transliteration word pairs for transliteration mining based on features derived from a Bayesian process that simultaneously co-segments and force-aligns grapheme sequences within the words. Our approach is simple and symmetrical with respect to the two languages involved, and will operate on grapheme sequences in the native scripts of the languages involved. It is not dependent on the existence of a method for romanizing either language. Furthermore, our method performs automatic co-segmentation of both source and target sequences, eliminating any requirement for language specific segmentation schemes.

We evaluated our approach on all of the transliteration mining tracks of the NEWS2010 Named Entity Workshop shared task. Our system in spite of its simplicity, achieved performance comparable to the state of the art systems on this task, indicating the features derived from the Bayesian forced alignment are strongly predictive in classifying transliteration pairs. This paper also contributes a new set of results on an English-Japanese data set we constructed in a similar manner to the NEWS workshop datasets. Our results indicate that mining English-Japanese transliteration pairs should be possible at high levels of precision and recall using the techniques proposed in this paper.

In future research we would like to extend the scope of our work to integrate it into a broader framework to be used for mining named entity pairs (including but not limited to transliteration pairs) that will be used to improve a named entity translation system, and integrate this into an end-to-end machine translation system. In addition we intend to enhance the Bayesian model used to align the grapheme sequences.

[2] http://www.csse.monash.edu.au/~jwb/edict_doc.html

References

Slaven Bilac and Hozumi Tanaka. 2005. Extracting transliteration pairs from comparable corpora. In *In Proceedings of the Annual Meeting of the Natural Language Processing Society*, Japan.

Eric Brill, Gary Kacmarcik, and Chris Brockett. 2001. Automatically harvesting katakana-english term pairs from search engine query logs.

Corinna Cortes and Vladimir Vapnik. 1995. Support-vector networks. In *Machine Learning*, pages 273–297.

Kareem Darwish. 2010. Transliteration mining with phonetic conflation and iterative training. In *Proceedings of the 2010 Named Entities Workshop*, pages 53–56, Uppsala, Sweden, July. Association for Computational Linguistics.

Andrew Finch and Eiichiro Sumita. 2010. A Bayesian Model of Bilingual Segmentation for Transliteration. In Marcello Federico, Ian Lane, Michael Paul, and François Yvon, editors, *Proceedings of the seventh International Workshop on Spoken Language Translation (IWSLT)*, pages 259–266.

Yun Huang, Min Zhang, and Chew Lim Tan. 2011. Nonparametric Bayesian Machine Transliteration with Synchronous Adaptor Grammars. In *ACL (Short Papers)*, pages 534–539.

Sittichai Jiampojamarn, Kenneth Dwyer, Shane Bergsma, Aditya Bhargava, Qing Dou, Mi-Young Kim, and Grzegorz Kondrak. 2010. Transliteration generation and mining with limited training resources. In *Proceedings of the 2010 Named Entities Workshop*, pages 39–47, Uppsala, Sweden, July. Association for Computational Linguistics.

Mitesh Khapra, Raghavendra Udupa, A. Kumaran, and Pushpak Bhattacharyya. 2010. Pr + rq □ pq: Transliteration mining using bridge language.

A Kumaran and Haizhou Li, editors. 2010. *Proceedings of the 2010 Named Entities Workshop*. Association for Computational Linguistics, Uppsala, Sweden, July.

A Kumaran, Mitesh M. Khapra, and Haizhou Li. 2010a. Report of news 2010 transliteration mining shared task. In *Proceedings of the 2010 Named Entities Workshop*, pages 21–28, Uppsala, Sweden, July. Association for Computational Linguistics.

A Kumaran, Mitesh M. Khapra, and Haizhou Li. 2010b. Whitepaper of news 2010 shared task on transliteration mining. In *Proceedings of the 2010 Named Entities Workshop*, pages 29–38, Uppsala, Sweden, July. Association for Computational Linguistics.

Chun-Jen Lee and Jason S. Chang. 2003a. Acquisition of english-chinese transliterated word pairs from parallel-aligned texts using a statistical machine transliteration model. In *Proceedings of the HLT-NAACL 2003 Workshop on Building and using parallel texts: data driven machine translation and beyond - Volume 3*, HLT-NAACL-PARALLEL '03, pages 96–103, Stroudsburg, PA, USA. Association for Computational Linguistics.

Chun-Jen Lee and Jason S. Chang. 2003b. Acquisition of english-chinese transliterated word pairs from parallel-aligned texts using a statistical machine transliteration model. In *Proceedings of the HLT-NAACL 2003 Workshop on Building and using parallel texts: data driven machine translation and beyond - Volume 3*, HLT-NAACL-PARALLEL '03, pages 96–103, Stroudsburg, PA, USA. Association for Computational Linguistics.

Haizhou Li, Min Zhang, and Jian Su. 2004. A joint source-channel model for machine transliteration. In *ACL '04: Proceedings of the 42nd Annual Meeting on Association for Computational Linguistics*, page 159, Morristown, NJ, USA. Association for Computational Linguistics.

Daichi Mochihashi, Takeshi Yamada, and Naonori Ueda. 2009. Bayesian unsupervised word segmentation with nested pitman-yor language modeling. In *ACL-IJCNLP '09: Proceedings of the Joint Conference of the 47th Annual Meeting of the ACL and the 4th International Joint Conference on Natural Language Processing of the AFNLP: Volume 1*, pages 100–108, Morristown, NJ, USA. Association for Computational Linguistics.

Peter Nabende. 2010. Mining transliterations from wikipedia using pair hmms. In *Proceedings of the 2010 Named Entities Workshop*, pages 76–80, Uppsala, Sweden, July. Association for Computational Linguistics.

Sara Noeman and Amgad Madkour. 2010. Language independent transliteration mining system using finite state automata framework. In *Proceedings of the 2010 Named Entities Workshop*, pages 57–61, Uppsala, Sweden, July. Association for Computational Linguistics.

Jong-Hoon Oh and Hitoshi Isahara. 2006. Mining the web for transliteration lexicons: Joint-validation approach. In *Proceedings of the 2006 IEEE/WIC/ACM International Conference on Web Intelligence*, WI '06, pages 254–261, Washington, DC, USA. IEEE Computer Society.

Keita Tsuji and Kyo Kageura. 2006. Automatic generation of japanese□english bilingual thesauri based on bilingual corpora. *J. Am. Soc. Inf. Sci. Technol.*, 57:891–906, May.

Product Name Identification and Classification in Thai Economic News

Nattadaporn Lertcheva
Department of Linguistics
Chulalongkorn University
nattadaporn@gmail.com

Wirote Aroonmanakun
Department of Linguistics
Chulalongkorn University
awirote@chula.ac.th

Abstract

The purpose of this research is to analyze the patterns of the product names used in Thai economic news and to find clues that could be used to identify the product names' boundaries and their categories. It is found that the patterns of Thai product names are quite varied. Thirty two patterns are found in this study. While some clues like collocation and the context of names can be used for identifying product names, many of them cannot be identified by these means. This indicates that the task of product named entity recognition is an interesting task for Thai language processing.

1 Introduction

Most named entity recognition research has been focused on person, location, and organization names. Though other proper names, such as biomedical names and product names, are important in language processing, only a little research has been done on recognizing these names in Thai such as Lertcheva and Aroonmanakun (2009). Since different types of names have different patterns and characteristics, basic linguistic knowledge of the names is needed for imposing any rules or features for any rule-based or statistical-based named entity recognition systems. This paper presents basic knowledge of Thai product names. A corpus of Thai economic news is used in analyzing product names. Patterns and variations of their forms in texts are analyzed. In this paper, background information of product names and relevant research will be presented first. Then, the corpus and annotation used in marking Thai product names will be described in section 3. The results of the analysis will be presented in sections 4 and 5 followed by the conclusion.

2 Background Knowledge

Unlike a person name, an organization name, or a location name, which is normally used to refer to one unique referent, a product name is used to refer to many referents categorized under the same product. Product names are a kind of proper name because each is created to refer to a certain product produced by a company. This section describes the definition of product names and product categories used in this study. Although product named entity recognition has been analyzed in Lertcheva and Aroonmanakun (2009) which focused on linguistic analysis of the product names for solving product name identification, this paper furthers the study by analyzing product names in detail using a larger corpus. Moreover, we will propose the pattern of product names and describe the components used to classify different types of product.

2.1 Definition of Product Names

To distinguish one product from the same products produced by other companies, trademarks or brand names are usually used in the product names. However, previous research used the terms "product names"with different meanings. For example, Liu et al. (2005) defined a product name as a name consisting of a trade mark and product type, e.g. Nokia 3310. Nilsson and Malmgren (2005) defined a product name as a term under brand names. In other words, a brand name consists of a trademark, a product name, and a service name. Trademarks have a broader scope than product names or service names. For example, Volvo is regarded as a trademark while Volvo C70 is considered a product name. Boonpaisarnsatit (2005) used the

Proceedings of the 2011 Named Entities Workshop, IJCNLP 2011, pages 58–64,
Chiang Mai, Thailand, November 12, 2011.

term "product names" differently from Liu et al. (2005) and Nilsson and Malmgren (2005). What is called "product name" in Boonpaisarnsatit (2005) is actually a generic noun indicating a category of product. He referred to "brand names" as the combination of product name and trademark. For example, รถยนต์|โตโยต้า is analyzed as consisting of a product name รถยนต์ -'car' and a trademark โตโยต้า -'Toyota'. The use of a generic noun when referring to a product is a characteristic of referring to products in Thai. In this study, we use the term product name as defined in Lertcheva and Aroonmanakun (2009) which is a linguistic expression consisting of a generic noun, a brand name indicator, a brand name, a product type indicator, and a product type.

2.2 Product Categories

In product named entity recognition, the task includes not only identifying the boundary but also the type of the product. However, there is no standard classification of product category. In this paper, we use the classification listed by the Department of Export Promotion, Ministry of Commerce of Thailand and Wikipedia as a basis of classification and divide the products into 26 categories as follows:

1. Foods
2. Medical devices
3. Pharmaceutical
4. Cosmetic and spa products
5. Eyewear brands
6. Electrical products and parts / Electronics
7. Automotive / auto parts and accessories
8. Building materials and hardware items
9. Chemicals and plastic resins
10. Printing products, paper and packaging
11. Machinery and equipment
12. Gems and jewelry
13. Watches/Clocks
14. Bags/Footwear/Leather Products
15. Textiles, garments and fashion accessories
16. Sporting goods
17. Furniture and parts
18. Gift and decorative items/handicrafts
19. Household products
20. Home textiles
21. Toys and games
22. Stationery/Office supplies and Equipment
23. Tobacco
24. Farming products
25. Cleaning products
26. Miscellaneous

3 Corpus and Annotation

To reveal patterns of product names in Thai, a corpus of Thai economic news is used. The corpus size is 178,474 words, in which 2,463 product names are found.[1] Since the language used in the headlines usually has different style from the body text, in this study, we analyze only the product names found in the body text of the news. TEI annotation style is used in marking up product names. A product name is tagged by using<productNametype="Product's_Category" >…</productName>. The annotation of the components in product names is as follows.

1. <genericNoun>.....</genericNoun> is used for tagging words used to describe the type of product. For example, โทรศัพท์มือถือ|โนเกีย consists of a compound noun, โทรศัพท์มือถือ-'mobile phone', and a brand name "Nokia". Although the corpus is collected from Thai economic news, generic nouns are not always written in Thai script. Even though English names can be transliterated using Thai script, they are often written in English. For example, the product name "LCD TV รุ่นAN-LT 322 DU" begins with a generic noun in English "LCD TV" followed by a product type indicator in Thai รุ่น-'model' and then the product type in English "AN-LT 322 DU". Generic nouns can be a simple word, a compound, or a phrase e.g.อาหารทะเลแช่แข็ง-'frozen sea food'.

2. <brandIndicator>.....</brandIndicator> is used to mark a brand indicator, or a word indicating the brand name. Brand indicators found in the corpus are limited to words like ตรา-'brand', ยี่ห้อ-'brand', ตระกูล-'family', เครื่องหมายการค้า-'trademark', ชื่อ-'name', ผลิตภัณฑ์-'product', and แบรนด์-'brand'. Brand indicators can be preceded by some prepositions like ภายใต้-'under', e.g. ภายใต้|ผลิตภัณฑ์ = 'under'+'product', or it can be modified by an adjective like ใหม่-'new', e.g. แบรนด์|ใหม่= 'brand'+'new'.

3. <brandName>.....</brandName> is used to mark the brand name of the product. The brand name is normally a trademark named for the products. Brand names are sometimes found

[1] The corpus can be downloaded from http://pioneer.chula.ac.th/~awirote/Data-Nattadaporn.zip

written in English, such as, เครื่องสำอาง|**DHC** = a generic noun 'cosmetic' + a brand name '**DHC**'

4. <proIndicator>..... </proIndicator> is the markup for the product type indicator used to identify the product type. Product type indicators found in the corpus are รุ่น-'type', ซีรีย์-'series', สูตร-'formula', กลิ่น-'scent', รส/รสชาติ-'taste', ชนิด-'type',ครอบครัวตระกูล-'family'. These product type indicators sometimes can be modified by an adjective, such as รุ่น+ใหม่= 'type'+'**new**'.

5. <productType>.....</productType> is for tagging product subtype under the same brand name. It is found that either common nouns or proper nouns can be used as a product type. In food product names, a common noun related to taste is likely to be used indicating its subtype, e.g. มาม่า+รส+ต้มยำกุ้ง– 'Mama'+'taste'+'**spicy lemongrass with shrimp**'. For technology products, a proper noun is usually used to identify the subtype, e.g. the name ยาริส-'Yaris' is used to indicate a specific model of the car, โตโยต้า+ยาริส–'Toyota'+ 'Yaris'

4 Product Name Identification

Product names in Thai consist of five components as stated in the previous section. However, the patterns can be varied. To identify a product name, its patterns and contextual clues have to be examined. In this study, we found 32 patterns of product names. These patterns can be categorized into 4 groups, head only, head-initial, head-centre, and head-final (section 4.1). Then, a study of context clues for identifying product names is presented in section 4.2.

4.1 Pattern of Product Names

Of the 32 patterns, brand name and product type are the core part of the product name. A brand name is used to distinguish the product from the same one produced by other companies. A product type is usually used to differentiate similar products under the same brand name. Every pattern of product name would have the brand name as its core part. If the brand name is omitted, the product type would be used as the core part of the product name. These two components are essential in uniquely identifying the product. Therefore, 'head' in this paper refers to a brand name or a product type.

The symbols used in the pattern of product names are described as follows.

1. (...) indicates the component that can be omitted in the product name.

Example: A + (B) + C = A + B + C or A + C

2. [...] indicates that the component is required in the pattern.

Example: [+brand] means that a brand indicator must be present in this pattern and must be the word 'brand'.

3. {...} indicates that at least one element in the braces must be present.

Example: {A + B} + C = A + C or B + C or A + B + C

4. | is used for marking the selection of only one choice.

Example: A|B + D = A + D or B + D

From the 32 patterns found in the 2,463 product names, we can categorize them into 4 groups as follows:

1. Head Structures

This pattern consists of one component, brand name or product type, functioning as the head word. From all the product names, the pattern with the brand name as head is found in 39.26% of the product names while the pattern with product type as head is found in 4.06% of the product names.

- Brand name

This pattern is found when the product name is used continuously in the text or in an illustration sentence. For example, <product Name type="cosSpa" ID="P03"><brandName> จุยซ์บิวตี้</brandName></productName> is a name consisting of only the brand name "Juice Beauty".

- Product type

This pattern is found when the product name is continuously referred to in the text. The product type can be either a common noun or a proper noun. For example, <product Nametype ="Elec"><productType>ธิงค์แพดเอ็กซ์100อี</product Type></productName>has a proper name as the product type, "ThinkPad X 100E." In the example, <productNametype="food"><product Type>หมูสับ</productType></productName>, the product type is a common noun referring to "minced pork". This pattern, in which only a common word functions as the product type, is acceptable only if the same product is previously referred to using a product name pattern containing a brand name. This is because, unlike a proper noun, a common noun by itself cannot specify what the product is. For example, we can use the product type "Jazz" without mentioning a brand name because the reader can understand what we are referring to. In contrast, we cannot use a common word likeหมูสับ – "minced pork" as the product name when first introduced in the text since the readers cannot understand what the product is.

2. Head-Initial Structures

This is the pattern in which the head is located at the beginning. This pattern consists of 4 sub-patterns which account for 10.19% of the product names.

▪ **Brand name** + {brand name indicator [+brand] + generic noun }

Example: <productName type="gems"><brandName>ดามิอานิ </brandName><brandIndicator>แบรนด์ </brandIndicator><genericNoun>เครื่องประดับ </genericNoun></productName>

This example consists of a brand name "Damiani", a brand indicator "brand" and a generic noun "jewelry".

▪ **Brand name** + {generic noun + product type indicator}+ product type

Example: <productName type="Elec" ID="P02"> <brandName> แบล็กเบอร์รี่ </brand Name> <proIndicator>รุ่น</proIndicator><productType> โบลด์</productType> </productName>

This example consists of a brand name "Blackberry", a product type indicator "type" and a product type "Bold".

▪ **Brand name** + product type + (generic noun)

Example: <productName type="food"> <brandName>ไวตามิ้ลค์</brandName> <productType>โลว์ชูการ์</productType> </productName>

This example consists of a brand name "Vitamilk" and a product type "Low sugar".

▪ **Product type** + product type indicator

Example: <productName type="Elec"> <productType>ธิงค์แพด</productType> <proIndicator>ซีรีส์</proIndicator> </productName>

This example consists of a product type "ThinkPad" and a product type indicator "series".

3. Head-Centre Structures

This is the pattern in which the head is located at the centre of the structure. This pattern consists of 5 sub-patterns which account for 5.08% of the product names.

▪ Generic noun | brand name indicator + **brand name** + generic noun

Example: <productName type="food" ID="P02"><brandIndicator>แบรนด์ </brandIndicator><brandName>อาร์ทรี </brandName><genericNoun>ชาพร้อมดื่ม </genericNoun></productName>

This example consists of a brand indicator "brand", a brand name "Artea" and a generic noun "tea".

▪ {Generic noun + brand name indicator | product type indicator}+ **brand name** + product type

Example: <productName type="cosSpa"> <genericNoun>ยาสีฟัน</genericNoun> <brandIndicator>ยี่ห้อ</brandIndicator> <brandName>ฟลูโอคารีล</brandName> <productType>40 พลัส</productType> </productName>

This example consists of ageneric noun "toothpaste", a brand indicator "brand", a brand name "Fluocaril" and a product type "40 plus".

▪ Generic noun + **brand name** + product type + generic noun

Example:<productName type="Auto"> <genericNoun>รถ</genericNoun><brandName> เชฟโรเลต</brandName><productType>โคโลราโด </productType><genericNoun>ปิคอัพอเมริกันพันธุ์แกร่ง </genericNoun></productName>

This example consists of a generic noun "car", a brand name "Chevrolet", a product type "Colorado" and a generic noun "American pick-up".

▪ Brand name indicator + **brand name** + brand name indicator + generic noun

Example: <productName type="fashion"> <brandIndicator>ไฟติ้งแบรนด์ชื่อ</brandIndicator> <brandName>จีแอนด์จี</brandName> (Guy&Girl) <brandIndicator>แบรนด์</brandIndicator> <genericNoun>ชุดชั้นใน</genericNoun> </productName>

This example consists of a brand indicator "fighting brand", a brand name "G&G", a brand indicator "brand" and a generic noun "underwear".

▪ Generic noun + (brand name indicator) + **brand name** + (product type) + product type indicator + product type

Example: <productName type="Auto"> <genericNoun>รถ</genericNoun> <brandName>ฮอนด้า</brandName> <productType>ซิตี้</productType><proIndicator> รุ่น</proIndicator><productType>ปี2008 </productType></productName>

This example consists of a generic noun “car”, a brand name “Honda”, a product type “City” a product type indicator “type” and a product type “year 2008”

4. Head-Final Structures

Besides the pattern head only structure, this is the most commonly used structure in product names. The pattern has the head located at the final part of the structure. This pattern consists of 4 sub-patterns which account for 41.41% of the product names.

▪ (generic noun) + brand name indicator + **brand name**

Example: <productName type=“Elec”>
<genericNoun>โทรศัพท์เคลื่อนที่</genericNoun>
<brandIndicator>ภายใต้แบรนด์</brandIndicator>
<brandName>แบล็กเบอร์รี่</brandName>
</productName>

This example consists of a generic noun “mobile phone”, a brand indicator “under brand” and a brand name “Blackberry”.

▪ (generic noun) + brand name indicator + generic noun + brand name indicator + **brand name**

Example: <productName type="food" ID="P01">
<genericNoun>ข้าวสารบรรจุถุง</genericNoun>
<brandIndicator>ภายใต้แบรนด์</brandIndicator>
<genericNoun>ข้าว</genericNoun>
<brandIndicator>ตรา</brandIndicator>
<brandName>ฉัตร</brandName></productName>

This example consists of a generic noun “a bag of rice”, a brand indicator “under brand”, a generic noun “rice”, a brand indicator “brand” and a brand name “Chut”

▪ (brand name indicator [+brand]) + generic noun + **brand name**

Example:<productName type="food">
<brandIndicator>แบรนด์</brandIndicator>
<genericNoun>น้ำผลไม้</genericNoun>
<brandName>แบรี่</brandName></productName>

This example consists of a brand indicator “brand”, a generic noun “juice” and a brand name “Berri”.

▪ {Generic noun + product type indicator} + **product type**

Example: <productName type=“Auto”>
<proIndicator>รุ่น</proIndicator> <productType>
ซีรีส์ 7 ซีดาน</productType> </productName>

This example consists of a product type indicator “type” and a product type “Series 7 Sedan”.

Thai product names tend to be used with head structure and head-final respectively. Head-structure can be used without causing any confusion because normally the product is previously referred to in the text. The preference for the head-final structure conforms to the structure of a proper name in Thai, in which a proper name is preceded by a common noun indicating its class, e.g. โรงเรียน|สวนกุหลาบ= school+ ‘Suankularp’, วัด|บัวขวัญ= temple+‘Buakhwan’, etc. Therefore, readers will perceive the kind of product before the name of products. e.g., ปลาราดพริก|ตรา|ปลายิ้ม = fish with a chili sauce + a brand indicator ‘brand’ + a brand name ‘PlaYim’

4.2 Clues for Identifying Product Names

To find contextual clues that would be useful in identifying product names, words collocated with the product names and specific sentence patterns are examined as follows:

1. Word collocations

This section emphasizes the study of words collocated with the product names. A preliminary observation shows that some words located in front of product names tend to have a meaning related to products such as ‘seller’, ‘buyer’, ‘importer’, ‘sell’, ‘produce’, ‘import’ etc. To determine the efficacy of these words as an indicator of the product names, we analyzed the occurrence of every word found in front of a product name within the span of four words. Words occurring in the corpus less than 6 times were excluded. Then, a percentage of how often the words collocated with product names was calculated and sorted. In this study, words with more than 50% co-occurrence with a product name are considered useful. Only three words are found with this criterion. They are ผู้ผลิต - ‘a producer’, แนะนำ - ‘introduce’ and ผู้แทนจำหน่าย - ‘a dealer’. When the span is set to be three words before the product name, only two words are found useful, namely แนะนำ - ‘introduce’ and ผู้แทนจำหน่าย - ‘a dealer’.

Although a preliminary observation intuitively indicates the close relation between the product name and its collocations, the result does not confirm that observation because the percentages of co-occurrences for most of the collocates are lower than 50%.

2. Illustration sentences

A sentence pattern that is found to be useful for identifying a product name is the sentence with illustration. In this pattern, product names are found as a list of illustrations after the words ได้แก่ - ‘for example’,and เช่น- ‘such as’. The last product name usually comes after the conjunction และ- 'and'. In this example, ผู้จัดหาเสื้อผ้า|<u>แบรนด์</u> |**<u>เช่น</u>**|ลีวายส์ |และ |แรงเลอร์ (clothing dealer + <u>brand</u> + **<u>such as</u>** + Levi's + and + Wrangler), two product names are listed after the word เช่น-'such as'.

5 Product Category Identification

The task of product named entity recognition includes not only identifying product name boundaries but also product categories. In this section, we describe the criteria used for identifying product categories. From 2,463 product names, we found that only 1,603 product names (65%) can be assigned to a product category by considering either the components in the product name or contextual clues.

1. Components in the product name

Of those 1,603 names, the product categories can be determined for 1,172 by considering the components within the product names. Components that are useful are generic nouns, brand names, and product types.

- Generic noun

Product categories can be easily determined from the generic noun in the product name. For example,วิทยุ|โซนี่ = **a radio** + a brand name 'Sony' is categorized as 'Electrical products' because 'radio' is a subclass of electrical products. In this example,น้ำดื่ม|สิงห์ = **drinking water** + a brand name 'Singha' is categorized as 'Foods' because 'drinking water' is a subtype of food.

- Brand name

For some names, a part of the brand name can be useful in identifying its category. For example, the brand name ไวตามิลค์ (Vita**milk**) is categorized as 'Foods' because there is a word 'milk' within the brand name. In this example, ไอโฟน (i**phone**) is categorized as 'Electronic products' because of the word 'phone.' The brand name เนสท์กาแฟ (Nescafé) is used to categorize the product as 'Foods' because the word 'café' in Thai means coffee.

- Product type

In some cases, product category can be inferred from the product type. For example, มาม่า|รส|หมูสับ= a brand name 'Mama' + a product type indicator 'taste' + a product type **'minced pork'** can be categorized as 'Foods' because of the product type 'minced pork'.

2. Contextual clues

When components in the product name cannot be used to identify the product category, a contextual clue, which comes from a previous mention of the product name in the text, is used. It is found that the categories for 431 product names can be identified by referring back to the same product names previously presented in the text. If a product is referred to more than once in the text, its category is usually identified by considering the components inside the first mention of the name. When the same product is referred to again using a reduced form, its category can be inferred from the previous mention.

In sum, based on the analysis of 2,463 product names, we found that categories can be identified for only 65% of them by analyzing the components inside the product name (1,172) or by referring to a previous mention of the product name (431). The rest, 860 product names (35%), cannot be assigned to their categories using these means. It seems that background knowledge is needed in identifying the product category. These are usually a product which is well known, e.g. โค้ก= 'Coke', แพนทีน= 'Pantene', etc. Thus, product category identification is not an easy task.

6 Conclusion

This study concerns both product name and product category identification. A linguistic analysis of Thai product names is carried out to reveal patterns of product names and clues that would be useful for product named entity recognition in Thai.

Though there is some preference for the head-only and head-final structures in Thai product names, it is found that the patterns of Thai product names are quite varied. In addition, there is no explicit clue for identifying a product name. Using collocates alone seems to be insufficient for identifying the product name.

For product category identification, some inner clues can be found from the components in the product names. Keeping track of products referred to in the discourse can also help in identifying the category when the name is used in a reduced form. However, categories cannot be identified for a number of product names by this means.

Therefore, the problem of Thai product named entity recognition is not an easy task. Further research on this topic is needed. A general named entity recognition model should be implemented to verify whether the model that has been used in Thai named entity recognition could resolve this problem. We think that a named entity recognition that uses both word forms and part-of-speech sequences should suffice for identifying the product name boundaries. But identifying product category, if it is needed, should be implemented separately by keeping track of product names found previously and creating semantic relations between the product names and contextual words.

Acknowledgments

This research is supported by The Thailand Research Fund (TRF) under grant no MSG53Z0007, and partially supported by Chulalongkorn University Centenary Academic Development Project.

References

Boonpaisarnsatit, N. 2005.*Semantic analysis of Thai Products' Brand names*.Unpublished master's thesis, Chiang Mai University, Thailand.

Department of Export Promotion.Ministry of Commerce.*Product's information*.Retrieved from: http://www.depthai.go.th[accessed 11 March 2009]

Lertcheva, N. and Aroonmanakun, W. 2009.A Linguistic Study of Product Names in Thai Economic News.In *Proceeding of the 8th international symposium on natural language processing*. October 20-21, 2009. Bangkok. Thailand

Liu, F., Zhao, J., Lv, B., Xu, B., and Yu, H. 2005.Product Named entity Recognition Based on Hierarchical Hidden Markov Model.In *Proceedings of the 4thSIGHAN Workshop on Chinese Language Processing*.

Nilsson, K., and Malmgren, A. 2005. Towards automatic recognition of product names: An exploratory study of brand names in economic texts. In *Proceedings of the15th NODALIDA conference*, Joensuu.

Settels, B. 2004.*Biomedical Named Entity Recognition Using Conditional Random Fields and Rich Feature Sets*.

Wikipedia.*Category:Brands by product type*. Retrieved from: http://en.wikipedia.org/wiki/Category:Brands_by_product_type [accessed 25 December 2008]

Mining Multi-word Named Entity Equivalents from Comparable Corpora

Abhijit Bhole
Microsoft Research India
Bangalore, India
v-abbhol@microsoft.com

Goutham Tholpadi
Indian Institute of Science
Bangalore, India
gtholpadi@gmail.com

Raghavendra Udupa
Microsoft Research India
Bangalore, India
raghavu@microsoft.com

Abstract

Named entity (NE) equivalents are useful in many multilingual tasks including MT, transliteration, cross-language IR, etc. Recently, several works have addressed the problem of mining NE equivalents from comparable corpora. These methods usually focus only on single-word NE equivalents whereas, in practice, most NEs are multi-word. In this work, we present a generative model for extracting equivalents of multi-word NEs (MWNEs) from a comparable corpus, given a NE tagger in only one of the languages. We show that our method is highly effective on three language pairs, and provide a detailed error analysis for one of them.

1 Introduction

NEs are important for many applications in natural language processing and information retrieval. In particular, NE equivalents, i.e. the same NE expressed in multiple languages, are used in several cross-language tasks such as machine translation, machine transliteration, cross-language information retrieval, cross-language news aggregation, etc. Recently, the problem of automatically constructing a table of NE equivalents in multiple languages has received considerable attention from the research community. One approach to solving this problem is to leverage the abundantly available comparable corpora in many different languages of the world (Udupa et al., 2008; Udupa et al., 2009a; Udupa et al., 2009b). While considerable progress has been made in improving both recall and precision of mining of NE equivalents from comparable corpora, most approaches in the literature are applicable only to single-word NEs, and particularly to transliterations (e.g. Tendulkar and तेन्डुलकर). In this work, we consider the more general problem of MWNE equivalents from comparable corpora.

In the MWNE equivalents mining problem, a NE in the source language could be related to a NE in the target language by, not just transliteration, but a combination of transliteration, translation, acronyms, deletion/addition of terms, etc. To give an example, Figure 1 shows a pair of comparable articles in English and Hindi. 'Sachin Tendulkar' and 'सचिन तेन्डुलकर' are MWNE equivalents, and both words have been transliterated. Another example is the pair 'Siddhivinayak Temple Trust' and 'सिद्धिविनायक मन्दिर siddhivinayak mandir'. Here, the first word has been transliterated, the second one translated, and the third omitted in Hindi. The task is to (a) identify these MWNEs as equivalents, (b) infer the word correspondence between the MWNE equivalents, and (c) identify the type of correspondence (transliteration, translation, etc.).

Such NE equivalents would not be mined correctly by the previously mentioned approaches as they would mine only the pair (Siddhivinayak, सिद्धिविनायक). In practice, most NEs are multi-word and hence it makes sense to address the problem of mining MWNE equivalents.

To the best of our knowledge, this is the first work on mining MWNEs in a language-neutral manner.

In this work, we make the following contributions:

- We perform an empirical study of MWNE occurrences, and the issues involved in mining (Section 2).
- We define a two-tier generative model for MWNE equivalents in a comparable corpus (Section 4).
- We propose a modified Viterbi algorithm for identifying MWNE equivalents, and

Proceedings of the 2011 Named Entities Workshop, IJCNLP 2011, pages 65–72,
Chiang Mai, Thailand, November 12, 2011.

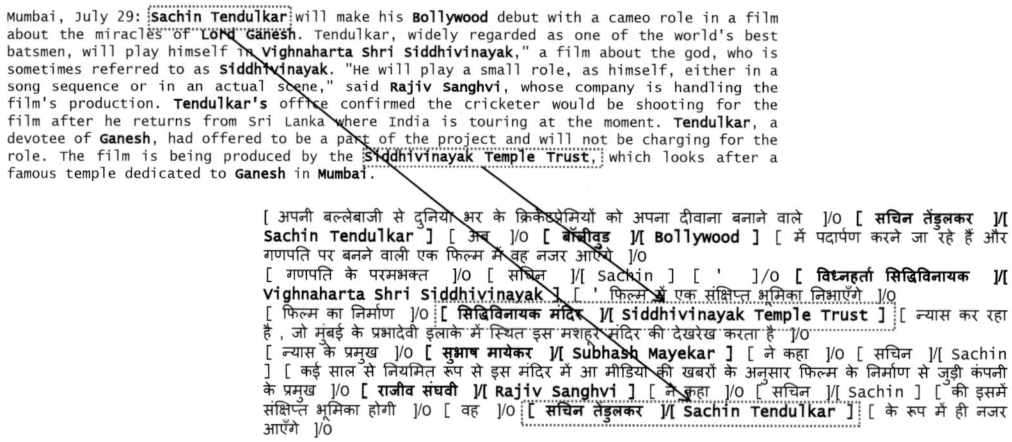

Figure 1: An example of MWNE mining.

for inferring correspondence information (Section 4.3).

- We evaluate the method on three language pairs (involving English (En), Arabic (Ar), Hindi (Hi) and Tamil (Ta)) (Section 6).

In our method, we assume the existence of the following linguistic resources: a NE tagger, a translation model, a transliteration model, and a language model. We show good mining performance for En-Hi and En-Ta. We perform error analysis for En-Ar, and identify sources of error (Section 6.5).

2 Empirical Study of Multi Word NE Equivalents

To understand the various issues in mining MWNE equivalents from comparable corpora, we took a random sample of 100 comparable En-Hi news article pairs from the Indian news portal WebDunia [1]. The English articles had 682 unique NEs of which 252 (37%) were person names, 130 (19%) were location names, and 300 (44%) were organization names. A substantial percentage of the names comprised of more than one word: locations 25%, person names 96%, and organizations 98%. For each English MWNE, we manually identified its equivalent (if any) in the comparable Hindi article. We observed that the MWNEs studied usually conformed to one/some of the following characteristics:

1. Each word in the Hindi MWNE is a transliteration of some word in the English MWNE. E.g. (Mahatma Gandhi, महात्मा गाँधी) where (Mahatma, महात्मा) and (Gandhi, गाँधी) are transliterations.

2. At least one word in the Hindi MWNE is a translation of some word in the English MWNE while the remaining words are transliterations. E.g. (New Delhi, नई दिल्ली `nai dillee`) where (New, नई) is a translation and (Delhi, दिल्ली) is a transliteration.

3. MWNEs contain abbreviations (initials). E.g. (M. K. Gandhi, एम. के. गाँधी) where (M, एम) and (K, के) are initials.

4. One-to-one correspondence between the words in the English and Hindi MWNEs. E.g. (New Delhi, नई दिल्ली)

5. One-to-many correspondence between the words in the English and Hindi MWNEs. E.g. (Card, प्रशस्ती पत्र `prashasti patr`).

6. Many-to-one correspondence between the words in the two MWNEs. E.g. (Air force, वायुसेना `vayusena`).

7. Sequential correspondence between words in the two MWNEs. E.g. (High Court, उच्चतम न्यायालय `ucchatam nyayalay`) where (High, उच्चतम) and (Court, न्यायालय) are equivalents.

8. Non-sequential correspondence between words in the two MWNEs. E.g. (Battle Honour Gurais, गुराइस युद्ध सम्मान `gurais`

[1] http://www.webdunia.com

yuddha sammaan) where the correspondence is (Battle, युद्ध), (Honour, सम्मान) and (Gurais, गुराइस).

9. Some words in the English MWNE do not have an equivalent in the Hindi MWNE. E.g. (Department of Telecommunication, दूरसंचार विभाग doorsanchaar vibhaag) where 'of' does not have an counterpart in the Hindi MWNE.

10. Acronym transliteration by transliterating each character separately. E.g. (IRRC, आईआरआरसी ai aar aar si) and (RBC, आर बी सी aar bi si).

11. Acronym transliteration by transliterating as a whole. E.g. (SAARC, सार्क saark) and (TRAI, ट्राई traai).

Our study revealed that each of the above characteristics is statistically important. Nearly 37% of location names and 77% of organization names involved both transliteration and translation. 12% of person names, 30% of location names and 45% of organization names had either one-to-many or many-to-one correspondence between words. 36% of organization names had non-sequential correspondence between words. These statistics clearly indicate that MWNEs need special treatment and any non-trivial MWNE equivalent mining technique must take into account the characteristics described above.

3 Problem Description

Given a pair of comparable documents in different languages, we wish to extract a set of pairs of MWNEs, one in each language, that are equivalent to each other. We are given a NE tagger in one of the languages, dubbed the *source* language, while the other language is called the *target* language (denoted with subscripts s and t). We are given a document pair (d_s, d_t) and the NEs in d_s i.e. $\{N_i\}_{i=1}^{m}$ and we want to find all possible NEs in d_t which are equivalent to some N_i. The problem now reduces to finding sequences of words in d_t that are equivalent to some N_i's.

In the example in Figure 1, $\{N_i\}_{i=1}^{m}$ = {(Sachin, Tendulkar), (Lord, Ganesh), (Siddhivinayak, Temple, Trust), ...}. We want to extract the set { (Sachin Tendulkar, सचिन तेंडुलकर), (Siddhivinayak Temple Trust, सिद्धिविनायक मंदिर), ...}.

4 Mining algorithm

4.1 Key idea

We model the problem of finding NE equivalents in the target sentence T using source NEs as a generative model. Each word t in the target sentence is hypothesized to be either part of a NE, or generated from a target language model (LM). Thus, in the generative model, the source NEs N's plus the target language model constitute the set of hidden states. The t's are the observations. We want to *align* states and observations, i.e. determine which state generated which observation, and choose the alignment that maximizes the probability of the observations. The probability of generating a target word t from a source NE state N is dependent on

- whether N is itself multi-word; if so, each word in N acts as a substate and can generate t.
- the context (the words preceding t in T); note that the length of the context window for t depends on the length of the source NE generating t, and is not a fixed parameter.
- the relationship (transliteration or translation) the state/substate and the target word.[2]

Dynamic programming (DP) approaches are usually used to compute the best alignment, but it fails here as the context size varies for each NE. Hence, we posit the generative model at two levels:

1. A sentence-level generative model (SGeM), where each word in the target sentence is generated either by the target LM or by one of the source NEs.

2. A generative model for the NE (NEGeM), where each word in the target NE is generated by one of the substates of the source NE.

This is illustrated by the example in Figure 2. The portions 'मंगलवार को' and 'के छात्रो ने अपने' of the Hindi sentence is generated by the language model. 'साउथेम्पटन युनिवर्सिटी' is generated by the English NE 'University of Southampton'. Note that without using the language model, 'के' would have been incorrectly aligned with 'of'. Another example is 'एम के

[2]We also use another relationship for letters in acronyms that are transliterated.

गाँधी . . . ' which is equivalent to the NE "M. K. Gandhi". Here, 'के' is likely to be a part of the NE. The language model not only reduces false positives but also disambiguates NE boundaries.

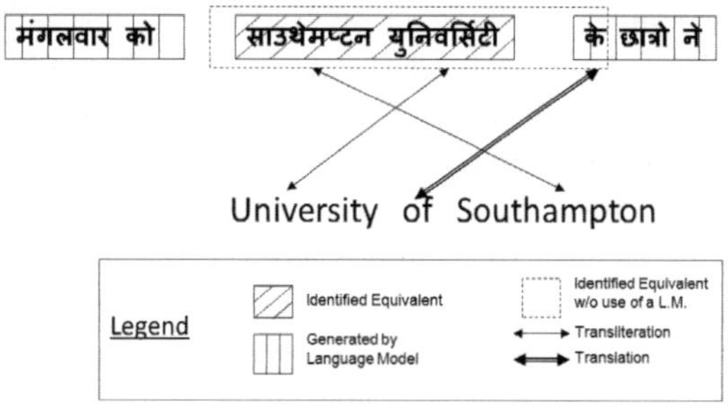

Figure 2: Generation of a Hindi sentence from an English NE.

4.2 Generative Model

SGeM Let $T = t_1 \dots t_n$ be the target sentence and $N = \{N_i\}_{i=0}^{m}$ be the hidden states (as before), where N_0 is the target LM state. In the SGeM, we want to predict the hidden state used to produce the next target term t_i. Let $a_i = j$ if t_i is generated by N_j. We find an alignment $A = a_1 \dots a_n$ which maximizes

$$P(T, A\,|N) = \prod_{i=1}^{n} P\left(a_i\,|a_1^{i-1}, N_{a_i}\right) P\left(t_i\,|t_1^{i-1}, N_{a_i}\right) \quad (1)$$

By choosing which source NE generates each target term, this model also controls the length of the target NE equivalent to a source NE.

Let $t_{k_i} \dots t_{i-1}$ be the *context* for t_i (all these terms are aligned to N_{a_i}). Then

$$P\left(t_i\,|t_1^{i-1}, N_{a_i}\right) = P\left(t_i \middle| t_{k_i}^{i-1}, N_{a_i}\right)$$

NEGeM To model the generation of the target term t_i given the context t_1^{i-1} and the substates of the source NE N_j, we let $N_j = \left(n_{j1}, \dots, n_{jL_j}\right)$ where n_{jp} is a substate. The *internal* alignment $B = b_{k_i}, \dots, b_i$ is defined such that $b_p = s$ if t_p is generated by n_{js}. We get

$$P\left(t_i \,\middle|\, t_{k_i}^{i-1}, N_{a_i}\right) = \sum_{B} \prod_{p=k_i}^{i} P\left(b_p\,|b_{p+1}^{i}\right) P\left(t_p\,|n_{a_i b_p}\right) \quad (2)$$

To model the relationship between the source and target terms, we introduce variables in a fashion similar to the introduction of B in (2). Let $R = r_{k_i}, \dots, r_i$ where $r_p \in$ {transliteration, translation, acronym, none} such that t_p and n_{jb_p} have the relationship r_p. Then [3]

$$\begin{aligned} &P\left(t_j\,|n_{a_i b_j}, r_j\right) \\ &= m_{tlat} P_{tlat}\left(t_j\,|n_{a_i b_j}\right)^{r_{tlat}} && \text{if } r_j = \text{translation} \\ &= m_{tlit} P_{tlit}\left(t_j\,|n_{a_i b_j}\right)^{r_{tlit}} && \text{if } r_j = \text{transliteration} \\ &= \delta\left[t_j \equiv n_{a_i b_j}\right] && \text{if } r_j = \text{acronym} \\ &= P_{lm}\left(t_j\right) && \text{if } r_j = \text{none} \end{aligned}$$

The four probability terms on the right are obtained, respectively, from a translation model, a transliteration model [4], an acronym model [5], and a language model.

Controlling target NE length In the SGeM, $P\left(a_i\,|a_1^{i-1}, N_{a_i}\right)$ is the probability that N_{a_i} will generate t_i. To compute this, we first note that, for a given term t_i, either $a_i = a_{i+1}$ i.e. N_{a_i} continues to generate beyond t_i, or $a_i \neq a_{i+1}$ i.e. N_{a_i} terminates at t_i. The probability of continuation depends on the length L of N_{a_i} and the length l of the target NE generated so far by N_{a_i}. Based on empirical observations, we defined a function $f(l, L)$ as

$$\begin{aligned} f(l, L) &= 0 \text{ for } l \notin \{L-2, L+2\} \\ &= 1 - \epsilon \text{ for } l \in \{L-1, L\} \\ &= \epsilon \text{ for } l \in \{L+1, L+2\} \end{aligned}$$

where $f\,(l, L)$ is the probability of continuation, and $1 - f\,(l, L)$ is the probability of termination. ϵ is a very small number. We now define

$$\begin{aligned} &P\left(a_i\,|a_1^{i-1}, N\right) \\ &= p_{NE} && \text{if } a_{i-1} = 0 \\ &= f\left(i - k_i, l_{a_i}\right) && \text{if } a_{i-1} \neq 0, k_i < i \\ &= 1 - f\left(i - k_{i-1}, l_{a_{i-1}}\right) && \text{if } a_{i-1} \neq 0, k_i = i \end{aligned}$$

where the probabilities on the right are for beginning an NE, continuing an NE, and terminating a previous NE, respectively.

[3] $\delta\,[\mathbf{x}] = 1$ if condition $\mathbf{x}$ is true

[4] A character-level extended HMM described in (Udupa et al., 2009a).

[5] A mapping from source language alphabets to target language transliterations of the alphabets.

4.3 Modified Viterbi algorithm

We use the dynamic programming framework to do the maximization in (1). For each target term t_i, for each source NE N_j, the subproblem is to find the best alignment $a_1 \ldots a_i$ such that $a_{i+1} \neq a_i$ i.e. t_i is the last term in the equivalent of N_j.

$$\texttt{subproblem}\,[i, j] =$$
$$\max_{a_1^i} P\left(a_i = j \neq a_{i+1} \left| a_1^{i-1}, N_j\right.\right) P\left(t_i \left| t_1^{i-1}, N_j\right.\right)$$

Let l be the length of the target NE ending at t_i, based on the alignment so far. The first probability term becomes

$$P\left(a_{i-l-1} \neq a_{i-l}^{i} = j \neq a_{i+1} \left| N_j\right.\right)$$
$$= \alpha \times f\left(l, L_j\right)\left(1 - f\left(l+1, L_j\right)\right)$$

This is non-zero only for certain values of l, for which we can construct the solution to $\texttt{subproblem}\,[i, j]$ using solutions for $i = l$. Denote $k = i - l$, then

$$\texttt{subproblem}\,[i, j] =$$
$$\max_{j \neq i} \texttt{subproblem}\,[k-1, j] \times \texttt{negem}\left(t_k^p, N_i\right)$$

where the procedure negem computes the probability that a given sequence of target words is an equivalent of the given source NE. This procedure solves a second (independent) DP problem (for the NEGeM), constructed in a similar fashion. It also models conditions such as "If a target term is a transliteration, it cannot map to more than one source substate."

The output of the system is a set of MWNE pairs. For each pair, we also give the internal alignment between the words of the two NEs.

5 Parameter Tuning

The MWNE model has five user-set parameters. These need to be tuned appropriately in order to be able to compare probabilities from different models. In the following, we describe the parameters and a systematic way to go about tuning them.

- $p_{NE} \in (0, +\infty)$ specifies how likely are we to find an NE in a target sentence
- Given a probability p returned by the transliteration model, the probability value used for comparisons p'_{tlit} is calculated as $p'_{tlit} = m_{tlit}\ p^{r_{tlit}}$ where $r_{tlit} \in R$, $m_{tlit} \in (0, +\infty)$. r_{tlit} is tuned to boost/suppress p; m_{tlit} is also used similarly, but to get more fine-grained control.
- Similarly, for a probability p given by the translation model, we calculate $p'_{tlat} = m_{tlat}\ p^{r_{tlat}}$ where $r_{tlat} \in R$, $m_{tlat} \in (0, +\infty)$

In our experiments, we found that transliteration probabilities were quite low compared to the others, followed by the translation probabilities. So, we used the following procedure to tune these parameters use a small hand-annotated set of document pairs.

1. Initially set $p_{NE} = +\infty$, and all other parameters to zero.
2. Tune r_{tlit} to find as many of the transliterations as possible. Then, use m_{tlit} to fine-tune it to improve precision without losing too much on recall.
3. Next, tune r_{tlat} to find as many of the translations as possible. Then, use m_{tlat} to fine-tune it to improve precision without losing too much on recall.
4. The system is now finding as many NEs as possible, but it is also finding noise. Keep lowering p_{NE} to allow the language model LM to absorb more and more noise. Do this until NEs also begin to get absorbed by LM.

6 Empirical Evaluation

In this section, we study the overall precision and recall of our algorithm for three different language pairs. English (En) is the source language, and Hindi (Hi), Tamil (Ta) and Arabic (Ar) are the target languages. Hindi belongs to the Indo-Aryan family, Tamil belongs to Dravidian family, and Arabic belongs to the Semitic family of languages. The results show that the method is applicable for a wide spectrum of languages.

6.1 Linguistic Resources

Models We need four models (translation, transliteration, language, and acronym) in order to run the proposed algorithm. For a language pair, we learnt these models using the following kinds of data, which was available to us:

- A set of pairs of NEs that are transliterations, to train the transliteration model
- A set of parallel sentences, to learn a translation model

Lang. pairs	Translit. pairs	Word pairs	Monolin. corpus
En-Hi	15K	634K	23M words
En-Ta	17K	509K	27M words
En-Ar	30K	8.2M	47M words

(1K = 1 thousand, 1M = 1 million)

Table 1: Training data for the models.

- A monolingual corpus in the target language, to train a language model
- A dictionary mapping English alphabets to their transliterations in the target language.

One can get an idea of the scale of linguistic resources used by looking at Table 1.

Source language NER The Stanford NER tool (Finkel et al., 2005) was used for obtaining a list of English NEs from the source document.

6.2 Corpus for MWNE mining

For each language pair, a set of comparable article pairs is required. The article pairs each for En-Hi and En-Ta were obtained from news websites[6], where the article correspondence was obtained using a method described in (Udupa et al., 2009b). En-Ar article pairs were extracted from Wikipedia using inter-language links.

Preprocessing The Stanford NER tags each word in the source document as a person, location, organization or other. A continuous sequence of identical tags was treated as a single MWNE. Completely capitalized NEs were treated as acronyms. For each acronym (e.g. "FIFA"), both the acronym version ("FIFA") as well as the abbreviation version ("F I F A") were included in the list of source NEs. Each target document was sentence-separated and tokenized using simple rules based on the presence of newlines, punctuation, and blank spaces. If a word can be constructed by concatenating strings from the acronym model, it is treated as an acronym, and the acronym strings are separated out (e.g. 'एमके' `emke` is changed to 'एम के' `em ke`).

6.3 Experimental Setup

Annotation Given an article pair, a human annotator looks through the list of source NEs, and identifies transliterations in the target document. For MWNEs, the annotator also marks which word in the source corresponds to each word in the target MWNE. This constitutes gold standard data that can be used to measure performance. 120 article pairs were annotated for En-Hi, 120 for En-Ta, and 36 for En-Ar.

Evaluation The NEs mined from one article pair are compared with the gold standard for that pair, and one of three possible judgements is made:

- Fully matched (if it fully matches some annotated NE (both source and target)).
- Partially matched (if source NEs match, and the mined target NE is a subset of the gold target NE).
- Incorrect match (in all other cases).

The algorithm is agnostic of the type of the NE (*Person*, *Organization*, etc.). So, reporting the precision and recall for each NE type does not provide much insight into the performance of the method. Instead, we report at different levels of match—full or partial, and for different categories of MWNEs—single word transliteration equivalents (SW), multi word transliteration equivalents (including acronyms) (MW-Translit) and multi word NEs having at least one translation equivalent (MW-Mixed). We compute the numbers for each article pair and then average over all pairs.

Parameter Tuning Parameter tuning was done following the procedure described in Section 5. For En-Hi and En-Ta, the following values were used: $p_{NE} = 1, m_{tlit} = 100, r_{tlit} = 7, m_{tlat} = 1, r_{tlat} = 1$. For En-Ar, $m_{tlit} = 1, r_{tlit} = 14$ was used, the other parameters remaining the same. For the tuning exercise, 40 annotated article pairs were used for En-Hi, 40 pairs for En-Ta, and 26 pairs for En-Ar.

6.4 Results and Analysis

We evaluated the algorithm on 80 article pairs for En-Hi, 80 pairs for En-Ta, and 11 pairs for En-Ar. The results are given in Table 2.

We observe that the results for both types of precision (and recall) are nearly identical. This is so because, in most cases, the system is able to mine the entire NE. This validates our intuition of using

[6]En-Hi from *Webdunia*, En-Ta from *The New Indian Express*.

Lang Pair	Prec. (full)	Prec. (part.)	Recall (full)	Recall (part.)
En-Hi	0.84	0.86	0.89	0.89
En-Ta	0.78	0.80	0.61	0.63
En-Ar	0.42	0.44	0.63	0.66
En-Ar*	0.43	0.44	0.60	0.62

* including the data used for tuning

Table 2: Precision and recall of the system

Category	En-Hi	En-Ta	En-Ar
SW	0.90	0.82	0.69
MW - Translit	0.91	0.64	0.63
MW - Mixed	0.77	0.40	0.66

Table 3: Category-wise recall of the system

language models to disambiguate NE boundaries. (The false negatives are mostly due to limitations of transliteration model and the dictionary.) The precision is relatively low in Arabic, even when we include the tuning data. This suggests that the problem is not because of incorrect parameter values. The error analysis for Arabic is discussed in Section 6.5.

We also report recall of the system for various categories of NEs in Table 3.[7] Note that the MW cases and the SW case are mutually exclusive.

6.5 Error Analysis for Arabic

The system performed relatively poorly in Arabic than in the other languages. Detailed error analysis revealed the following sources of error.

Source NER The text of the English articles automatically extracted from Wikipedia was not very clean, as compared to the newswire text used for En-Hi and En-Ta. As a result, the source NER wrongly identified many words as NEs, which were mapped to words on the target side, affecting precision. E.g. words such as "best", "foxe" were marked as NEs, and words with similar meaning or sound were found in the target. But since the annotator had ignored these words, the evaluation marked them as false positives.

Translation model Many words were ignored by the translation model because of the presence of diacritics, or affixes (e.g. 'ال' `al` in Arabic is frequently prefixed to words; also, in Arabic, different sources of text may have different levels of diacritization for the same words). E.g. The target document contained الجمهوريه `al-jamhooriyah` "republic"; the dictionary contained الجمهوريات `al-jamhooriyat`, which has a different suffix, and hence was not found.

Transliteration model The non-uniform usage of diacritics and affixes (across training and test data) as mentioned above affected the performance of transliteration too. E.g. The model is trained on data where the 'ال' prefix usually occurs in the Arabic NE, but not in the English NE. As a result, it maps the 'new' in 'new york' to النيو `al-nyoo`. The annotator had mapped 'new' to نيو `nyoo` (i.e. without the prefix), causing the evaluation program to mark the system's output as a false positive.

Generative Model Some errors occurred due to deficiencies in the generative model. The model requires every word in the source NE to be mapped to a unique word in the target NE. This causes problems when there are function words in the source NE, or when two source words are mapped to the same target word. E.g. 'yale school of management' corresponds to the 3-word NE 'الاداره مدرسه ييل' where 'of' has no Arabic counterpart. 'al azhar' corresponds to the single word الازهر `al-azhar`(which can be split as ال ازهر `al azhar`, but is never done in practice).

7 Related work

Automatic learning of translation lexicons has been studied in many works. Pirkola et al. (Pirkola et al., 2003) suggest learning transformation rules from dictionaries and applying the rules to find cross lingual spelling variants. Several works (Fung, 1995; Al-Onaizan and Knight, 2001; Koehn and Knight, 2002; Rapp, 1999) suggest approaches to learn translation lexicons from monolingual corpora. Apart from single word approaches, some works (Munteanu and Marcu, 2006; Chris Quirk, 2007) focus on mining parallel sentences and fragments from 'near parallel' corpora.

On the other hand, out-of-vocabulary words are transliterated to the target language. Approaches have been suggested for automatically learning transliteration equivalents. Klementiev et al. (Klementiev and Roth, 2006) proposed the use of similarity of temporal distributions for identifying NEs

[7] Since we cannot determine the category of false positives, we do not report the precision here.

from comparable corpora. Tao et al. (Tao et al., 2006) used phonetic mappings for mining NEs from comparable corpora, but their approach requires language specific knowledge which limits it to specific languages. Udupa et al. (Udupa et al., 2008; Udupa et al., 2009b) proposed a language-independent mining technique for mining single-word NE transliteration equivalents from comparable corpora. In this work, we extend this approach for mining NE equivalents from comparable corpora.

8 Conclusion

Through an empirical study, we motivated the importance and non-triviality of mining multi-word NE equivalents in comparable corpora. We proposed a two-tier generative model for mining such equivalents, which is independent of the length of NE. We developed a variant of the Viterbi algorithm for finding the best alignment in our generative model. We evaluated our approach for three language pairs, and discussed the error analysis for English-Arabic.

Currently, unigram approaches are popular for most tasks in NLP, CLIR, MT, topic modeling, etc. tasks. Phrase-based approaches are limited by their efficiency and complexity, and also show limited improvement. We hope that this work will motivate researchers to explore principled methods that make use of NE phrases to significantly improve the state-of-the-art in these areas. The two-tier generative model is applicable to any problem where the context of an observed variable does not depend on a fixed number of past observed variables.

References

Yaser Al-Onaizan and Kevin Knight. 2001. Translating named entities using monolingual and bilingual resources. In *ACL '02: Proceedings of the 40th Annual Meeting on Association for Computational Linguistics*, pages 400–408, Morristown, NJ, USA. Association for Computational Linguistics.

Arul Menezes Chris Quirk, Raghavendra Udupa U. 2007. Generative models of noisy translations with applications to parallel fragments extraction. In *MT Summit XI*, pages 377–284. European Association for Machine Translation.

Jenny Rose Finkel, Trond Grenager, and Christopher Manning. 2005. Incorporating non-local information into information extraction systems by gibbs sampling. In *ACL '05: Proceedings of the 43rd Annual Meeting on Association for Computational Linguistics*, pages 363–370, Morristown, NJ, USA. Association for Computational Linguistics.

Pascale Fung. 1995. A pattern matching method for finding noun and proper noun translations from noisy parallel corpora. In *IN PROCEEDINGS OF THE 33RD ANNUAL CONFERENCE OF THE ASSOCIATION FOR COMPUTATIONAL LINGUISTICS*, pages 236–243.

Alexandre Klementiev and Dan Roth. 2006. Weakly supervised named entity transliteration and discovery from multilingual comparable corpora. In *ACL-44: Proceedings of the 21st International Conference on Computational Linguistics and the 44th annual meeting of the Association for Computational Linguistics*, pages 817–824, Morristown, NJ, USA. Association for Computational Linguistics.

Philipp Koehn and Kevin Knight. 2002. Learning a translation lexicon from monolingual corpora. In *Proceedings of the ACL-02 workshop on Unsupervised lexical acquisition*, pages 9–16, Morristown, NJ, USA. Association for Computational Linguistics.

Dragos Stefan Munteanu and Daniel Marcu. 2006. Extracting parallel sub-sentential fragments from non-parallel corpora. In *ACL-44: Proceedings of the 21st International Conference on Computational Linguistics and the 44th annual meeting of the Association for Computational Linguistics*, pages 81–88, Morristown, NJ, USA. Association for Computational Linguistics.

Ari Pirkola, Jarmo Toivonen, Heikki Keskustalo, Kari Visala, and Kalervo Järvelin. 2003. Fuzzy translation of cross-lingual spelling variants. In *SIGIR '03*, pages 345–352, New York, NY, USA. ACM.

Reinhard Rapp. 1999. Automatic identification of word translations from unrelated english and german corpora. In *ACL*, pages 519–526.

Tao Tao, Su youn Yoon, Andrew Fister, Richard Sproat, and Chengxiang Zhai. 2006. Unsupervised named entity transliteration using temporal and phonetic correlation.

Raghavendra Udupa, K. Saravanan, A. Kumaran, and Jagadeesh Jagarlamudi. 2008. Mining named entity transliteration equivalents from comparable corpora. In *CIKM '08*, pages 1423–1424. ACM.

Raghavendra Udupa, K. Saravanan, Anton Bakalov, and Abhijit Bhole. 2009a. "they are out there, if you know where to look": Mining transliterations of oov query terms for cross-language information retrieval. In *ECIR*, volume 5478, pages 437–448. Springer.

Raghavendra Udupa, K. Saravanan, A. Kumaran, and Jagadeesh Jagarlamudi. 2009b. Mint: A method for effective and scalable mining of named entity transliterations from large comparable corpora. In *EACL*, pages 799–807.

An Unsupervised Alignment Model for Sequence Labeling: Application to Name Transliteration

Najmeh Mousavi Nejad
Department of Engineering,
Islamic Azad University, Science
& Research Branch, Punak,
Ashrafi Isfahani, Tehran, Iran
najme.mousavi@gmail.com

Shahram Khadivi
Department of Computer
Engineering, Amirkabir University
of Technology 424 Hafez Ave,
Tehran, Iran 15875-4413
khadivi@aut.ac.ir

Abstract

In this paper a new sequence alignment model is proposed for name transliteration systems. In addition, several new features are introduced to enhance the overall accuracy in a name transliteration system. Discriminative methods are used to train the model. Using this model, we achieve improvements on the transliteration accuracy in comparison with the state-of-the-art alignment models. The 1-best name accuracy is also improved using a name selection method from the 10-best list based on the contents of the web. This method leads to a relative improvement of 54% over 1-best transliteration. The experiments are conducted on an English-Persian name transliteration task. Furthermore, we reproduce the past studies results under the same conditions. Experiments conducting on English to Persian transliteration show that new features provide a relative improvement of 5% over previous published results.

1 Introduction

Transliteration is a phonetic translation that finds the phonetic equivalent in target language given a source language word. The quality of name transliteration plays an important role in a variety of applications such as machine translation, as proper nouns are usually not in the dictionary and also new ones are introduced every day (e.g. scientific terms).

The transliteration process consists of training stage and testing stage. In the training stage the model learns segment alignment and produces transformation rules with a probability assigned to each of them. In the test stage it uses these transformation rules to generate the target name. Obviously the alignment process highly affects the results. There are some alignment tools which produce alignments from a bilingual corpus such as GIZA++ (Och and Ney, 2003).

Previous studies can be divided into two categories according to their alignment process: those which apply alignment tools or predefined algorithms in their transliteration process and those that propose new algorithms for aligning word pairs.

There has been an exploration on several alignment methods for letter to phoneme alignment (Jiampojamarn and Kondrak, 2010). M2M-aligner, ALINE which performs phonetic alignment, constraint-based alignment and Integer Programming were investigated. The system was evaluated on several data sets such as Combilex, English Celex, CMUDict, NETTalk, OALD and French Brulex.

Furthermore transliteration based on phonetic scoring has been studied using phonetic features (Yoon et al., 2007). This method was evaluated for four languages – Arabic, Chinese, Hindi and Korean – and one source language – English. The name pairs were aligned using standard string alignment algorithm based on Kruskal.

Substring-based transliteration was investigated applying GIZA++ for aligning name pairs and using open-source CRF++ software package for training the model (Reddy and Waxmonsky, 2009). The model was tested from English to three languages - Hindi, Kannada and Tamil.

English-Japanese transliteration was performed using a maximum entropy model (Goto et al., 2003). First the likelihood of a particular choice of letter chunking into English

Proceedings of the 2011 Named Entities Workshop, IJCNLP 2011, pages 73–81,
Chiang Mai, Thailand, November 12, 2011.

conversion units is calculated and the English word is divided into conversion units that are partial English character strings in an English word. Second each English conversion unit is converted into a partial Japanese character strings called katakana. In this process the English and Japanese contextual information are considered simultaneously to calculate the plausibility of conversion from each English conversion unit to various Japanese conversion candidate units using a single probability model.

There are a few researches which do not use alignment in the transliteration process. For example in recent years two discriminative methods corresponding to local and global modeling approaches were proposed (Zelenko and Aone, 2006). These methods do not require alignment of names in different languages and the features for discriminative training are extracted directly from the names themselves. An experimental evaluation of these methods for name transliteration was performed from three languages (Arabic, Korean, and Russian) into English.

The language pair we perform our tests on, is Persian-English and vice versa. There have been a few researches on Persian language (Karimi et al., 2007). The quality of transliterated names has been improved in the past studies. However, the proposed method is language specific and the algorithm is designed for Persian language. The best general language independent model in the mentioned paper is CV-MODEL3. To compare our new method, we have reproduced its results under similar conditions. In both systems the same corpus was used and both experiments are 10-fold cross-validation.

In this paper, the openNlP maximum entropy package is used for training the model[1]. We define new features for discriminative training. Moreover a new approach for aligning name pairs is proposed. In the case studies, we investigate the effect of each feature by adding it to and removing it from training process. As a result, the best combination of features is achieved for English-Persian language pair. In addition, we compare our proposed alignment method to GIZA++. Our main concern is finding an alignment model for transliteration. We have found that the most common word alignment tool for transliteration alignment is GIZA++ (Hong, et al., 2009; Karimi, et al., 2007; Sravana Reddy and Sonjia Waxmonsky, 2009). The proposed language-independent alignment method performs similar to GIZA++ results in Top-1 for English-Persian transliteration and improves the accuracy and MRR[2] in Top-5 and Top-10. For reverse transliteration (Persian to English), new alignment shows a significant improvement over GIZA++ outcome. Furthermore an approach based on name frequencies in the web contents is applied to choose one name from 10 best possible transliterations. Since the dominant language of web is English, the experiments were performed for Persian-to-English transliteration and not English-to-Persian.

The rest of this paper is organized as follows: The feature set is described in Sec. 2. The proposed alignment method is described in Sec. 3. In Sec. 4 our experimental study is described. Choosing one name from 10 best transliterations is described in Sec. 5 and the conclusion is described in Sec. 6.

2 Feature Set

Maximum entropy models use features for maximizing log likelihood. Consequently defining proper features has a high impact on the final results. We define two types of features which are binary-valued vectors. For both types of features (consonant-vowel and n-gram), current context (current letter), two past and two future contexts (neighboring letters) are used. We choose a window with a length of 5, since experiments show that lower length or higher length would have degrade the results.

2.1 Consonant-Vowel Features

Every language has a set of consonant and vowel letters. The consonant letters can be divided into different groups based on their types (Table 1).

Plosive (stop)	p , b , t , d , k , g , q
Fricative	f , v , s , z , x , h
Plosive-Fricative	j , c
Flap (tap)	r
Nasal	m , n
Lateral approximant	l , y

Table 1. Six group of consonants

Most combinations of consonant-vowel features were tested for English-Persian language pair. We have found the following consonant-vowel features are the most effective ones for

[1] Available at http://incubator.apache.org/opennlp/

[2] Mean Reciprocal Rank

generating current target letter (t_n). S_i is used to represent the source name characters and t_i represents the target name characters. CV is an abbreviation for consonant- vowel.

$f1_{cv}: CV_{s_n}$
$f2_{cv}: CV_{s_{n-1}}\ CV_{s_n}$
$f3_{cv}: CV_{t_{n-1}}\ CV_{s_{n-1}}\ CV_{s_n}$
$f4_{cv}: CV_{s_{n-1}}\ CV_{s_n}\ CV_{s_{n+1}}$
$f5_{cv}: CV_{s_{n-2}}\ CV_{s_{n-1}}\ CV_{s_n}$
$f6_{cv}: CV_{s_n}\ CV_{s_{n+1}}\ CV_{s_{n+2}}$
$f7_{cv}: CV_{t_{n-1}}\ CV_{s_{n-1}}\ CV_{s_n}\ CV_{s_{n+1}}$
$f8_{cv}: CV_{t_{n-1}}\ CV_{s_{n-2}}\ CV_{s_{n-1}}\ CV_{s_n}$

We have defined three types of CV features. CV-TYPE1 is some basic features to reproduce past studies results. These features consist of $f1_{cv}, f2_{cv}, f5_{cv}$ and $f6_{cv}$. To achieve better results, some new features are presented called CV-TYPE2 which is an augmented set of features including $f1_{cv}$ to $f8_{cv}$. Finally to track the effect of new consonant grouping strategy, CV-TYPE3 is defined which is similar to CV-TYPE2 except that the consonant letters are divided according to Table 1.

Table 1 can be used for categorizing any language letters as well, by replacing each English letter with its corresponding letter in the target language. These features improve transliteration, but still are not sufficient. Therefore we need n-gram features.

2.2 N-gram Features

In n-gram features for source name, two past and two future contexts are used (a window with a length of 5). For target name however, only two past contexts are used (because we don't have future context yet). Since the maximum entropy is used for training, the whole approach for target name can be considered as Maximum Entropy Markov Model (MEMM) which is a simple extension of the ME classification and is useful for modeling sequences as it takes into account the previous classification decision. But for source name the future letters are known and are used for feature extraction. So the MEMM concept cannot be broadcast to source name as well.

Using S to demonstrate the source name and T to demonstrate the target name, the n-gram features for each name can be summarized as:

$s_{n-2}\ s_{n-1}\ s_n\ s_{n+1}\ s_{n+2}$
$t_{n-2}\ t_{n-1}\ \times\ \times\ \times$

For any language pair, all combinations of s_i and t_i can be used to define a feature. In our model, the following set of features has been used:

f1: s_n
f2: $s_{n-1}\ s_n$
f3: $s_n\ s_{n+1}$
f4: $s_{n-2}\ s_{n-1}\ s_n$
f5: $s_{n-1}\ s_n\ s_{n+1}$
f6: $s_n\ s_{n+1}\ s_{n+2}$
f7: t_{n-1}
f8: $t_{n-2}\ t_{n-1}$

The best sequence of above features, varies from one language pair to another. We report the best combination for English-Persian language pair in Sec. 4.

3 The Proposed Alignment Method

Features explained in the previous section, are extracted from the aligned names. In other words, first the alignments of source and target names should be produced. Our proposed alignment method is a two-dimensional Cartesian coordinate system. The horizontal axis is labeled with the source name and the vertical axis is labeled with the target name (or vice versa). A line is drawn from the coordinate (0,0) to the point with coordinate (source_name_length , target_name_length). We mark the corresponding cell in each column of the alignment matrix which has the less distance to the line (Figure 1). Considering Figure 1 the following alignments are achieved:

(a,ا) , (b,ب) , (r,ر) , (a,ا) , (m,م) , (s,ز)

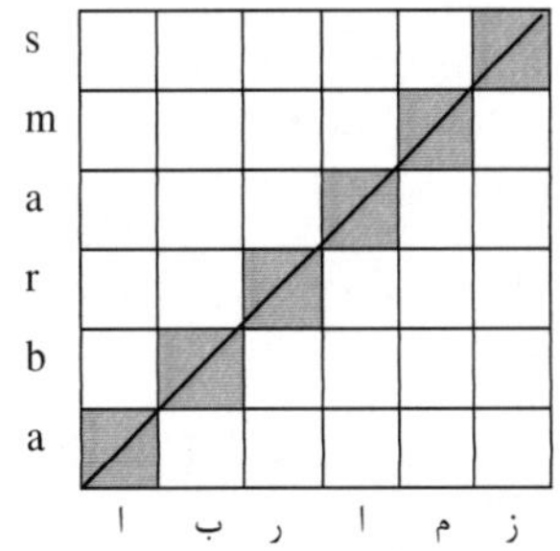

Figure 1. Alignment matrix of (abrams,ابرامز)

The name pair in Figure 1 has a simple alignment. For more complex alignments, some fixed points are needed in order to draw the lines. These fixed points are coordinates of segments that are known to be always alignments of each other. For instance in English-Persian, "ب" is always aligned to "b" or "bb". If there exists any fixed point in the name pair, one line is drawn from origin to the fixed point coordinate and the other one is drawn from the fixed point to the point with (source_name_length , target_name_length) coordinate. In other words if there are n fixed points in the name pair, there will be n+1 lines in the plane. In Figure 2, (bb,ب) and (n,ن) are fixed points. So the following alignments are achieved:

(g,گ) , (i,ی) , (bb,ب) , (o,و) , (n,ن) , (i,ی)

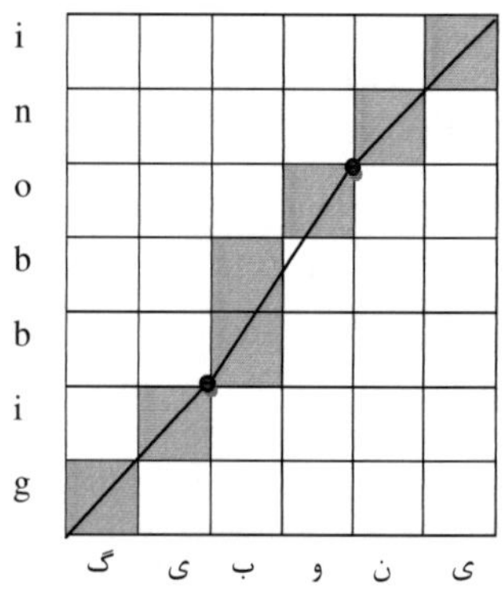

Figure 2. Alignment matrix of (gibboni,گیبونی)

These fixed points help us to perform the alignment process more accurately. The more accurate they are, the better the final results are.

Finding fixed points is difficult for some language pairs, especially for the ones about which we have no knowledge. Based on the fact that our goal is to design a language independent transliteration system, an automatic way to find the fixed points is of interest.

We investigate two approaches for finding the fixed points. In the first one, Moses, a statistical machine translation system is used to define the fixed points. Moses trains translation models for any language pair automatically (Koehn, et al., 2007). In translation process, it produces a phrase table which contains source and target phrases with different lengths and the conditional probability of those phrases. If each letter in transliteration is considered as a word and each name as a sentence, Moses can be used to find the fixed points automatically.

To produce the phrase table, Moses should be run on a bilingual corpus. Any corpus containing name pairs can be used. Then the phrase table is parsed and the phrases with the maximum probabilities are extracted. The length of the phrases is usually between 1 and 3, since for most natural languages, the maximum length of corresponding phonemes of each grapheme is a digraph (two letters) or at most a trigraph (three letters). Once a set of fixed points are found for a language pair, they stay constant for all other transliterations and do not change. In other words it is sufficient to run Moses one time and use produced fixed points for any transliteration task related to that language pair.

In the second approach the training dataset helps the system find the fixed points set. We introduce FPA algorithm which is an unsupervised approach that adopts the concept of EM training. In the expectation step the training name pairs are aligned using current model and in the maximization step the most probable alignments are added to the fixed points set. The algorithm is as follows:

1. An initial and inaccurate alignment is considered, assuming just one line in the alignment matrix.
2. The discriminative model learns the mapping between source and target names using maximum entropy.
3. Using the trained model (ME) and extracting the most probable mappings, an initial set of fixed points are nominated. This process is repeated until the algorithm converges.

A brief sketch of FPA algorithm is presented in Figure 3. In line 2 we initialize the fixed points with an empty set. Line 3 shows the convergence of the algorithm. It means when the fixed points set do not change, the final set is found. In line 6 name pairs with equal lengths are only considered. The corresponding consonant-vowel sequences of the name pairs are generated. If the CV sequences are exactly similar to each other, the name pair is included in the training stage. Although the whole training data can be used in the first iteration, this condition produces a reasonable result with the advantage of ignoring a large amount of training data and saving the time in the first iteration. Line 11 to 21 shows the process of updating the fixed points set. In line 14 forcedAlignment means using current ME model to transliterate source name with the condition in which the produced transliterations should be the same as the target name. This condition guarantees the convergence of the algorithm. Suppose the source name length is J and the target name length is I, then the decoding process is as follows:

1. For each letter of the source name choose top N transformation rules with highest probabilities which lead to producing the

target name.

2. Build a search tree: add N 3-tuple (current letter, generated transliteration, transformation probability) to an N-complete tree.
3. Do beam search to find the best path in the tree. (Best path is the highest multiplication of edges probability).
4. Update set A:

$$FP(S_1^J, T_1^I, A) = \{ (S_{j1}^{j2}, T_i): \forall j_1 \le j \le j_2 : (j, i) \in A \}$$

$$FP(S_1^J, T_1^I, A) = \{ (S_j, T_{i1}^{i2}): \forall i_1 \le i \le i_2 : (j, i) \in A \}$$

We change the value of N between 1 and 5. Results show that there is no significant improvement after N = 3 (N > 3). Also time complexity and memory usage increases exponentially. Therefore the best value for N is 3. Line 17 and 18 are final steps in producing fixed points set. |k| is the number of distinct segments in the best path set and $p(\tilde{T}_k|\tilde{S}_k)$ is the probability of $\tilde{T}_k|\tilde{S}_k$ transformation rule. Once the probabilities are calculated, they are compared to a predefined threshold. If they are bigger than threshold, they are added to the fixed points set. We change the value of threshold between 0.7 and 1, and find out the best value for threshold is 0.9. The test stage starts after finding the final fixed points set. The decoding process in test stage is similar to forcedAlignment, but here the condition for generated transliteration (forcing algorithm to produce target name) is meaningless. So any transliteration can be added to Top-N results.

A good method for finding the fixed points generates a set similar to other methods. For example both approaches introduced in this section, lead to similar results. That's why we present only the second approach results in the experiment section. From another point of view, it is sufficient to find the fixed points set for each language pair only once. Because the fixed points set which is found by a proper corpus, is very similar to the set produced by a different corpus on the same language pair. Therefore if more than one set are produced using different corpora, the intersection of these sets is considered as the final fixed points set for other transliteration tasks regarding that language pair.

```
1: Algorithm FPA
2: fixedPoints = {} , oldFixedPoints = {}
3: while( fixedPoints != oldFixedPoints) {
4:    oldFixedPoints = fixedPoints;
5:    if( first iteration){
6:       fixedPoints = updateFixedPoints(names_with_equal_CV_sequence)
7:    }else{
8:       fixedPoints = updateFixedPoints(whole_training_corpus)
9:    }
10: }
11: Function updateFixedPoints(training_data){
12:    bestPathEdges = {};
13:    for( all name pairs) do {
14:       A = forcedAlignment(sourceName, targetName, currentModel)
15:    }
16:    for (all segment pairs in A) do{
17:       p(T̃k|S̃k) = Σp(T̃k,S̃k) / Σ_T́ p(T́,S̃k)
18:       p(S̃k|T̃k) = Σp(T̃k,S̃k) / Σ_Ś p(Ś,T̃k)
19:    }
20:    if (p > threshold) { add transformation rule to the fixedPoints }
21: }
```

Figure 3. Sketch of FPA algorithm

We present a list of most common fixed points for English to Persian transliteration which is sorted in descending order of the probability values.

{ (م mm) , (د dd) , (ب bb) , (و wh) , (ر rr) , (کس x) , (ن kn) , (ن nn) , (ف ff) , (ت tt) , (پ pp) , (ل ll) , (ه h) , (ن n) , (ر r) , (د d) , (گ g) , (ب b) , (ت t) , (ش sh) , (پ p) , (ل l) , (م m) , (ج j) , (ف ph) , (س ss) , (ز z) , (و w) , (ک q) , (ف f) , (و v) , (ی y) , (س s) , (ک k) }

There is a study on statistical machine translation which combines discriminative training and Expectation-Maximization (Fraser and Marcu, 2006). The proposed EMD algorithm uses discriminative training to control the contributions of sub-models. Furthermore, EM is applied to estimate the parameters of sub-models. In contrast to their method, we generate fixed points set by Expectation-Maximization and no parameter estimation is done during EM. The new fixed points set, updated in EM step, improves the alignment quality and consequently causes the model to reestimates its parameters.

4 Case Studies

Two types of experiments have been performed, one for effectiveness of different features and the other for the effectiveness of alignment process. A corpus consisting of 16760 word pairs has been used. These words are names of geographical places, people and companies. This is the same corpus which previous study experiments were performed on (Karimi et al., 2007). Each name has only one transliteration. Many words of different language origins (such as Arabic, French, and Dutch) were included in the corpus. This corpus is referred to as B^+. The experiments apply 10-fold cross-validation in which the whole corpus is partitioned into 10 disjoint segments. This type of experiment is an alternative method for controlling over-fitting.

4.1 Effectiveness of Features

All combinations of f1 to f8 for English-Persian language pair were tested. Table 2 shows mean word accuracy in 10-fold, for English-Persian transliteration. The first row in Table 2 shows reproducing CV-MODEL3 results using some basic features. Extending CV-TYPE1 features to CV-TYPE2 improves the accuracy (second row). Similarly applying the new grouping of consonant letters (CV-TYPE3), leads to a relative improvement of 1% over CV-TYPE2 (third row). CV-TYPE1, CV-TYPE2 and CV-TYPE3 are explained in Sec. 2.2.

The best word accuracy in Table 3 is 58.4%. Comparing word accuracies, it can be concluded that for English-Persian transliteration, the following features are the most effective ones:

f1: s_n
f2: $s_{n-1}\ s_n$
f3: $s_n\ s_{n+1}$
f5: $s_n\ s_{n+1}\ s_{n+2}$
f7: t_{n-1}

As we can see, t_{n-2} does not help in better transliteration. Because written Persian omits short vowels, and only long vowels appear in texts. So t_{n-2} is completely irrelevant for generating current Persian letter. Using f2 and f3 simultaneously, improves the results much more than f4, f5 or f6 alone. Since each of them has the power of bigram feature and together, they provide trigram features.

Experimental results for English to Persian transliteration show that CV-TYPE3 has the best word accuracy among all other consonant-vowel grouping strategy. Therefore, we use this type of consonant-vowel features for the reverse direction as well. Furthermore English-Persian experiments imply n-gram features with a distance of two letters are not useful for Persian names. This is due to Persian language nature. This fact reduces the number of experiments, since it removes f4, f5 and f6 from n-gram features. Table 3 shows the effect of several feature combinations on mean word accuracy in Top-1 for Persian-English transliteration task. The best word accuracy in Table 3 is 20.6%. Therefore, the following features result in best performance.

f1: s_n
f2: $s_{n-1}\ s_n$
f3: $s_n\ s_{n+1}$
f7: t_{n-1}
f8: $t_{n-2}\ t_{n-1}$

Persian-English transliteration is more difficult than English-Persian. Because moving from the language with smaller alphabet size to the one with larger size, increases the ambiguity. Using web page contents improves the transliteration. The strategy is explained in Sec. 5.

f1	f2	f3	f4	f5	f6	f7	f8	CV-TYPE1	CV-TYPE2	CV-TYPE3	Mean WA
√	√	√	×	×	√	×	×	√	×	×	55.3
√	√	√	×	×	√	×	×	×	√	×	56.7
√	√	√	×	×	√	×	×	×	×	√	57.2
√	×	×	×	√	×	√	×	×	×	√	57.3
√	√	√	×	×	×	×	×	×	×	√	57.3
√	√	√	√	√	√	√	√	×	×	√	57.3
√	√	√	√	×	×	√	×	×	×	√	57.4
√	×	×	×	√	√	√	×	×	×	√	57.5
√	√	√	×	×	×	√	√	×	×	√	58.0
√	√	√	×	√	√	√	×	×	×	√	58.2
√	√	√	×	×	×	√	×	×	×	√	58.4
√	√	√	×	×	√	√	×	×	×	√	58.4

Table 2. The effect of several feature combinations on mean word accuracy in Top-1 for English-Persian transliteration

f1	f2	f3	f7	f8	CV-TYPE3	WA
√	√	√	×	×	×	17.1
√	√	√	√	×	√	19.3
√	√	×	√	√	√	19.8
√	×	√	√	√	√	20.5
√	√	√	√	√	√	20.6

Table 3. The effect of several feature combinations on mean word accuracy in Top-1 for Persian-English transliteration

4.2 Effectiveness Of Alignment

The proposed alignment (FixedPointsAlign) results are compared to GIZA++ alignment. The settings of important parameters of GIZA++ are as follows: five iterations for each IBM1 model and HMM and three iterations for each IBM3 and IBM4 models. We checked GIZA++ output for name pairs and discovered the alignments are always monotone, except for rare cases. That's why it is used in past studies as well (Hong, et al., 2009; Karimi, et al., 2007; Sravana Reddy and Sonjia Waxmonsky, 2009). The approaches using GIZA++ utilize symmetrized alignments in both directions. All of the experiments are done on B^+ corpus, using 10-fold cross validation. The results are compared to CV-MODEL3 (Karimi et al., 2007). The most effective features, founded in the previous section, are included in the training stage. These combinations are specifically appropriate for English-Persian language pair. For other languages if the best combination is not known, all the features, f1 to f8 should be included in the feature extraction.

For each fold, word accuracy and MRR is computed. Table 4 and Table 5 show mean word accuracy and mean MRR in Top-1, Top-5 and Top-10 for English to Persian. Persian to English results are presented in Table 6 and Table 7.

The transliteration systems that use GIZA++ in their alignment differ from each other by transliteration generation process. Since GIZA++ has a unique strategy for aligning sentences or name pairs. CV-MODEL3 is a language-independent model which uses GIZA++ for aligning name pairs. Since our experiment conditions are exactly the same as CV-MODEL3 experiments conditions, the results are comparable.

Table 4 shows that our proposed alignment method is a proper replacement for GIZA++ tool. It has an equal accuracy in Top-1 and also improves accuracy in Top-5 and Top-10 transliterations. SLA (single line align) is the proposed method with an empty fixed points set. As can be seen from Table 4, defining a proper set of fixed points significantly improves the results. Furthermore Table 6 and Table 7 show that for Persian to English transliteration, our proposed alignment algorithm significantly improves the results. The outcomes lead us to the conclusion that although GIZA++ provides good results in English to Persian transliteration, it does not produce a reasonable result in the reverse direction. This is due to parameters setting. Unlike our proposed alignment, GIZA++ alignment is highly dependent to its parameters.

N-Best	SLA	CV-MODEL3	GIZA++	FPA
Top-1	50.7	55.3	58.4	58.4
Top-5	77.0	84.5	86.8	88.7
Top-10	84.0	89.5	90.8	92.6

Table 4. Mean word accuracy of 10-fold on B^+ corpus for English to Persian transliteration

N-Best	GIZA++	FPA
Top-1	58.4	58.4
Top-5	70.2	70.9
Top-10	70.7	71.5

Table 5. Mean MRR of 10-fold on B^+ Corpus for English to Persian.

N-Best	SLA	CV-MODEL3	GIZA++	FPA
Top-1	19.4	17.6	14.6	20.6
Top-5	41.6	36.2	32.7	44.9
Top-10	50.4	46.0	38.4	53.2

Table 6. Mean word accuracy of 10-fold on B+ corpus for Persian to English transliteration

N-Best	GIZA++	FPA
Top-1	14.6	20.6
Top-5	21.3	29.7
Top-10	22.1	30.8

Table 7. Mean MRR of 10-fold on B+ Corpus for Persian to English

5 N-Best Reranking

Generating 10 best transliterations instead of one name definitely has a better word accuracy, because if the target name exist in one of the 10 names, the word accuracy is equal to one for that name pair. But an efficient transliteration system should produce only the correct ones.

A large corpus containing several names can be considered as a reference to choose one name from possible transliterations. First the unigram probability of each transliteration is calculated. Then the transliteration with the max probability is chosen as the final result. Since the dominant language in the web is English, it is the best corpus for Persian to English transliteration. As a result, in this section the experiments were performed for Persian-to-English transliteration and not English-to-Persian.

We calculate the probabilities of Top-10 for each source name and the one with the maximum probability is chosen as the final transliteration. A test file consisting of 1676 name pairs was produced. We extract 10% of the train file randomly to generate the test file. The word accuracy of this approach is **32.1%** and the accuracy for the same test and train files, generating only one transliteration (Top-1) is **20.8%**. It means that this approach leads to a relative improvement of **54%** over Top-1 results.

6 Conclusions

In this paper, we presented a language-independent alignment method for transliteration. Discriminative training is used in our system. The proposed method has improved transliteration generation compared to GIZA++. Furthermore we defined a number of new features in the training stage.

For Persian to English transliteration, web pages contents are used to choose one name from 10-best hypothesis list. This approach leads to a relative improvement of 54% over simple Top-1 transliteration.

References

Fraser, A., Marcu, D., Semi-Supervised Training for Statistical Word Alignment, Proceedings of ACL-2006, pp. 769-776, Sydney, Australia

Goto, I., Kato, N., Uratani, N., Ehara, T., Transliteration Considering Context Information Based on the Maximum Entropy Method, In Proc. Of IXth MT Summit. (2003)

Hong, G., Kim, M., Lee, D., Rim, H., A Hybrid to English-Korean Name Transliteration, Proceedings of the 2009 Named Entities Workshop, ACL-IJCNLP 2009, pages 92–95, Suntec, Singapore, 7 August 2009.

Jiampojamarm, S., Kondrak, G., Letter-Phoneme Alignment: An Exploration, Proceedings of the 48th Annual Meet-ing of the Association for Computational Li-nguistics, pages 780–788, Uppsala, Sweden, 11-16 July 2010.

Josef, F., Ney. H., Discriminative Training and Maximum Entropy Models for Statistical Machine Translation, Proceedings of the 40th Annual Meeting of the Association for Computational Linguistics (ACL), Philadelphia, July 2002, pp. 295-302.

Josef, F., Ney. H., A Systematic Comparison of Various Statistical Alignment Models, Computational Linguistics, vol.29 (2003), pp. 19-51

Karimi, S., Scholer, F., Turpin, A., Collapsed Consonant and Vowel Models: New Approaches for English-Persian Transliteration and Back-Transliteration, The 45th Annual Meeting of the Association for Computational Linguistics (ACL'07), pages 648-655, Prague, Czech Republic, June 2007.

Karimi, S., Machine Transliteration of Proper Names between English and Persian, A thesis submitted in fulfillment of the requirements for the degree of Doctor of Philosophy, BEng. (Hons.), MSc.

Koehn, P., Hoang, H., Birch A., CallisonBurch, C., Federico, M., Bertoldi, N., Cowan, B., Shen, W., Moran, C., Zens, R., Dyer C., Bojar, O., Constantin, A., Herbst E., 2007. Moses: Open source toolkit for statistical machine translation. In Proceedings of the 45th Annual Meeting of the Association for Computational Linguistics (ACL'07) – Companion Volume, June.

Microsoft Web N-gram Services available at http://research.microsoft.com/en-us/collaboration/focus/cs/web-ngram.aspx

Reddy, S., Waxmonsky, S., Substring-based Transliteration with Conditional Random Fields, Proceedings of the 2009 Named Entities Workshop, ACL-IJCNLP 2009, pages 92–95, Suntec, Singapore, 7 August 2009.

Yoon, S., Kim, K., Sproat, R., "Multilingual Transliteration Using Feature based Phonetic Method", Proceedings of the 45th Annual Meeting of the Association of Computational Linguistics, pages 112–119, Prague, Czech Republic, June 2007, Association for Computational Linguistics.

Zelenko, D., Aone. C., Discriminative Methods for Transliteration, Proceedings of the 2006 Conference on Empirical Methods in Natural Language Processing (EMNLP 2006), pages 612–617, Sydney, July 2006.

Forward-backward Machine Transliteration between English and Chinese Based on Combined CRFs

Ying Qin
Department of Computer Science,
Beijing Foreign Studies University
qinying@bfsu.edu.cn

Guohua Chen
National Research Centre for Foreign Language Education, Beijing Foreign Studies University
professorchenguohua@yahoo.com.cn

Abstract

The paper proposes a forward-backward transliteration system between English and Chinese for the shared task of NEWS2011. Combined recognizers based on Conditional Random Fields (CRF) are applied to transliterating between source and target languages. Huge amounts of features and long training time are the motivations for decomposing the task into several recognizers. To prepare the training data, segmentation and alignment are carried out in terms of not only syllables and single Chinese characters, as was the case previously, but also phoneme strings and corresponding character strings. For transliterating from English to Chinese, our combined system achieved Accuracy in Top-1 0.312, compared with the best performance in NEWS2011, which was 0.348. For backward transliteration, our system achieved top-1 accuracy 0.167, which is better than others in NEWS2011.

1 Introduction

The surge of new named entities is a great challenge for machine translation, cross-language IR, cross-language IE and so on. Transliteration, mostly used for translating personal and location names, is a way of translating source names into target language with approximate phonetic equivalents (Li et al., 2004), while backward transliteration traces back to the foreign names (Guo and Wang, 2004). Phonetic-based and spelling-based approaches are popularly applied in machine transliteration (Karimi et al. 2011). Recently direct orthographical mapping (DOM) between two languages, a kind of spelling-based transliteration approach, outperforms that of phonetic-based methods. Most systems in NEWS2009 and NEWS2010 utilized this approach to automatic transliteration (Li et al., 2009; Li et al., 2010).

In previous researches, syllable segmentation and alignment were done in terms of single syllables in training a transliteration model. (Yang et al., 2009; Yang et al., 2010; Aramaki and Abekawwa, 2009; Li et al., 2004). Sometimes, however, it is hard to split an English word and align each component with a single Chinese character, which is always monosyllabic. For instance, when *TAX* is transliterated into 塔克斯 (Ta Ke Si) in Chinese, no syllable is mapped onto the characters 克 and 斯, for *X* is pronounced as two phonemes rather than a syllable. In this paper, we try to do syllable segmentation and alignment on a larger unit, that is, phoneme strings.

Conditional Random Fields (CRF) was successfully applied in transliteration of NEWS2009 and NEWS2010 (Li et al. 2009; Li et al. 2010). Transliteration was viewed as a task of two-stage labeling (Yang et al. 2009; Yang et al., 2010; Aramaki and Abekawwa, 2009). Syllable segmentation was done at the first stage, and then target strings were assigned to each chunk at the next stage. The huge amounts of features in the second stage made model training time-consuming. Thirteen hours on an 8-core server were expended to train the CRF model in the work done by Yang et al. (2010).

To reduce training time and requirement of high-specification hardware, we adopt a combined CRF transliteration system by dividing the training data into several pools and each being used to train a recognizer to predict the target characters. The final transliteration results are the arranged according to the probabilities of all CRF outputs.

In the following, section 2 describes how segmentation and alignment are done on the unit of phoneme strings. Section 3 explains how the forward-backward transliteration system between English and Chinese is built. Performances of the

Proceedings of the 2011 Named Entities Workshop, IJCNLP 2011, pages 82–85,
Chiang Mai, Thailand, November 12, 2011.

system on all the metrics of NEWS2011 are listed in section 4, which is followed by discussions. The last section is the conclusion.

2 Segmentation and Alignment

Lack of gold standard syllable segmentation and alignment data is an obstacle to transliteration model training. Yang et al. (2009) applied N-gram joint source-channel and EM algorithm, while Aramaki and Abekawwa (2009) made use of word alignment tool in GIZA++ to obtain a syllable segmentation and alignment corpus from the training data given. Neither of them reported how precise their alignments were. Yang et al. (2010) proposed a joint optimization method to reduce the propaganda of alignment error.

Pinyin is known as romanized pronunciation of Chinese characters. Due to the nature of *pinyin*, there are many similarities between English orthography and Chinese *pinyin*. Of the 24 English consonants, 17 have almost the same pronunciation in *pinyin*. Since English orthography has a close relationship with phonetic symbols, we believe that consonants in *pinyin* can also provide clues for syllable segmentation and alignment. In the following example, the consonant sequence in English is same as that in *pinyin*.

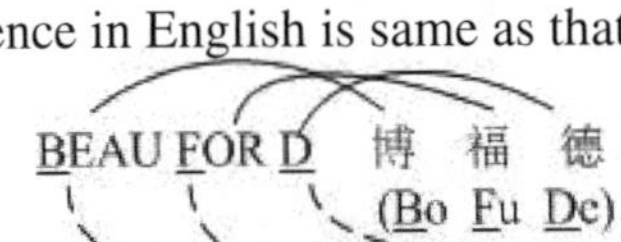

Therefore we can do syllable segmentation with the help of pronunciations of Chinese characters. Segmentation is carried out from the second character, for there is no need to split from the initial letter of a string.

However not all mappings between spelling and phoneme are involved in this approach. The following cases are insolvable.

Case 1: there is no corresponding consonant. For instance, ARAD 阿拉德 (A La De).

Case 2: several letters occupy one phoneme. For instance, BAECK 贝克 (Bei Ke).

Case 3: duplicate letters cause ambiguity. For instance, ANNADA LE 安娜代尔 (An Na Dai Er).

Case 4: consonants are sometimes mismatched. For instance, ACQUARELLI 阿奎雷利 (A Kui Lei Li).

Case 5: there are inconsistencies complicating the situation. For instance: ADDINGTON 阿丁顿 (A Ding Dun).

Therefore *pinyin*-based segmentation is only treated as a preliminary result.

To deal with case 1, we take a two-step matching—strict matching and then loose matching—between the consonant in *pinyin* and the English word. If the same consonant is not available, strings of a similar pronunciation are sought. For instance, the consonant in *pinyin* Fu is *f*, if there is no letter *f* in the English transliteration, *v, ph, gh* are adopted for segmentation.

We apply transformation rules to optimize the syllable alignment result. The rules are induced manually by observation of segmentation errors. We believe gold alignment training corpora are the foundation of good performance no matter which algorithms is applied.

However, we find that some chunks in English correspond to Chinese strings in most translations. Some of such chunks are given in Table 1 as examples. We keep the alignment between these chunks and corresponding Chinese character strings, calling it phoneme strings based alignment.

SKIN 斯金	SKI 斯基	SCO 斯科
MACA 麦考	MACA 麦卡	MACC 麦克
MACKI 麦金	X 克斯	SKEW 斯丘

Table 1. Alignment of English chunks and corresponding Chinese character strings

The alignment of phoneme strings has advantages over single phoneme alignment. Since each English syllable string may be mapped onto several possible Chinese characters, there will be fewer choices if the alignment is based on phoneme strings when an English syllable sequence is finally transliterated into Chinese character strings. For example, *s* can be mapped onto the Chinese characters 斯(Si), 丝(Si) and 思(Si), *ky* can be mapped onto 基(Ji), 吉(Ji) and 季(Ji), but for *sky*, it is usually transliterated into 斯基(Si Ji), not others sequences serve as alternatives. Therefore, we think phoneme strings alignment is better than single phoneme alignment. The following is an example of alignment based on phonemes strings.

As to the backward transliteration, segmentation and alignment are also based on phoneme strings. Following are two columns of aligned data for CRF model training.

哈 HA
克斯 X

3 Forward and Backward Transliteration System

CRF is a discriminative model and makes a global optimum prediction according to the conditional probability (Lafferty et al., 2001). When applying CRF to transliteration, the task is treated as labeling source words with target language strings. Similar to previous works (Yang et al., 2010; Aramaki and Abekawwa, 2009), we build a two-stage CRF transliteration system between English and Chinese. The first stage CRF decoder splits the source words into several chunks. Outputs of the first stage are then sent to the second CRF to label what target characters are transliterated. The final transliteration of the source word is the sequence of all the target characters.

For training the CRF chunker with the given corpora segmented and aligned, each character is labeled with the *BI* scheme, that is, *B* for the beginning character of a chunk, *I* for the characters in other position. For example, in English to Chinese training data, *ABBE* is segmented and aligned as follows.

A	阿
BBE	贝

The two-column data for training the CRF chunker is,

A	*B*
B	*B*
B	*I*
E	*I*

The window size is set as 3, the same as the experiment by Aramaki and Abekawwa (2009).

Though a larger window is propitious to provide more contextual information, there are too many features for training the second stage CRF. We have to reduce the window size. In the second stage of CRF training, the window size is 2, that is, features used are C_{-2}, C_{-1}, C_0, C_1, C_2, $C_{-1}C_0$, C_0C_1, $C_{-2}C_{-1}C_0$ and $C_0C_1C_2$, which C_0 denotes the current chunk. Still the time it takes to train a model on a normal PC is intolerably long[1].

Even the training data aligned on phoneme strings are checked manually, errors are still sometimes somewhere. To reduce the risk of local errors in segmentation and alignment, we divide the training data randomly and evenly into several pools. The size of the pools is set simply according to the capability of our PCs. If some errors occur in some pools but not in all, a correct predication can still be made by the CRFs trained on correct pools.

The combined CRF recognizers are both used for forward and backward transliterations at the second stage. The workflow of our transliteration system is depicted in Figure 1.

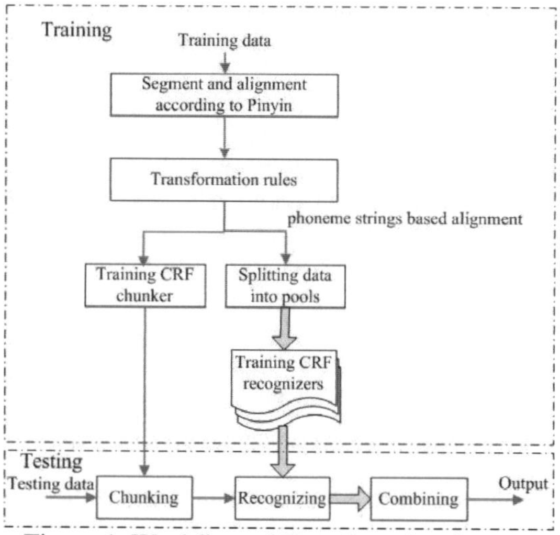

Figure 1. Workflow of Transliteration System

4 Performances and Discussion

We use the open CRF++[2] toolkits to build the two-stage CRF transliteration with all given data of NEWS2011.

4.1 Performances

The number of recognizers may affect the performance of the whole system. To suit the best capacity of our PC, we train 10 forward and 20 backward recognizers. We also train another forward transliteration consisting of 20 recognizers for comparison. Due to time limit, we do not try other numbers in backward and forward transliteration during NEWS2011. Because the test data of NEWS2011 are reserved for future use, we can not try other numbers to build transliteration systems for comparison.

Table 2 shows the common evaluation of our transliteration system between English (E) and Chinese (C). We can see that the performance of E->C transliteration varies slightly with different numbers of combination on all evaluation metrics. The performance of backward transliteration is lower than that of the forward direction on ACC but is better on Mean F score.

[1] Using the same parameters setting of CRF learner as Aramaki and Abekawwa (2009), the training time on a PC (2.3GHZ, 4GB) with NEWS2011 data (37753 English names) reaches 4800 hours.

[2] http://crfpp.sourceforge.net/

	CRFs	ACC	Mean F	MRR	MAP_{ref}
E->C	10	0.312	0.669	0.339	0.310
	20	0.308	0.666	0.337	0.306
C->E	20	0.167	0.765	0.202	0.167

Table 2. Performance of Combined Transliteration System

4.2 Discussions

- Granularity of syllable segmentation and alignment

Preprocessing training data on phoneme strings alignment is our approach in attempting to improve transliteration between English and Chinese. In backward transliteration, our system is better than others in the shared task of NEWS2011. Can we assume that larger granularity alignment is better than a smaller one? Which granularity is optimum?

- Number of CRF recognizer

With more data, the time it takes to train a model based on CRF increases sharply. We train transliteration models with the same algorithm but different usage of data and then combine the results of all recognizers. In this way, training time is reduced. However we can see from the result of testing that the performance of transliteration varies with the number of recognizers. What is the comparison between combined system and single system? Which number of combinations is the best? We will need to explore these questions with more data.

5 Conclusion

Two-stage CRFs are applied to transliterating between English and Chinese. We try to improve the performance from two directions, one is training data processing, which is segmented and aligned based on phoneme strings; another is system building, in which several models on different parts of data are trained and their outputs are combined. The final results of the transliteration are arranged in sequential order in accordance with the degree of probability of all the recognizers.

In future work, we will focus on good standard data and methods of combination to further improve the performance of forward-backward transliteration system.

Acknowledgments

The work is supported by the National Social Science Fund (No. 10CYY024). Thanks are due to the support of National Research Centre for Foreign Language Education, BFSU.

We are grateful to all anonymous reviewers.

References

Eiji Aramaki and Takeshi Abekawa. 2009. Fast decoding and easy implementation: Transliteration as a sequential labeling. *Proceeding of ACL/IJCNLP*. Named Entities Workshop Shared Task. 65-68.

Yuqing Guo, Haifeng Wang. 2004. Chinese-to-English Backward Machine Transliteration. Companion Volume to *Proceedings of the 1st International Joint Conference on Natural Language Processing (IJCNLP 04)*. 17-20.

Sarvnaz Karimi, Falk Scholer and Andrew Turpin. 2011. *Machine Transliteration Survey*. ACM Computing Surveys, 43(4): 1–57.

John Lafferty, Andrew McCallum, and Fernando Pereira. 2001. Conditional random fields: Probabilistic models for segmenting and labeling sequence data. *International Conference on Machine Learning (ICML01)*.

Chun-Jen Lee and Jason S. Chang. 2003. Acquisition of English-Chinese Transliterated Word Pairs from Parallel-Aligned Texts Using a Statistical Machine Transliteration Model. *Proceedings of HLT-NAACL*. 96-103.

Haizhou Li, Min Zhang, and Jian Su. 2004. A joint source-channel model for machine transliteration. *Proceedings of 42nd ACL Annual Meeting*. 159–166.

Haizhou Li, A Kumaran, Vladimir Pervouchine and Min Zhang. 2009. Report of NEWS 2009 Machine Transliteration Shared Task. *Proceedings of the 2009 Named Entities Workshop, ACL-IJCNLP*. 1–18.

Haizhou Li, A Kumaran, Min Zhang and Vladimir Pervouchine. 2010. Report of NEWS 2010 Transliteration Generation Shared Task. *Proceedings of the 2010 Named Entities Workshop, ACL 2010*. 1–11.

Dong Yang, Paul Dixon, Yi-Cheng Pan, Tasuku Oonishi, Masanobu Nakamura and Sadaoki Furui. 2009. Combining a Two-step Conditional Random Field Model and a Joint Source Channel Model for Machine Transliteration. *Proceedings of the 2009 Named Entities Workshop, ACL-IJCNLP*. 72–75.

Dong Yang, Paul Dixon and Sadaoki Furui. 2010. Jointly optimizing a two-step conditional random field model for machine transliteration and its fast decoding algorithm. *Proceedings of the ACL 2010. Conference Short Papers*. 275–280.

English-to-Chinese Machine Transliteration using Accessor Variety Features of Source Graphemes

Mike Tian-Jian Jiang
Department of Computer Science, National Tsing Hua University
Institute of Information Science, Academia Sinica
tmjiang@iis.sinica.edu.tw

Chan-Hung Kuo
Institute of Information Science,
Academia Sinica
laybow@iis.sinica.edu.tw

Wen-Lian Hsu
Institute of Information Science,
Academia Sinica
hsu@iis.sinica.edu.tw

Abstract

This work presents a grapheme-based approach of English-to-Chinese (E2C) transliteration, which consists of many-to-many (M2M) alignment and conditional random fields (CRF) using accessor variety (AV) as an additional feature to approximate local context of source graphemes. Experiment results show that the AV of a given English named entity generally improves effectiveness of E2C transliteration.

1 Introduction

Transliteration is a subfield of computation linguistics, and is defined as the phonetic translation of names across languages. Transliteration of named entities is essential in numerous applications, such as machine translation, corpus alignment, cross-language information retrieval, information extraction, and automatic lexicon acquisition. The transliteration modeling approaches can be classified as phoneme-based, grapheme-based, and a hybrid of phoneme and grapheme.

Numerous studies focus on the phoneme-based approach (Knight and Graehl, 1998; Virga and Khudanpur, 2003). Suppose that E is an English name and C is its Chinese transliteration, the phoneme-based approach first converts E into an intermediate phonemic representation p, and then converts p into its Chinese counterpart C. The idea is to transform both the source and target names into comparable phonemes so that the phonetic similarity between the two names can be measured easily. The grapheme-based approach, which treats the transliteration as a statistical machine translation problem under monotonic constraint, has also attracted much attention (Li *et al.*, 2004). This approach aims to obtain the bilingual orthographical correspondence directly to reduce the possible errors introduced in multiple conversions. The hybrid approach attempts to utilize both phoneme and grapheme information for transliteration. Oh and Choi (2006) proposed a strategy to include both phoneme and grapheme features in a single learning process.

This work presents a grapheme-based approach of English-to-Chinese (E2C) transliteration using many-to-many alignment (M2M-aligner) (Jiampojamarn *et al.*, 2007) and conditional random fields (CRF) (Lafferty *et al.*, 2001) with additional features of accessor variety (AV) (Feng *et al.*, 2004). The remainder of this article is organized as follows. Section 2 briefly introduces related works involving M2M-aligner, CRF, and AV. The concept of this work for transliteration using M2M-aligner, CRF, and AV are explained in Section 3. Section 4 describes the experiment results and discussion. Finally, the conclusion is presented in Section 5.

2 Related Works

2.1 CRF-based Transliteration

Yang *et al.* (2009) proposed a two-step CRF model for direct orthographical mapping (DOM) machine transliteration, in which the first CRF segments a source word into chunks and the second CRF maps the chunks to a word in the target language. Reddy and Waxmonsky (2009) presented a phrase-based translation system that characters are grouped into substrings to be mapped atomically into the target language, which showed how substring representation can be incorporated into a CRF model with local context and phonemic information. Shishtla *et al.* (2009) adopted a statistical transliteration technique that consists of alignment model of GIZA++ (Och and Ney, 2003) and CRF model.

Proceedings of the 2011 Named Entities Workshop, IJCNLP 2011, pages 86–90,
Chiang Mai, Thailand, November 12, 2011.

The approach of this work is similar to the technique of Shishtla *et al.*, yet this work focuses on the additional AV feature of CRF and uses M2M-aligner, which will be described in Section 2.2, instead of GIZA++.

2.2 M2M-Aligner

Jiampojamarn *et al.* (2007) argued that previous work has generally assumed one-to-one alignment for simplicity, but letter strings and phoneme strings are not typically in the same length, so null phonemes or null letters must be introduced to make one-to-one-alignments possible. Furthermore, two letters frequently combine to produce a single phoneme (double letters), and a single letter can sometimes produce two phonemes (double phonemes). For example, the English word "ABERT" with its Chinese transliteration "阿贝特", which Jaimpojamarn *et al.* referred as "phonemes", is aligned as:

A	BE	RT
|	|	|
阿	贝	特

The letters "BE" are an example of the double letter problem which mapping to the single phoneme "贝." These alignments provide more accurate grapheme-to-phoneme relationships for a phoneme prediction model. Hence the M2M-aligner is for alignments between substrings of various lengths and based on the expectation maximization (EM) algorithm. For more details of the algorithm, readers are encouraged to explore previous works of Ristad and Yianilos (1998), and Jiampojamarn *et al.* (2007).

Despite ambiguity between Chinese transliteration and phoneme, the above paragraph of the opinion of Jaimpojamarn *et al.* indicates a particular problem of E2C transliteration, that the training data comprised pairs of names written in source and target scripts lacks explicit grapheme-level alignment. This work uses M2M-aligner as an unsupervised method for generating alignments of the training data, which provide hypotheses of DOM without null graphemes.

2.3 Accessor Variety

Feng *et al.* (2004) proposed accessor variety (AV) to measure how likely a character substring is a Chinese word. Another similar measurement of English and Chinese words called boundary entropy or branching entropy (BE) was used in several works (Tung and Lee, 1994; Chang and Su, 1997; Cohen and Adams, 2001; Cohen *et al.*, 2002; Huang and Powers, 2003; Tanaka-Ishii, 2005; Jin and Tanaka-Ishii, 2006; Cohen *et al.*, 2007). The basic idea behind these measurements is closely related to one particular perspective of *n*-gram and information theory of cross entropy or perplexity. Zhao and Kit (2007) induced that AV and BE both assume that the border of a potential word is located where the uncertainty of successive characters increases, where AV and BE are regarded as the discrete and continuous versions, respectively, of the fundamental work of Harris (1970), and then chose to adopt AV as the additional feature of CRF-based Chinese Word Segmentation (CWS). The AV of a string *s* is defined as:

$$AV(s) = \min\{L_{av}(s), R_{av}(s)\} \tag{1}$$

In Eq. (1), L_{av}(s) and R_{av}(s) are defined as the number of distinct preceding and succeeding characters, except when the adjacent character is absent due to a sentence boundary, and then the pseudo-character of the beginning or end of a sentence is accumulated indistinctly. Feng *et al.* (2004) also developed more heuristic rules to remove strings that contain known words or adhesive characters. For the strict meaning of unsupervised features and for simplicity, this study does not include those additional rules.

The necessity of AV is primarily on the demand for semi-supervised learning. Since AV can be extracted from large corpora without any manual segmentation or annotation, hidden variables underlying frequent surface patterns of languages may be captured via an inexpensive and unsupervised algorithm such as suffix array. Unsupervised feature selection of AV or similar features has generally improved effectiveness of supervised CWS on cross-domain and unlabeled data (Jiang *et al.*, 2010), and this work consequently considers that AV of un-segmented English names from training, development, and test data might help enhancing E2C transliteration.

3 Transliteration using EM and CRF

3.1 CRF Alignment Labeling

In the work, M2M-aligner first maximizes the probability of the observed source-target word pairs using the EM algorithm and subsequently sets the grapheme alignments via maximum a posteriori estimation. CRF is then conditioned on the grapheme alignments to produce globally optimal solutions. However, the performance of the EM algorithm is frequently affected by the initialization. To obtain better alignment results of M2M-aligner, this work empirically sets the "maxX" parameter for the maximum size of sub-alignments in the source side to 8, and sets the "maxY" parameter for the maximum size of sub-alignments in the target side to 1 (denoted as X8Y1 in short), since one of the well known *a priori* of Chinese is that almost all Chinese characters are monosyllabic, which reflects the situation of "double phoneme" mentioned in Section 2.2. Notably, this work follows the definition of grapheme described by Oh and Choi (2005) to prevent from confusion of phoneme, grapheme, character, and letter, that graphemes refer to the basic units (or the smallest contrastive units) of written language: for example, English has 26 graphemes or letters or characters, Korean has 24, and German has 30. Table 1 is an example of M2M-aligner results. With aligned training data, a transliteration model can be then trained by CRF to generate names in the target language from names in the source language. This work uses Wapiti (Lavergne *et al.*, 2010) as CRF toolkit. Table 2 is an example of training data for a CRF alignment labeling, where the tags *B* and *I* indicate whether the grapheme is in the starting position of the sub-alignment.

This work tests several combinations of conventional CRF features along with their abbreviated notations for E2C transliteration, as shown in Table 3, where C_i represents the input graphemes bound individually to the prediction label at its current position *i*. Take Table 2 as an example, if the current position is at the label "*B* 迪", features generated by C_{-1}, C_0 and C_1 are "A" "D" and "I" respectively. Note that a prediction label may either comprise a positioning tag and a Chinese grapheme, or just be the positioning tag itself.

Source	Target	M2M-Aligner Result	
ABBADIE	阿巴迪	A:B|B:A|D:I:E|	阿|巴|迪|

Table 1. An Example of M2M Alignment

Character	Label
A	*B*阿
B	*I*
B	*B*巴
A	*I*
D	*B*迪
I	*I*
E	*I*

Table 2. Example of a CRF labeling format for E2C transliteration

Context			
Function	C_0, C_{-1}, C_1, C_0C_1, $C_{-1}C_0$,	C_0, C_{-1}, C_1, C_{-2}, C_2 C_0C_1, $C_{-1}C_0$, $C_{-2}C_1$, C_1C_2	C_0, C_{-1}, C_1, C_{-2}, C_2 C_{-3}, C_3 C_0C_1, $C_{-1}C_0$, $C_{-2}C_1$, C_1C_2 $C_{-3}C_{-2}$, C_2C_3
Notation	1UB	2UB	3UB
Positioning Tag of Prediction Label			
Function	*B, I*		*B, I, E*
Notation	P_{BI}		P_{BIE}
Chinese Grapheme of Prediction Label			
Function	On *B* only		On *B* and *I*
Notation	G_B		G_{BI}

Table 3. Conventional CRF Features

3.2 CRF with AV

This work extends the work of Zhao and Kit (2008) into a unified representation for AV features of English graphemes. The representation accommodates both the position of a string and the string's likelihood ranking by the logarithm. Formally, the ranking function for a string, *s,* with a score, *x,* counted by AV is defined as:

$$f(s) = r, if\, 2^r \leq x < 2^{r+1} \quad (2)$$

The logarithm ranking mechanism in Eq. (2) is inspired by Zipf's law to alleviate the potential data sparseness of infrequent strings. The rank *r* and the corresponding positions of a string are then concatenated as feature tokens. To provide readers with a clearer picture of the appearance of feature tokens, a sample representation for AV is presented and explained in Table 4.

For example, considering strings with two graphemes, one of the strings "AB" is ranked $r = 3$; therefore, the column of di-grapheme feature tokens has "A" denoted as *3B* and "B" denoted as *3E*. If another di-grapheme string, "BA,"

Input	AV Feature					Label
	1 char	2 char	3 char	4 char	5 char	
A	*7S*	*3B*	*2B*	*0B*	*1B*	*B*阿
B	*5S*	*3E*	*2B*	*0B*	*1B*	*I*
B	*5S*	*3B*	*2B*	*0B*	*1B*	*B*巴
A	*7S*	*4B*	*2B*	*1B*	*1B*	*I*
D	*7S*	*4E*	*3B*	$1B_1$	*1E*	*B*迪
I	*5S*	*4E*	$3B_1$	$1B_2$	*0E*	*I*
E	*7S*	*3E*	*3E*	*1E*	*0E*	*I*

Table 4. Example of AV features

competes with "AD" at the position of "A" with a higher rank of $r = 4$, then *4B* is selected for feature representation of the token at a certain position. Notably, when the string "AD" conflicts with the string "DI" at the position of "D" with the same rank of $r = 4$, the corresponding position with the ranking of the leftmost string, which is *4E* in this case, is applied arbitrarily.

4 Results and Discussions

4.1 E2C Transliteration Results

In the interest of brevity, only the 3rd and the 4th standard runs that exceed 0.3 in terms of top-1 accuracy (ACC) are listed in Table 5. Numerous models of pilot tests have been trained using both the training set and the development set, and then evaluated on the development set for optimizing CRF feature combinations, as shown in Table 6.

4.2 Error Analysis and Discussions

Based on observations of the pilot tests, there is a clear trend that AV features improve performances significantly. However, improvements on the test set are not as good as expected. After carefully investigating NEWS-2011 data, one particular phenomenon has been noticed: only the development set contains phrasal named entities. Furthermore, some E2C word pairs are not pure transliterations and aligned in very different character lengths, such as the word pair of "COMMONWEALTH OF THE BAHAMAS" and "巴哈马联邦," and this phenomenon is noted as "semi-semantic transliteration" for convenience. In fact, the M2M parameter "maxX" of this work has been designed for these phrasal structure to be relatively larger and less symmetrical to the parameter "maxY" than previous works that usually set both X and Y to 2 as default values. Since the M2M and the CRF models might over-fit the development set, phrasal structure and semi-semantic transliterations that only appeared in the development set probably became noises according to the test set.

ID	Configuration	ACC	Mean F-score
4	X8Y1, 3UB, P_{BIE}, G_B, AV	0.327	0.688
3	X8Y1, 2UB, P_{BI}, G_{BI}, AV	0.303	0.675

Table 5. Selected E2C standard runs

Configuration	ACC	Mean F-score
X8Y1, 1UB, P_{BI}, G_B	0.001	0.151
X8Y1, 1UB, P_{BI}, G_B, AV	0.000	0.078
X8Y1, 2UB, P_{BI}, G_B	0.001	0.122
X8Y1, 2UB, P_{BI}, G_B, AV	0.000	0.064
X8Y1, 3UB, P_{BI}, G_B, AV	0.569	0.860
X8Y1, 1UB, P_{BI}, G_{BI}	0.454	0.762
X8Y1, 1UB, P_{BI}, G_{BI}, AV	0.547	0.813
X8Y1, 2UB, P_{BI}, G_{BI}	0.547	0.814
X8Y1, 2UB, P_{BI}, G_{BI}, AV	0.753	0.910
X8Y1, 1UB, P_{BIE}, G_B	0.182	0.586
X8Y1, 1UB, P_{BIE}, G_B, AV	0.273	0.656
X8Y1, 2UB, P_{BIE}, G_B	0.347	0.708
X8Y1, 2UB, P_{BIE}, G_B, AV	0.483	0.800
X8Y1, 3UB, P_{BIE}, G_B	0.449	0.771
X8Y1, 3UB, P_{BIE}, G_B, AV	0.597	0.857

Table 6. Selected E2C pilot tests

To analyze semi-semantic transliterations, NEWS-2011 Chinese-to-English (C2E) back-transliteration corpus have been acquired, and the corresponding standard runs have been submitted owing to the policy of NEWS shared task. The C2E experiments, however, encountered a serious problem of CRF L-BFGS training requirement on space complexity, therefore the submitted results are actually incomplete and erroneous, since C2E transliteration using the proposed approach produces too many labels and features to train a CRF model with the whole training set. In authors' experiences, even a workstation with 24GB memory spaces is insufficient for such training. Notably, the similar hardware constraint makes the 4th standard run of E2C, which is the primary one, to regress to the simpler Chinese grapheme labeling strategy, namely G_B, while introducing deeper contexts and more specific positioning tags, to trade efficiency of CRF training phases.

5 Conclusion and Future Work

This work proposes to use AV of source grapheme for E2C transliteration. Experiments indicate the AV features generally improve the performance in terms of ACC. Recommended future investigations would be features of target graphemes or source-channel models (Li *et al.*, 2004) that are efficient and capable of recognizing semi-semantic transliteration.

Acknowledgements

This research was supported in part by the National Science Council under grant NSC 100-2631-S-001-001, and the research center for Humanities and Social Sciences under grant IIS-50-23. Wallace Academic Editing service is appreciated for their editorial assistance. The authors would like to thank anonymous reviewers for their constructive criticisms.

References

Jing-Shin Chang and Keh-Yih Su. 1997. An unsupervised iterative method for Chinese new lexicon extraction. *Computation Linguistics and Chinese language Processing*, 2(2):97-148.

Paul Cohen and Niall Adams. 2001. An Algorithm for Segmenting Categorical Time Series into Meaningful Episodes. *Advances in Intelligent Data Analysis*, 198-207.

Paul Cohen, Niall Adams and Brent Heeringa. 2007. Voting Experts: An Unsupervised Algorithm for Segmenting Sequences. *Intelligent Data Analysis*, 11(6):607-625.

Paul R Cohen, B Heeringa and Niall M Adams. 2002. An Unsupervised Algorithm for Segmenting Categorical Timeseries into Episodes. *Proceedings of the ESF Exploratory Workshop on Pattern Detection and Discovery*, 49-62.

Haodi Feng, Kang Chen, Xiaotie Deng, and Wiemin Zheng. 2004. Accessor Variety Criteria for Chinese Word Extraction. *Computational Linguistics*, 30(1):75-93.

Zellig Sabbetai Harris. 1970. Morpheme boundaries within words. *Papers in Structural and Transformational Linguistics*, 68-77.

Jin Hu Huang and David Powers. 2003. Chinese Word Segmentation based on contextual entropy. *Proceedings of the 17th Asian Pacific Conference on Language, Information and Computation*, 152-158.

Sittichai Jiampojamarn, Grzegorz Kondrak and Tarek Sherif. 2007. Applying Many-to-Many Alignments and Hidden Markov Models to Letter-to-Phoneme Conversion. *Proceedings of the Annual Conference of the North American Chapter of the Association for Computational Linguistics*, 372-379.

Tian-Jian Jiang, Shih-Hung Liu, Cheng-Lung Sung and Wen-Lian Hsu. 2010. Term Contributed Boundary Tagging by Conditional Random Fields for SIGHAN 2010 Chinese Word Segmentation Bakeoff. *Proceeding of the First CIPS-SIGHAN Joint Conference on Chinese Language Processing*, 266-269.

K. Knight and J. Graehl. 1998. Machine Transliteration. *Computational Linguistics*, 24(4):599-612.

John Lafferty, Andrew McCallum, Fernando Pereira. 2001. Conditional Random Fields Probabilistic Models for Segmenting and Labeling Sequence Data. *Proceedings of ICML*, 591-598.

Thomas Lavergne, Olivier Cappé and François Yvon. 2010. Practical Very Large Scale CRFs. *Proceedings the 48th ACL*, 504-513.

Haizhou Li, Min Zhang and Jian Su. 2004. A Joint Source Channel Model for Machine Transliteration. *Proceedings of the 42nd ACL*, 159-166.

Franz Josef Och and Hermann Ney. 2003. A Systematic Comparison of Various Statistical Alignment Models. *Computational Linguistics*, 29(1):19-51.

J. H. Oh and K. S. Choi. 2006. An Ensemble of Transliteration Models for Information Retrieval. *Information Processing and Management*, 42:980-1002.

Eric Sven Ristad and Peter N. Yianilos. 1998. Learning String Edit Distance. *IEEE Transactions on Pattern Recognition and Machine Intelligence*, 20(5):522-532.

Sravana Reddy and Sonjia Waxmonsky. 2009. Substring-based transliteration with conditional random fields. *Proceedings of the 2009 Named Entities Workshop,* 92-95.

Praneeth Shishtla, V. Surya Ganesh, Sethuramalingam Subramaniam and Vasudeva Varma. 2009. A language-independent transliteration schema using character aligned models at NEWS 2009. *Proceedings of the 2009 Named Entities Workshop,* 40-43.

Kumiko Tanaka-Ishii. 2005. Entropy as an Indicator of Context Boundaries: An Experiment Using a Web Search Engine. *Proceedings of International Joint Conference on Natural Language Processing* , 93-105.

Cheng-Huang Tung and His-Jian Lee. 1994. Identification of unknown words from corpus. *Computational Proceedings of Chinese and Oriental Languages*, 131-145.

P. Virga and S. Khudanpur. 2003. Transliteration of Proper Names in Cross-lingual Information Retrieval. In the *Proceedings of the ACL Workshop on Multi-lingual Named Entity Recognition.*

Dong Yang, Paul Dixon, Yi-Cheng Pan, Tasuku Oonishi, Masanobu Nakamura, Sadaoki Furui. 2009. Combining a two-step conditional random field model and a joint source channel model for machine transliteration. *Proceedings of the 2009 Named Entities Workshop,* 72-75.

Hai Zhao and Chunyu Kit. 2007. Incorporating Global Information into Supervised Learning for Chinese Word Segmentation. *Proceedings of the 10th Conference of the Pacific Association for Computation Linguistics,* 66-74.

Hai Zhao and Chunyu Kit. 2008. Unsupervised Segmentation Helps Supervised Learning of Character Tagging for Word Segmentation and Named Entity Recognition. *Proceedings of the Sixth SIGHAN Workshop on Chinese Language Processing.*

The Amirkabir Machine Transliteration System for NEWS 2011: Farsi-to-English Task

Najmeh Mousavi Nejad
Department of Engineering, Islamic Azad University, Science & Research Branch, Punak, Ashrafi Isfahani , Tehran, Iran
najme.mousavi@gmail.com

Shahram Khadivi
Department of Computer Engineering, Amirkabir University of Technology
424 Hafez Ave, Tehran, Iran 15875-4413
khadivi@aut.ac.ir

Kaveh Taghipour
Department of Computer Engineering, Amirkabir University of Technology
424 Hafez Ave, Tehran, Iran 15875-4413
k.taghipour@aut.ac.ir

Abstract

In this paper we describe the statistical machine transliteration system of Amirkabir University of Technology, developed for NEWS 2011 shared task. This year we participated in English to Persian language pair. We use three systems for transliteration: the first system is a maximum entropy model with a new proposed alignment algorithm. The second system is Sequitur g2p tool, an open source grapheme to phoneme convertor. The third system is Moses, a phrased based statistical machine translation system. In addition, several new features are introduced to enhance the overall accuracy in the maximum entropy model. The results show that the combination of our maximum entropy system with Sequitur g2p tool and Moses lead to a considerable improvement over each system result.

1 Introduction

This paper describes the statistical machine transliteration system used for participation in the NEWS 2011 shared task workshop. We participated in English to Persian task and used three different systems for transliteration generation.

There have been a few researches on Persian language (Karimi et al., 2007). The quality of transliterated names has been improved in the past studies. However, the proposed method is language specific and the algorithm is designed for Persian language. We present two combined transliteration systems. The first system is a combination of a maximum entropy model along with our proposed alignment algorithm and Sequitur g2p tool. The second system is a combination of our maximum entropy system and Moses. Our training and test data is English to Persian set from NEWS 2011 Name Transliteration Shared Task (Zhang et al., 2011). We use openNlP maximum entropy package to train our system. We define new features for discriminative training. Moreover a new approach for aligning name pairs is proposed.

2 The Transliteration Process

Our Maximum Entropy transliteration system has the following steps:

1. Preprocessing
2. Alignment of name pairs
3. Definition of proper features for aligned names
4. Training the model to produce features weight

2.1 Preprocessing

Preprocessing plays an important role in many NLP Applications. The amount and kind of processing done depends on the nature of the language. Since there are some letters in Persian language which have more than one Unicode (for example "ی"), we run a normalization tool on the training set to uniform the letters.

2.2 Alignment of Name Pairs

The features for maximum entropy training are extracted from aligned names. Our proposed alignment method is a two-dimensional Cartesian coordinate system. The horizontal axis is labeled with the source name and the vertical axis is labeled with the target name (or vice versa). A line is drawn from the coordinate (0,0) to the point with coordinate (source_name_length , target_name_length). We mark the

Proceedings of the 2011 Named Entities Workshop, IJCNLP 2011, pages 91–95,
Chiang Mai, Thailand, November 12, 2011.

corresponding cell in each column of the alignment matrix which has the less distance to the line. A single line is not enough for a name pair and is only suitable for names with equal length. For more complex alignments, some fixed points are needed in order to draw the lines. In Figure 1, (bb,ب) and (n,ن) are fixed points and the following alignments are achieved:

(g,گ) , (i,ی) , (bb,ب) , (o,و) , (n,ن) , (i,ی)

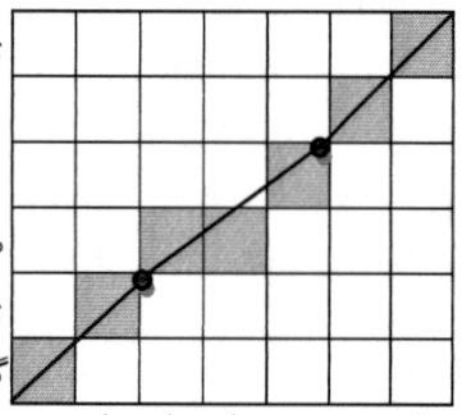

Figure 1.Alignment matrix of (gibboni,گیبونی)

Based on the fact that our goal is to design a language independent transliteration system, an automatic way to find the fixed points is of interest. We introduce FPA algorithm (Fixed Points Alignment) which is an unsupervised approach that adopts the concept of EM training. In the expectation step the training name pairs are aligned using the current model and in the maximization step the most probable alignments are added to the fixed point set. A brief sketch of FPA algorithm is presented in Figure 2. Line 5 to 11 shows the process of updating the fixed points set. In line 7 forcedAlignment means using the current ME model to transliterate source name with the condition that the produced transliterations should be the same as the target name. This condition guarantees the convergence of the algorithm. Line 9 is the last step in producing fixed point set. |k| is the number of distinct segments in the best path set and $p(\tilde{T}_k|\tilde{S}_k)$ is the probability of the $\tilde{T}_k|\tilde{S}_k$ transformation rule. Once the probabilities are calculated, they are compared to a predefined threshold (in our case threshold is 0.9).

2.3 Definition of Proper Features for Aligned Names

We define two types of features: consonant-vowel and n-gram. For both types current context (letter), two past and two future contexts are used. We choose a window with a size of 5, since lower or higher length would have degraded the results.

2.3.1 Consonant-Vowel Features

Every language has a set of consonant and vowel letters. The consonant letters can be divided into different groups based on their types (Table 1).

Plosive (stop)	p , b , t , d , k , g , q
Fricative	f , v , s , z , x , h
Plosive-Fricative	j , c
Flap (tap)	r
Nasal	m , n
Lateral approximant	l , y

Table 1. Six group of consonants

Most combinations of consonant-vowel features were tested for English to Persian transliteration. We have found the following consonant-vowel features are the most effective ones for generating current target letter (t_n). S_i is used to represent the source name characters and t_i represents the target name characters. CV is an abbreviation for consonant- vowel. Note that the consonant letters are divided according to Table $CV_{S_{n-2}}, CV_{S_{n-1}}, CV_{S_n}, CV_{S_{n+1}}, CV_{S_{n+2}}, CV_{t_{n-1}}$.

The consonant-vowel features improve transliteration, but still are not sufficient. Therefore we need n-gram features.

```
1:  while( fixedPoints != oldFixedPoints) {
2:     oldFixedPoints = fixedPoints;
3:     fixedPoints = updateFixedPoints(whole_training_corpus)
4:  }
5:  Function updateFixedPoints(training_data){
6:     for( all name pairs) do
7:        A = forcedAlignment(sourceName, targetName, currentModel)
8:     for (all segment pairs in A) do
9:        p(T̃k|S̃k) = Σp(T̃k,S̃k) / Σ_T̃ p(T̃,S̃k) ,  p(S̃k|T̃k) = Σp(T̃k,S̃k) / Σ_S̃ p(S̃,T̃k)
10:    if (p > threshold) {  add transformation rule to the fixedPoints}
11: }
```

Line 9: $p(\tilde{T}_k|\tilde{S}_k) = \frac{\sum p(\tilde{T}_k,\tilde{S}_k)}{\sum_{\tilde{T}} p(\tilde{T},\tilde{S}_k)}$, $p(\tilde{S}_k|\tilde{T}_k) = \frac{\sum p(\tilde{T}_k,\tilde{S}_k)}{\sum_{\tilde{S}} p(\tilde{S},\tilde{T}_k)}$

Figure 2. Sketch of the FPA algorithm

2.3.2 N-gram Features

In n-gram features for source name, two past and two future contexts are used (a window with a size of 5). For the target name however, only two past contexts are used (since we don't have future context yet).

Using S to demonstrate the source name and T to demonstrate the target name, the n-gram features for each name can be summarized as:

$s_{n-2} s_{n-1}\ s_n\ s_{n+1}\ s_{n+2}$
$t_{n-2} t_{n-1}\ \times\ \times\ \times$

For any language pair, all combinations of s_i and t_i can be used to define a feature. We tested almost any combination of above features for English to Persian transliteration. The results show that t_{n-2} does not help in better transliteration. Because written Persian omits short vowels, and only long vowels appear in texts. So t_{n-2} is completely irrelevant for generating current Persian letter. But other contexts lead to a better transliteration.

The details of FPA algorithm and feature selection strategies are explained in our research paper which was accepted by NEWS 2011.

2.3 Training the Model and Producing Features Weight

As mentioned earlier, we use openNlP maximum entropy package in the training stage. The features which were extracted in the previous section are inputs for maximum entropy model. After a number of iterations, ME builds the model and produces the features weight. These weights will be used in the test stage.

Some names in the workshop dataset have more than one transliteration. Several experiments were done to study the effect of multi transliteration dataset on our system. Table 2 shows the results. The numbers and phases in the table are defined as follows:

Phase 1: updating the fixed points set
Phase 2: finding features weight
Approach 1: each Persian variant and corresponding English name is considered as one name pair. So if a line in the training file has one English name and 5 Persian transliterations, we will have 5 name pairs for that line. This approach causes many similar alignments to be added to the feature file for a single line in the training file.
Approach 2: This approach is similar to approach 1, except that we add distinct alignments to the feature file for each line in the training set. In other words all alignments of the first Persian transliteration are added to the feature file. For other variants only the alignments which were not seen in the previous Persian transliterations, are added to the file.
Approach 3: we assign an equal weight to each Persian transliteration of an English name. For example if an English name has 4 Persian transliteration, the value of each name weight will be 0.25.
Approach 4: only one Persian name is selected for training. The selection process uses the previous model to estimate the best Persian transliteration.

The best word accuracy in Table 2 belongs to the last row. So in the rest of the paper we use approach 2 for the first phase and approach 1 for the second phase.

Phase 1	Phase 2	WA	CA
Approach 1	Approach 2	65.7	82.4
Approach 1	Approach 1	66.8	82.5
Approach 3	Approach 1	66.8	82.5
Approach 4	Approach 2	67.2	82.7
Approach 2	Approach 2	67.3	82.7
Approach 4	Approach 1	68.2	82.9
Approach 2	Approach 1	68.3	82.9

Table 2. The Effect of multi transliteration dataset on word accuracy and character accuracy in Top-1 tested on the development set

3 System Combination

System combination is the method of combining stand alone systems to achieve a better result. We have three separate systems for transliteration which generate a reasonable output. The first System is the ME model along with our new alignment approach. The second system is the open source Sequitur G2P which is a grapheme to phoneme conversion tool (Bisani and Ney, 2010). Considering the transliteration direction, the names in the source language are regarded as graphemes and the names in the target language as phonemes. The third System is Moses, a phrased based statistical machine translation system. In order to have an accurate transliteration system with a phrase-based statistical translation model, Moses is trained with an unconstrained phrase length. Having no limit for the maximum phrase length is feasible in the transliteration case since the number of phrase pairs are much less when compared to the translation. Having no restriction for the phrase length enables the model to learn all proper phrases and also to perform as a translation memory. In addition, the decoder is not permitted to reorder the phrases by setting the distortion limit to zero. Moreover, the beam threshold, hypothesis stack size and the translation table limit is set to have maximum performance.

The final combined system should produce10 candidates for each name in the test data. To achieve this goal, the first combined system which is a combination of Sequitur g2p and MEM with FPA, has the following steps: First g2p produces 50 candidates for each name, ranked by the probability that the model assigns to them (P_1). Therefore if the number of test names are N, we will have N*50 name pairs. Then we apply forceAlignmnet to each pair which was described in Section 2.2. This process produces another probability for each pair (P_2), which is the multiplication of the best path edges in the search tree (see Figure 2 for further details). Now we can use a linear combination of P_1 and P_2. The final probability for each pair is:

$$P_{final} = \lambda * P_1 + (1 - \lambda) * P_2 \quad (3.1)$$

Once λ is found, 10 best transliterations which have highest P_{final}, are enumerated as final transliterations.

The second combined system is a combination of Moses and MEM with FPA. The process is similar to the first combined system. The difference is the value of λ. The values of λ for each combined system are reported in the next section.

4 Results

We report our results on the development data provided by the NEWS 2011 task. For the development runs, we use the training set for training and the development set for testing. The best combinations of features, founded in section 2.3, are included in the training stage.

We split development data into two half. The first half is used for tuning λ and the second half is used for systems evaluation. Table 3 shows word accuracy in Top-1 and MRR in Top-10 for the five systems. The value of λ for the forth system is set to 0.57 and for the fifth system is set to 0.7.

The workshop released train and development dataset have overlap and some names in the training set are repeated in the development set. Therefore a memory based approach will improve the results very much. In this approach if the test data is observed in the training set, its transliterations are put on top of the N-best list. The accuracy in Top-1 with memory based approach for the forth system is 86.4 and for the fifth system is 86.0.

ID	Systems	WA	MRR	F-Score	MAP_{ref}
1	MEM with FPA	66.5	77.5	94.6	65.5
2	Sequitur G2P	67.7	79.5	95.0	66.9
3	Moses	67.5	78.8	93.8	66.5
4	1 combined with 2	70.0	81.0	95.2	69.2
5	1 combined with 3	68.2	79.7	94.9	67.1

Table 3. Results on the second half of the development set (in %)

5 Conclusions

In this paper, we presented a language-independent alignment method for transliteration. Discriminative training is used in our system and numbers of new features are defined in the training stage. Furthermore a new grapheme to phoneme tool is recommended for transliteration task, assuming one side as graphemes and the other side as phonemes. Additionally, a phrase-based statistical translation model is configured to have maximum transliteration accuracy and is used as one of the independent components of the system combination process. Results showed that the combination of three systems improves overall accuracy.

Acknowledgments

This work has been partially supported by Iranian Research Institute for ICT (Ex. ITRC) under grant 500/1141. The authors wish to thank the anonymous reviewers for their criticisms and suggestions.

References

Bisani, M., Ney, H., Joint-Sequence Models for Grapheme-to-Phoneme Conversion, Speech Communication (2008), doi: 10.1016/j.specom.2008.01.002

Fraser, A., Marcu, D., Semi-Supervised Training for Statistical Word Alignment, Proceedings of ACL-2006, pp. 769-776, Sydney, Australia

Goto, I., Kato, N., Uratani, N., Ehara, T., Transliteration Considering Context Information Based on the Maximum Entropy Method, In Proc. Of IXth MT Summit. (2003)

Jiampojamarm, S., Kondrak, G., Letter-Phoneme Alignment: An Exploration, Proceedings of the 48th Annual Meet-ing of the Association for Computational Li-nguistics, pages 780–788, Uppsala, Sweden, 11-16 July 2010.

Josef, F., Ney. H., Discriminative Training and Maximum Entropy Models for Statistical Machine Translation, Proceedings of the 40th Annual Meeting of the Association for Computational Linguistics (ACL), Philadelphia, July 2002, pp. 295-302.

Karimi, S., Scholer, F., Turpin, A., Collapsed Consonant and Vowel Models: New Approaches for English-Persian Transliteration and Back-Transliteration, The 45th Annual Meeting of the Association for Computational Linguistics (ACL'07), pages 648-655, Prague, Czech Republic, June 2007.

Karimi, S., Machine Transliteration of Proper Names between English and Persian, A thesis submitted in fulfillment of the requirements for the degree of Doctor of Philosophy, BEng. (Hons.), MSc.

Koehn, P., Hoang, H., Birch A., CallisonBurch, C., Federico, M., Bertoldi, N., Cowan, B., Shen, W., Moran, C., Zens, R., Dyer C., Bojar, O., Constantin, A., Herbst E., 2007. Moses: Open source toolkit for statistical machine translation. In Proceedings of the 45th Annual Meeting of the Association for Computational Linguistics (ACL'07) – Companion Volume, June.

OpenNLP Maximum EntropyPackage Available at http://incubator.apache.org/opennlp/

Yoon, S., Kim, K., Sproat, R., "Multilingual Transliteration Using Feature based Phonetic Method", Proceedings of the 45th Annual Meeting of the Association of Computational Linguistics, pages 112–119, Prague, Czech Republic, June 2007, Association for Computational Linguistics.

Zelenko, D., Aone. C., Discriminative Methods for Transliteration, Proceedings of the 2006 Conference on Empirical Methods in Natural Language Processing (EMNLP 2006), pages 612–617, Sydney, July 2006.

Zhang, M., Kumaran, A. , Li, H., Whitepaper of NEWS 2011 Shared Task on Machine Transliteration, In Proceedings of the ACL-IJCNLP 2011 Named Entity Workshop

English-Chinese Personal Name Transliteration by Syllable-Based Maximum Matching

Oi Yee Kwong
Department of Chinese, Translation and Linguistics
City University of Hong Kong
Tat Chee Avenue, Kowloon, Hong Kong
Olivia.Kwong@cityu.edu.hk

Abstract

This paper reports on our participation in the NEWS 2011 shared task on transliteration generation with a syllable-based Backward Maximum Matching system. The system uses the Onset First Principle to syllabify English names and align them with Chinese names. The bilingual lexicon containing aligned segments of various syllable lengths subsequently allows direct transliteration by chunks. The official results suggest that our system could potentially be improved with a re-ranking module for English-to-Chinese transliteration, while its performance on Chinese-to-English back transliteration reached the state of the art.

1 Introduction

This paper describes our system participating in two tracks of the NEWS 2011 shared task on transliteration generation, including English-to-Chinese transliteration (EnCh) and Chinese-to-English back transliteration (ChEn).

Our system is essentially a syllable-based Backward Maximum Matching (BMM) system, which works bi-directionally for EnCh and ChEn. The Onset First Principle in phonology was used to syllabify English names and align them with the Chinese renditions. A bilingual lexicon containing segment pairs of various syllable lengths was then produced from the aligned names. This lexicon was subsequently used in transliteration, during which a source name was first syllabified and then segmented using BMM with syllables as the basic units. Target candidates were generated by looking up the bilingual lexicon and ranked by unigram probabilities.

We will briefly review related work in Section 2, and introduce the datasets used in this study in Section 3. The system will be described and its performance reported in Section 4, followed by future work and conclusion in Section 5.

2 Related Work

The reports of the shared task in NEWS 2009 (Li *et al.*, 2009) and NEWS 2010 (Li *et al.*, 2010) highlighted two particularly popular approaches for transliteration generation among the participating systems. One is phrase-based statistical machine transliteration (e.g. Song *et al.*, 2010; Finch and Sumita, 2010) and the other is Conditional Random Fields which treats the task as one of sequence labelling (e.g. Shishtla *et al.*, 2009). Besides these popular methods, for instance, Huang *et al.* (2011) used a non-parametric Bayesian learning approach in a recent study.

Regarding the basic unit of transliteration, traditional systems are mostly phoneme-based (e.g. Knight and Graehl, 1998). Li *et al.* (2004) suggested a grapheme-based Joint Source-Channel Model within the Direct Orthographic Mapping framework. Models based on characters (e.g. Shishtla *et al.*, 2009), syllables (e.g. Wutiwiwatchai and Thangthai, 2010), as well as hybrid units (e.g. Oh and Choi, 2005), are also seen. In addition to phonetic features, others like temporal, semantic, and tonal features have also been found useful in transliteration (e.g. Tao *et al.*, 2006; Li *et al.*, 2007; Kwong, 2009a).

3 Datasets

The transliteration data provided by the shared task organiser are mostly based on name pairs from Xinhua News Agency (1992). For EnCh, there are 37,753 English-Chinese name pairs in the training set, 2,802 pairs in the development set, and another 2,000 English names in the test set. For ChEn, there are 28,678 Chinese-English name pairs in the training set, 2,719 pairs in the development set, and another 2,266 Chinese names in the test set. The Chinese transliterations basically correspond to Mandarin Chinese pronunciations of the English names, as used by the media in Mainland China.

Proceedings of the 2011 Named Entities Workshop, IJCNLP 2011, pages 96–100,
Chiang Mai, Thailand, November 12, 2011.

In the current study, we focused entirely on personal name transliteration. The small proportion of place names in the data was not handled. Most of them contain multiple English words or otherwise are not entirely phonemically rendered in Chinese (e.g. Africa 非洲, transcribed as *feil zhoul* in Hanyu Pinyin). They are better dealt with by a specific lookup table of place names, but since we only participated in the standard runs and did not use any external resources, those cases were practically ignored.

All English names are in upper case letters, and all occurrences of "X" were replaced by "KS" before processing to facilitate subsequent syllabification, as a single letter "X" in an English word often corresponds to the consonant cluster /ks/ when pronounced.

4 System Description

Our system is motivated linguistically and for practical reasons. On the one hand, transliteration is to render a source name in a phonemically similar way in a target language, and syllable is an important concept in pronunciation. According to Ladefoged (2006), for alphabetic writing systems, syllables are systematically split into their components. A syllable is composed of an optional onset containing consonants and a mandatory rhyme. The rhyme comprises a mandatory nucleus containing vowels and an optional coda containing consonants. English has complex onsets and codas, whereas Mandarin Chinese has simple onsets and only allows nasal consonants in the coda. According to Dobrovolsky and Katamba (1996), native speakers of any language intuitively know that certain words that come from other languages sound unusual and they often adjust the segment sequences of these words to conform to the pronunciation requirements of their own language. These intuitions are based on a tacit knowledge of the permissible syllable structures of the speaker's own language. Hence, the complex onset in the English syllable "STEIN" (as in Figure 1) violates the onset constraints in Chinese and is therefore resolved into two Chinese syllables as "斯坦" (*si1 tan3*). Hence syllable is apparently the proper basic unit for machine transliteration.

On the other hand, during transliteration, people tend not to re-invent the wheel for a similar chunk of syllables in the source name. The examples in Table 1 illustrate this observation. As seen, "JACOB" is consistently rendered as "雅各布" (*ya3 ge4 bu4*) and "STEIN" as "斯坦" (*si1 tan3*) when they appear as part of different names. So based on the concept of translation memory, if a larger chunk can be matched, transliteration becomes easier and less uncertain. In this way, the context embedding a syllable is incorporated, and it might also reduce error propagation in the pipeline during syllabification and phoneme mapping.

With the above linguistic and practical considerations, a syllable-based Maximum Matching approach is thus adopted, and the following subsections explain the steps involved.

English	Chinese	Hanyu Pinyin
JACOB	雅各布	*ya3 ge4 bu4*
JACOBS	雅各布斯	*ya3 ge4 bu4 si1*
JACOBSEN	雅各布森	*ya3 ge4 bu4 sen1*
JACOBSTEIN	雅各布斯坦	*ya3 ge4 bu4 si1 tan3*
ARENSTEIN	阿伦斯坦	*a4 lun2 si1 tan3*
BARTENSTEIN	巴滕斯坦	*ba1 teng2 si1 tan3*
DUBERSTEIN	杜伯斯坦	*du4 bo2 si1 tan3*

Table 1. Examples of Transliteration by Chunks

4.1 Syllabification

The English names in the training data and development data were first syllabified with the Onset First Principle. According to Katamba (1989), the principle suggests that syllable-initial consonants are first maximised to the extent consistent with the syllable structure conditions of the language in question, followed by the maximisation of syllable-final consonants.

In English, written symbols do not necessarily bear a one-to-one relationship with phonological segments. So in practice, with reference to common phonics patterns, we drew up a list of possible onsets containing graphemic units which may correspond to simple phonemes (e.g. "CH", "TH") or complex onsets (e.g. "PL", "STR") to be used in syllabification.

During syllabification, all vowels were first marked as nucleus (N). The longest acceptable consonant sequences on the left of the vowels were then marked as onset (O), and finally all remaining consonants were marked as coda (C). From left to right, syllables are marked for each longest matching chain of ONC, ON, NC, or N. The top half of Figure 1 illustrates these steps.

Subsequently, the syllable chain was subject to sub-syllabification considering the difference in phonotactics between English and Chinese. In particular, Chinese syllables have no complex onsets and only allow nasal consonants for codas. So if the syllabification step produces fewer English syllables than Chinese syllables, the sub-syllabification process will try to expand the English syllables, with the number of syllables checked after each expansion. At any point if the English syllables outnumber the Chinese ones, the sub-syllabification process will try to contract the English syllables.

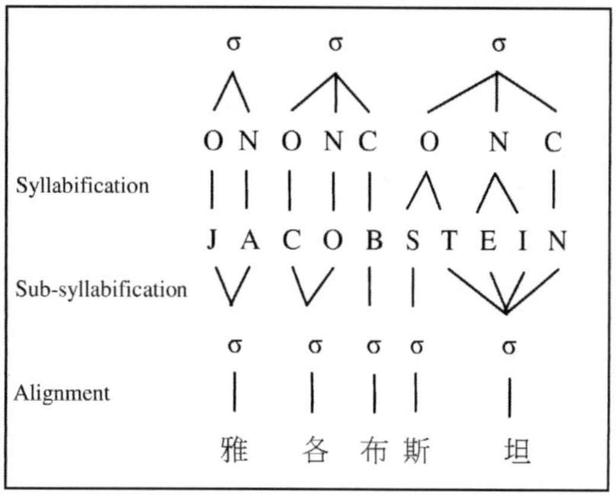

Figure 1. Syllabification and Alignment

The expansion process will thus follow the order of precedence below:

(1) From left to right, split up complex onsets. For example, "STEIN" is split up into "S/TEIN".

(2) From right to left, split up complex codas or separate coda from nucleus if the coda is not available in the target language. For example, "COB" is sub-syllabified as "CO/B".

(3) From right to left, separate liquids and glides ("L", "R", "W") from the nucleus if the Chinese rendition has "尔" (*er3*) or "夫" (*fu1*) in it. For example, with the pair "MINKOWSKI" and "明科夫斯基" (*ming2 ke1 fu1 si1 ji1*), initial syllabification produces three syllables, "MIN/KOW/SKI". During sub-syllabification, "SKI" will be split into "S/KI" with (1) above, but the English side is still one syllable short. So "KOW" will be split into "KO/W" in the next expansion.

(4) From left to right, expand diphthongs as necessary. For example, diphthongs like "IA" will be split up as in "A/ME/LI/A".

The contraction process will follow the order of precedence below:

(1) Contract the name-initial "M/C", if any, with the following syllable.

(2) From right to left, contract nasals, liquids and glides followed by "E" with the previous syllable. For example, "AALLIBONE" for "阿利本" (*a4 li4 ben3*) will be initially syllabified as "AA/LLI/BO/NE", which will then be contracted to "AA/LLI/BONE".

The middle part of Figure 1 illustrates the sub-syllabification process.

4.2 Alignment

Upon syllabification and sub-syllabification, if the number of English syllables equals the number of Chinese syllables, alignment can be done directly in a one-to-one manner. Otherwise some heuristics would be used to attempt some complex alignments. As long as Chinese syllables still outnumber English syllables, the next English syllable with four or more letters or starting with two different consonants will absorb two Chinese syllables, assuming such long segments are actually pronounced as two syllables. For example, "A/L/THOU/SE" does not have enough syllables to align with its Chinese rendition "奥尔特豪斯" (*ao4 er3 te4 hao2 si1*), so "THOU" will be forced to take up two Chinese syllables "特豪" (*te4 hao2*). At any point, if the remaining Chinese syllables fall short of English syllables, the rest will be aligned as a whole without further breaking into syllables. For example, "YON/GE" will simply be aligned with the Chinese name "扬" (*yang2*). The bottom part of Figure 1 shows the alignment step.

4.3 Lexicon Production

Based on the aligned names, segment pairs of various syllable lengths were extracted to produce a bilingual lexicon as follows:

```
For i = 1 to n (# of aligned segment pairs)
  For j = i to n
    Extract segment-i to segment-j
  Next j
Next i
```

Hence for the aligned name in Figure 1, the following segment pairs will enter into the lexicon: JA/雅 (*ya3*), JACO/雅各 (*ya3 ge4*), JACOB/雅各布 (*ya3 ge4 bu4*), JACOBS/雅各布斯 (*ya3 ge4 bu4 si1*), JACOBSTEIN/雅各布斯坦 (*ya3 ge4 bu4 si1 tan3*), CO/各 (*ge4*), COB/各布 (*ge4 bu4*), COBS/各布斯 (*ge4 bu4 si1*), COBSTEIN/各布斯坦 (*ge4 bu4 si1 tan3*), B/布 (*bu4*), BS/布斯 (*bu4 si1*), BSTEIN/布斯坦 (*bu4 si1 tan3*), S/斯 (*si1*), STEIN/斯坦 (*si1 tan3*), and TEIN/坦 (*tan3*). Note that we use "segment pairs" instead of "syllable pairs" here as the alignment may involve one or more syllables on either side.

4.4 Backward Maximum Matching

During transliteration, an English source name was first syllabified using the syllabification and sub-syllabification procedures described above, except the contraction part. The name was then segmented using Backward Maximum Matching with the lexicon. The matching was syllable-based, unless even the shortest syllable cannot be matched with the lexicon. In that case the syllable would be matched as a string of characters.

The same procedures were applied to EnCh and ChEn, as the lexicon contains bilingual segment pairs, and can be looked up bi-directionally. Maximum Matching can be done with the English segments or Chinese segments accordingly. Chinese source names do not need particular syllabification as Chinese characters are syllabic.

4.5 Candidate Generation and Ranking

With the segmented source name, target candidates were generated by looking up the lexicon for each segment and its rendition(s) in the target language. In the current study, the candidates were simply ranked by unigram probabilities. Figure 2 shows an example of Maximum Matching and candidate generation.

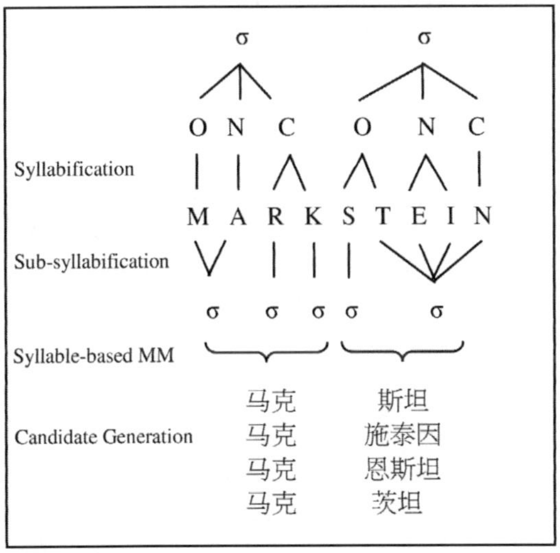

Figure 2. Max Matching and Candidate Generation

4.6 Official Results

Table 2 and Table 3 show the official results for the two standard runs we submitted and the best system in EnCh and ChEn respectively. The first run used segment pairs with frequency two or above, and the second run used those with frequency five or above. The evaluation metrics follow the definitions in the whitepaper of the shared task (Zhang *et al.*, 2011).

The performance of our system on EnCh is in the mid-range, and re-ranking with n-gram features is apparently important. For instance, VE/夫 (*fu1*) is more frequent than VE/维 (*wei2*), but the former is often restricted to the end of a name. This would not be realised for now, unless a longer segment can be matched, e.g. "VELO" could only be matched on single syllables, so "夫洛" (*fu1 luo4*) came before "维洛" (*wei2 luo4*), but "VELASCO" found a longer match with "维拉斯科" (*wei2 la1 si1 ke1*) as the first candidate. This suggests that Maximum Matching is useful, but re-ranking is needed for better performance.

ChEn is apparently more difficult, and scores are lower in general. Nevertheless, our system came in the top three, giving even better Mean F-score and MRR than the system with the best ACC. The more severe graphemic ambiguity for ChEn may make it a more difficult task. According to Kwong (2009b), on average one English segment (syllable) has 1.7 Chinese renditions but one Chinese character can be mapped to 10 different English segments. Another major problem for ChEn is unseen characters and the spelling conventions of English or other European languages. For example, "云" (*yun2*) was not found in the training and development data and therefore "云格" (*yun2 ge2*) could not be properly back transliterated. Also, some candidates end up with triple consonants which are obviously not acceptable in English and should be avoided.

Metric	Run 1	Run 2	Best
ACC	0.305	0.285	0.348
Mean F-score	0.672	0.660	0.700
MRR	0.378	0.349	0.462
MAP_{ref}	0.297	0.276	0.342

Table 2. Official EnCh Results on Test Data

Metric	Run 1	Run 2	Best
ACC	0.155	0.154	0.167
Mean F-score	0.766	0.757	0.765
MRR	0.215	0.206	0.202
MAP_{ref}	0.155	0.154	0.167

Table 3. Official ChEn Results on Test Data

5 Future Work and Conclusion

Thus the performance of our approach on EnCh has room for improvement, possibly with a re-ranking module, and that on ChEn is close to the state of the art. Forward and Backward Maximum Matching could potentially be used together to better handle overlapping ambiguity so as not to miss other possible candidates.

Acknowledgements

The work described in this paper was substantially supported by a grant from City University of Hong Kong (Project No. 7008004).

References

Dobrovolsky, M. and Katamba, F. (1996) Phonology: the function and patterning of sounds. In W. O'Grady, M. Dobrovolsky and F. Katamba (Eds.), *Contemporary Linguistics: An Introduction*. Essex: Addison Wesley Longman Limited.

Finch, A. and Sumita E. (2010) Transliteration using a phrase-based statistical machine translation system to re-score the output of a joint multigram model. In *Proceedings of NEWS 2010*, Uppsala, Sweden.

Huang, Y., Zhang, M. and Tan, C.L. (2011) Nonparametric Bayesian Machine Transliteration with Synchronous Adaptor Grammars. In *Proceedings of ACL-HLT 2011: Short Papers*, Portland, Oregon, pp.534-539.

Katamba, F. (1989) *An Introduction to Phonology*. Essex: Longman Group UK Limited.

Knight, K. and Graehl, J. (1998) Machine Transliteration. *Computational Linguistics, 24(4)*:599-612.

Kwong, O.Y. (2009a) Homophones and Tonal Patterns in English-Chinese Transliteration. In *Proceedings of the ACL-IJCNLP 2009 Conference Short Papers*, Singapore, pp.21-24.

Kwong, O.Y. (2009b) Graphemic Approximation of Phonological Context for English-Chinese Transliteration. In *Proceedings of NEWS 2009*, Singapore, pp.186-193.

Ladefoged, P. (2006) *A Course in Phonetics*. Thomson Wadsworth.

Li, H., Zhang, M. and Su, J. (2004) A Joint Source-Channel Model for Machine Transliteration. In *Proceedings of ACL 2004*, Barcelona, Spain, pp.159-166.

Li, H., Sim, K.C., Kuo, J-S. and Dong, M. (2007) Semantic Transliteration of Personal Names. In *Proceedings of ACL 2007*, Prague, Czech Republic, pp.120-127.

Li, H., Kumaran, A., Pervouchine, V. and Zhang, M. (2009) Report of NEWS 2009 Machine Transliteration Shared task. In *Proceedings of NEWS 2009*, Singapore.

Li, H., Kumaran, A., Zhang, M. and Pervouchine, V. (2010) Report of NEWS 2010 Transliteration Generation Shared Task. In *Proceedings of NEWS 2010*, Uppsala, Sweden.

Oh, J-H. and Choi, K-S. (2005) An Ensemble of Grapheme and Phoneme for Machine Transliteration. In R. Dale *et al.* (Eds.), *Natural Language Processing – IJCNLP 2005*. Springer, LNAI Vol. 3651, pp.451-461.

Shishtla, P., Ganesh, V.S., Sethuramalingam, S. and Varma, V. (2009) A language-independent transliteration schema using character aligned models. In *Proceedings of NEWS 2009*, Singapore.

Song, Y., Kit, C. and Zhao, H. (2010) Reranking with multiple features for better transliteration. In *Proceedings of NEWS 2010*, Uppsala, Sweden.

Tao, T., Yoon, S-Y., Fister, A., Sproat, R. and Zhai, C. (2006) Unsupervised Named Entity Transliteration Using Temporal and Phonetic Correlation. In *Proceedings of EMNLP 2006*, Sydney, Australia, pp.250-257.

Wutiwiwatchai, C. and Thangthai, A. (2010) Syllable-based Thai-English Machine Transliteration. In *Proceedings of NEWS 2010*, Uppsala, Sweden, pp.66-70.

Xinhua News Agency. (1992) *Chinese Transliteration of Foreign Personal Names*. The Commercial Press.

Zhang, M., Kumaran, A. and Li, H. (2011) Whitepaper of NEWS 2011 Shared Task on Machine Transliteration. In *Proceedings of NEWS 2011*, Chiang Mai, Thailand.

Statistical Machine Transliteration with Multi-to-Multi Joint Source Channel Model

Yu Chen, Rui Wang, Yi Zhang
Language Technology Lab
German Research Center for Artificial intelligence (DFKI)
Saarbrücken, Germany
{firstname.lastname}@dfki.de

Abstract

This paper describes DFKI's participation in the NEWS2011 shared task on machine transliteration. Our primary system participated in the evaluation for English-Chinese and Chinese-English language pairs. We extended the joint source-channel model on the transliteration task into a multi-to-multi joint source-channel model, which allows alignments between substrings of arbitrary lengths in both source and target strings. When the model is integrated into a modified phrase-based statistical machine translation system, around 20% of improvement is observed. The primary system achieved 0.320 on English-Chinese and 0.133 on Chinese-English in terms of top-1 accuracy.

1 Introduction

Machine transliteration has drawn a lot of attention in the previous years. In particular, the previous two shared tasks (Li et al., 2009; Li et al., 2010) attracted more than 30 participants. This year's task only focuses on the transliteration generation task. As our first attempt in this area, we participated in English-to-Chinese transliteration (En-Ch) and Chinese-to-English back transliteration (Ch-En) tasks.

For En-Ch and Ch-En transliterations, there was a discussion on whether to use the intermediate phonemic interpretation, i.e., Pinyin. Li et al. (2004) showed empirically that by skipping the intermediate phonemic interpretation (denoted as grapheme-based methods), the transliteration error rate was reduced significantly, since the mapping between Pinyin and Chinese characters was not trivial. Oh et al. (2009) had a more generalized version of Li et al. (2004)'s system as well as other previous work (e.g., (Knight and Graehl, 1998), denoted as phoneme-based methods) and showed that incorporating Pinyin as one of the features did help the transliteration performance finally. Li et al. (2007) included two other useful features, language of origin and the gender association. This is our first participation of this shared task, instead of considering the "best" setting, we aim at a basic but extensible architecture at first.

2 Systems

Transliteration can be viewed as a special case of the translation task, namely translation at a character level. State-of-the-art statistical machine translation systems were reported as being able to deliver satisfactory results for the transliteration task without additional knowledge on the languages (Knight and Graehl, 1998). However, general statistical machine translation systems do not consider the key features of the transliteration task, which, on the other hand, have been emphasized by the joint source channel models.

Our primary system is a standard phrase-based statistical machine translation (PBSMT) system with a modification based on the Multi-to-Multi Joint Source Channel model. We hope the combination could benefit from the simplicity of a joint source channel model without losing the flexibility of the PBSMT system.

2.1 Phrase-based SMT

The basic architecture of a phrase-based SMT system is an instance of the noisy-channel approaches (Brown et al., 1993). In the context of transliteration, the term "phrase" in phrase-based SMT would refer to a sequence of characters chosen by its statistical rather then any grammatical properties. The transliteration of a name s in the source language into a name t in the target language is modeled as:

Proceedings of the 2011 Named Entities Workshop, IJCNLP 2011, pages 101–105,
Chiang Mai, Thailand, November 12, 2011.

$$\arg\max_{\mathbf{t}} P(\mathbf{t}|\mathbf{s}) = \arg\max_{\mathbf{t}} (P(\mathbf{t})P(\mathbf{s}|\mathbf{t}));$$

The system involves a *phrase table*, a list of character sequences identified in a source name together with potential transliterations. These sequences derived from the source names may overlap and also have several correspondences in the target language. The process of searching for the target names starts with selecting a subset of the entries in the table. The members of the selected subset must then be arranged in a specific order to give a translation. These operations are determined by statistical properties of the target language enshrined in the so-called *language model.*

The segments in the source name and their counterparts in the target language should always be exactly in the same order, which is clearly not the case for general machine translation tasks. In addition to ordering, there are many other strict rules such that the transliteration task is relatively more deterministic than the translation process. For instance, although it is common that many Chinese characters have the same pronunciation, only a small set of Chinese characters can be used in the transliterated western names. Accordingly, for each source name, there are only a limited set of candidate transliterations, unlike the infinite target set for the general translation task.

It is critical to take into account these characteristics mentioned above when utilizing an SMT system for transliteration. First, the distortion model, one of the major components in a standard PBSMT system, is redundant for transliteration. Including the unnecessary model expands the search space and makes it more difficult to find the good candidates. Second, the word alignment model (Och and Ney, 2004) in a PBSMT system also assumes flexible ordering of correspondence to some extent. This could introduce additional noise to the translation models if applied directly to transliteration tasks without any modifications.

2.2 M2M Jonit Source-Channel Model

The joint source-channel machine transliteration model (Li et al., 2004) calculates the n-gram transliteration probability. More specifically, for a source name s, a target transliteration t, and an alignment α between the source and the target, we have the transliteration probability defined as:

$$P(s,t,\alpha) = \sum_{k=1}^{K} P(< e,c >_k \mid < e,c >_{k-n+1}^{k-1}) \tag{1}$$

where $< e,c >_k$ is the kth aligned pair of translation units. Therefore, forward and backward transliteration can be uniformly obtained by (2) and (3).

$$\bar{t} = \operatorname{argmax}_{s,\alpha} P(s,t,\alpha) \tag{2}$$

$$\bar{s} = \operatorname{argmax}_{t,\alpha} P(s,t,\alpha) \tag{3}$$

The alignment statistics can be obtained with an Expectation-Maximization procedure over the training corpus.

For English-Chinese bidirectional transliteration, Li et al. (2004) assumed that each Chinese character aligns with a sequence of one or more letters in English. This assumption drastically reduces the number of possible alignments. For a English source s and a Chinese target t, the number of possible alignment under this assumption is

$$\binom{|s|-1}{|t|-1} = \frac{(|s|-1)!}{(|t|-1)!(|s|-|t|)!}$$

While the assumption holds true in most of the cases, several obvious limitations arise. First, it is assumed that the source string is at least as long as the target which is not necessary true. Second, and more importantly, in some cases multiple Chinese characters should align with one single English letter (for example 'X'), and in others, multiple Chinese characters constitute one single transliteration unit. Therefore, instead of adopting the "one Chinese character per unit" assumption, we allow alignments between substrings of arbitrary lengths in both the source and the target. We call this a Multi-to-Multi Joint Source-Channel model (M2M-JSC). This constitutes a much larger model, with more possible transliteration units on the Chinese side. To simplify the calculation, we use the 1-gram model for the calculation of the transliteration probability, and hope that the larger transliteration units to compensate for the Markovian effect of mutual dependencies between alignment pairs. We use the similar Expectation-Maximization procedure to train the model on the corpus. One slight variation from Li et al. (2004) is that instead of choosing a random segmentation in the initialization step, we generate all possible multi-to-multi alignment hypotheses, and normalize the counts by the number of hypotheses of each transliteration pair. The segmentation alignment obtained is significantly different from the original Joint Source-Channel model. Table 1 shows some examples of the M2M-JSC alignment.

English	Chinese
A/JA/X	埃/甲/克斯
A/BA/STE/NIA	阿/巴/斯蒂/尼亚
AHL/BERG	阿尔/伯格

Table 1: Examples of M2M Joint Source-Channel Alignment Result

2.3 Combined system

In order to benefit from both previous described components, the M2MJSC model is integrated into the PBSMT system as a substitute of the translation model. Figure 1 illustrates the structure of the combined system.

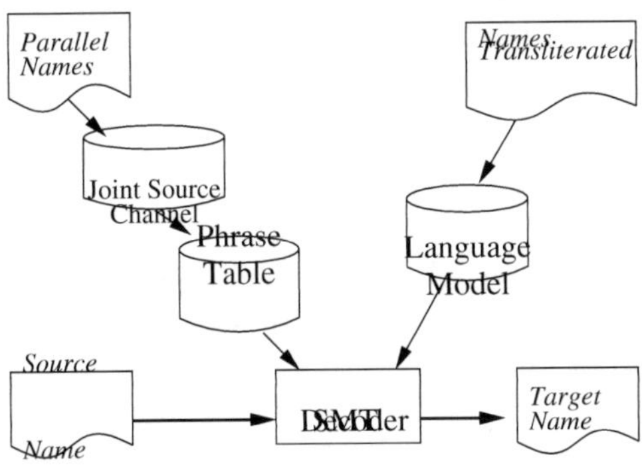

Figure 1: Phrase-based Transliteration System with Joint Source Channel Model

M2MJSC is first applied to the training set to divide each source name in parallel with the corresponding target name into the same number of segments. These segments are then considered as words that are one-to-one aligned. The PBSMT system takes multiple segments, namely phrases, as translation units. The phrase extraction follows the heuristic that starts with the given word alignment and expands to the adjacent alignment points (Koehn et al., 2003). The translation probabilities of the extracted phrases are estimated accordingly.

As the last step, we split all the segments in the translation model into characters to allow more straightforward integration into the original PBSMT system that relies on character based inputs.

3 Experiment setup

3.1 Preprocessing

We worked with the English data only in the uppercase form as provided in the training set. The names are tokenized into characters, but we did not perform any further phonetic mapping for both languages as the phonetic mapping requires additional knowledge which was not available in the training data.

Even though it is possible to combine the training sets for both English-to-Chinese and Chinese-to-English, we restrained ourselves to the set that are designated for the particular direction. In other words, the Chinese-to-English training set was not included for training of all the components of our English-to-Chinese system and vice versa.

3.2 SMT system for transliteration

3.2.1 Statistical models

Our system consists the following major statistical components:

- An n-gram language model;
- A translation model, including two phrase translation probabilities (both directions), two lexical weightings (both directions) induced from word translation probabilities, and a phrase penalty. This model is further decomposed into phrases;
- Word penalty used to penalize longer hypotheses.

The n-gram language model is estimated using the SRILM toolkit (Stolcke, 2002). The translation model is built from the character alignments given the M2MJSC model and we did not construct any distortion models.

3.2.2 Moses decoder

We used the open-source SMT decoder Moses (Koehn et al., 2007). Moses allows a log-linear model to combine various models and implements an efficient beam search algorithm that quickly finds the best translation among the large number of hypotheses. In order to adapt the SMT decoder to the transliteration task, we not only supplied the decoder with no reordering models, but also constrained the decoder in a monotone manner by setting distortion limit to 0.

Tasks	System	ACC	Mean F	MRR	Map_ref
English-to-Chinese	M2MJC+PBSMT	0.320	0.674	0.397	0.308
English-to-Chinese	M2MJC	0.260	0.638	0.340	0.251
Chinese-to-English	M2MJC+PBSMT	0.133	0.746	0.210	0.133
Chinese-to-English	M2MJC	0.117	0.731	0.177	0.117

Table 2: Official results

3.2.3 Parameter tuning

The system integrates all the models into a more complex discriminative model in a log linear formulation. The weights for the individual models can be optimized on development data so that the system outputs are as close as possible to correct candidates. Minimum error rate training (MERT) (Och, 2003) is one of the common method for balancing between features on different bases. We used Z-MERT (Zaidan, 2009) to search for the set of feature weights that maximizes the official f-score evaluation metric on the development set.

Moreover, we extracted a small development set of 500 names randomly from the official development set. The rest of the official development set served as a development test set, so we could run additional experiments on the provided data set apart from our submission. The feature weights we used for our submission are obtained from the complete development set.

4 Results

We participated in English-to-Chinese and Chinese-to-English transliteration tasks in NEWS2011. Table 2 lists the official evaluation scores for our submission to these two tracks. Our contrast system is the stand-alone M2MJSC system. It is clear that the final combined system has outperformed the M2MJSC system by around 20% for both directions.

We notice that there is a group of multi-word names in the development set that are particularly difficult for our system to transliterate correctly. Most of these names consists of parts that should be translated by the meanings instead of transliterated by the phonemes, for example, "DEMOCRATIC AND POPULAR REPUBLIC OF ALGERIA". To handle such cases, we need to include additional recognition and translation modules that clearly require knowledge beyond the provided training data set.

5 Conclusion

We successfully participated in this year's En-Ch and Ch-En machine transliteration shared tasks. We extended the original joint source-channel model proposed by Li et al. (2004) by allowing more possible transliteration units than single characters (in Chinese) and single letters (in English). When the M2M-JSC model is integrated into a modified phrase-based SMT system, around 20% of improvement is observed. In the future, we will further explore the M2M-JSC model with richer feature sets as well as the integration of other SMT approaches.

Acknowledgments

The first two authors were supported by the EuroMatrixPlus project (IST-231720) funded by the European Community under the Seventh Framework Programme for Research and Technological Development. The last was supported by the German Excellence Cluster of Multimodal Computing and Interaction.

References

Peter Brown, Stephen A. Della Pietra, Vincent J. Della Pietra, and Robert Mercer. 1993. The mathematics of statistical machine translation: Parameter estimation. *Computational Linguistics*, 19:263–311.

Kevin Knight and Jonathan Graehl. 1998. Machine transliteration. *Comput. Linguist.*, 24:599–612, December.

Philipp Koehn, Franz Josef Och, and Daniel Marcu. 2003. Statistical phrase-based translation. In *Proceedings of the 2003 Conference of the North American Chapter of the Association for Computational Linguistics on Human Language Technology - Volume 1*, NAACL '03, pages 48–54, Stroudsburg, PA, USA. Association for Computational Linguistics.

Philipp Koehn, Hieu Hoang, Alexandra Birch, Chris Callison-Burch, Marcello Federico, Nicola Bertoldi, Brooke Cowan, Wade Shen, Christine Moran, Richard Zens, Chris Dyer, Ondrej Bojar, Alexandra Constantin, and Evan Herbst. 2007. Moses:

Open Source Toolkit for Statistical Machine Translation. In *the 45th Annual Meeting of the Association for Computational Linguistics (ACL)*, Prague, Czech Republic, June.

Haizhou Li, Min Zhang, and Jian Su. 2004. A joint source-channel model for machine transliteration. In *The 42nd Annual Meeting of the Association for Computational Linguistics*, pages 160–167, Barcelona, Spain, July.

Haizhou Li, Khe Chai Sim, Jin-Shea Kuo, and Minghui Dong. 2007. Semantic transliteration of personal names. In *The 45th Annual Meeting of Association for Computational Linguistics*, pages 120–127, Prague, Czech Republic, June.

Haizhou Li, A Kumaran, Vladimir Pervouchine, and Min Zhang. 2009. Report of news 2009 machine transliteration shared task. In *Proceedings of the 2009 Named Entities Workshop*, pages 1–18, Singapore, Singapore, August.

Haizhou Li, A Kumaran, Min Zhang, and Vladimir Pervouchine. 2010. Report of news 2010 transliteration generation shared task. In *Proceedings of the 2010 Named Entities Workshop*, pages 1–11, Uppsala, Sweden, July.

Franz Josef Och and Hermann Ney. 2004. The alignment template approach to statistical machine translation. *Comput. Linguist.*, 30(4):417–449.

Franz Josef Och. 2003. Minimum error rate training in statistical machine translation. In *ACL '03: Proceedings of the 41st Annual Meeting on Association for Computational Linguistics*, pages 160–167, Morristown, NJ, USA. Association for Computational Linguistics.

Jong-Hoon Oh, Kiyotaka Uchimoto, and Kentaro Torisawa. 2009. Can chinese phonemes improve machine transliteration?:a comparative study of english-to-chinese transliteration models. In *Proceedings of the 2009 Conference on Empirical Methods in Natural Language Processing*, pages 658–667, Singapore, Singapore, August.

Andreas Stolcke. 2002. SRILM - an extensible language modeling toolkit. In *the 7th International Conference on Spoken Language Processing (ICSLP) 2002*, Denver, Colorado.

Omar F. Zaidan. 2009. Z-MERT: A fully configurable open source tool for minimum error rate training of machine translation systems. *The Prague Bulletin of Mathematical Linguistics*, 91:79–88.

Named Entity Transliteration Generation Leveraging Statistical Machine Translation Technology

Pradeep Dasigi
Computer Science Department
Columbia University
in the City of New York
pd2359@columbia.edu

Mona Diab
Center for Computational Learning Systems
Columbia University
in the City of New York
mdiab@ccls.columbia.edu

Abstract

Automatically identifying that different orthographic variants of names are referring to the same name is a significant challenge for processing natural language processing since they typically constitute the bulk of the out-of-vocabulary tokens. The problem is exacerbated when the name is foreign. In this paper we address the problem of generating valid orthographic variants for proper names, namely transliterating proper names in different scripts. We attempt to solve the problem for three different language pairs: English → Hindi, English → Persian, and Arabic → English. We adopt a unified approach to the problem. We frame the problem from a statistical Machine Translation perspective. We further post edit the output applying linguistically informed rules particular to the language pair and re-rank the output using machine learning methods.

1 Introduction

In a world of pervasive online media and globalization, we are flooded with streams of events where participants come from all over the world and they spell things in a myriad of ways especially where there are no orthographic standards. The problem is exacerbated for proper names especially when they are foreign. There are no standard spellings for such names. Accordingly orthographic variants are rampant. People typically rely on some form of phonetic transcription or what is referred to as transliteration. Humans have no issue identifying variants of names as the same, however for automatic algorithms in general and Natural Language Processing (NLP) in particular, proper name variants constitute a large portion of the out of vocabulary (OOV) phenomenon.

In this paper, we address the problem of generating valid transliterations for proper names in one language into some phonetic transcription (transliteration) in another language. The problem is not so bad if the two languages are phonetically close, share a script, and there exists an orthographic standard. However, if the two languages use different orthographic scripts and possess different phonetic inventories, we are faced with a much more complex situation.

We attempt to solve the problem for the latter case, namely for language pairs that are distant and that possess significantly different phonetic inventories. We target three language pairs: English → Hindi, English → Persian, and Arabic → English. English uses the Latin script, Arabic uses Arabic script, Persian uses an extended Arabic script to account for 6 extra sounds over Arabic, and Hindi uses Devanagari. We adopt a unified approach to the problem for the three language pairs. We leverage a statistical Machine Translation framework to address the problem. We apply linguistic expansion rules that are tailored for each language pair and transliteration direction. We view this as a generation problem, and we apply some post hoc filtering techniques to re-rank the output.

2 Linguistic Background

Hindi, Persian, Arabic, and English pertain to different language families but more importantly for the task at hand, they have different phonetic inventories. There are shared cognates between Hindi, Arabic and Persian due to historical reasons, however their sound repositories are significantly different from each other and in turn different from English. For instance, the /p/ and /v/ sounds in Persian do not exist in Arabic, the voiceless uvular plosive /q/ and the pharyngeal /h/ in Arabic have no real equivalents in English, the aspirated /b/ and /t/ in Hindi do not exist in English nor in Arabic or Persian for that matter. Such dis-

Proceedings of the 2011 Named Entities Workshop, IJCNLP 2011, pages 106–111,
Chiang Mai, Thailand, November 12, 2011.

tinctions in the sound inventories result in variable transcriptions, especially when a proper name in Hindi that has any of those aspirated letters such as the /b/, or the /q/ in Arabic. For example, the Arabic name *qAfy*[1] has a myriad of spelling variants such as **Kazafi, Qazafi, Kaddafi, Qadafy, Gaddafy, Gadaffy**, etc. This is partly a result of the lack of the phonetic sound in the inventory of English, but also due to the fact that different dialects of Arabic pronounce the /q/ sound differently affecting the foreign (in this case English) transliteration of it, for instance, in Egyptian Arabic, the /q/ sound is pronounced as a glottal stop, while in the Gulf it is pronounced as a /g/ sound.

The problem is further compounded for languages such as Arabic and Persian which have underspecified orthographies. In both languages, the short vowels and certain other phonetic markers such as consonantal gemination are underspecified in the surface orthography except when the genre of the text is liturgical such as in the Quran or the Bible, or in pedagogical materials for language learners, However the majority of text written for both languages lack short vowels which are typically expressed as diacritics. For instance the name *mHmd* in Arabic, as is evident in the transliteration, is expressed using only the consonants, and it corresponds to **Muhammad/Mohamed/Mohamad** etc., in English. We note the presence of the short vowels 'a, u, o' in the English transliteration, as well as the gemination of the medial letter 'm'.

Different considerations need to be paid attention to depending on the transliteration direction. Transliterating Arabic names into English is different from transliterating English names into Arabic. For instance, Arabic names when transliterated from English to Arabic, should lead to a smaller set of variants, than if an Arabic name is transliterated into English due to the underspecification of vowels inherent in the orthography of Arabic. For instance, the name **Bloomberg** can be spelled as **blwmbyrj/blmbrj/blwmbrj**, while a name such as **AbdAllTyf** would warrant at least the following variants in English **Abdel lateef, Abdallattif, Abdellatyff, Abd Allatif, Abd Allattyf**, etc. Accordingly in our algorithms we will be modeling for the language pair specifically bearing in mind the particularities of the transliteration direction.

3 Related Work

Automatic Transliteration has been well studied and various statistical approaches have been tried, starting from the seminal work by (Knight and Graehl, 1997). The noisy channel model has been extensively used by (Yuxiang et al, 2009) and the problem was dealt with in a manner similar to that of Statistical Machine Translation (SMT). Further, it has been modeled as a phrase based SMT problem in (Finch and Sumita, 2009), (Finch and Sumita, 2010), (Hong et al, 2009), (Noeman, 2009). (Finch and Sumita, 2009) reported accuracy of 0.788, F-score of 0.969 and Mean Reciprocal Rank of 0.788 on English $\rightarrow$ Hindi test data in NEWS 2009. (El-Kahky et al, 2011) modeled character sequence level alignments as bipartite graphs, and used graph reinforcement and link re-weighting to improve transliteration mining. They addressed two problems that arise from data sparsity - data coverage and erroneous translation probabilities due to ambiguous mappings. (Varadarajan and Rao, 2009) used Hidden Markov Models to derive substring alignments from training data and learn a weighted Finite State Transducer from these alignments. They reported an accuracy of 0.398, F-score of 0.855 and MRR of 0.515 on English $\rightarrow$ Hindi test data in NEWS 2009. (Noeman and Madkour, 2010) proposed a language independent technique for transliteration. They used Giza++ (2010) to model initial alignments. A Finite State Automaton (FSA) built from those alignments is used to generate transliterations at an edit distance of at most k from the source word. Their best performing system had an F-measure of 0.915 on English to Arabic transliteration task in NEWS 2010. In general, most of this work was to build an initial alignment and use statistical techniques in some form to generate better transliterations, and hence language independent. Our work differs in that it takes a more linguistically informed approach towards generating better transliterations by customizing the solutions per language pair and transliteration direction.

4 Approach and Experimental Design

In our basic approach, we model the problem as a noisy channel problem. We leverage Phrase Based Statistical Machine Translation (SMT) technology (Zens et al, 2002). Our statistical transliteration

[1]We use the Arabic Buckwalter transliteration scheme to express Arabic script throughout the paper. www.qamus.org.

system is implemented using Moses(Koehn et al, 2007). Each name is represented as a sentence for training, tuning and decoding. A name could be composite comprising multiple name units, such as **Michael Jackson** corresponding to **mAykyl jAkswn** in Arabic. Each character is treated as a separate token by the system, and name boundaries are marked using special characters. Accordingly, the sentence pair for the name **Michael Jackson** and it's Arabic counterpart will be represented as follows to the SMT system for training and tuning: **m i c h a e l # j a c k s o n** corresponding to **m A y k y l # j A k s w n**. Giza++ (Och and Ney, 2010) is used for building alignments between name pairs. For all the language pairs, the language scripts are represented in UTF-8 encoding. We further improve the output of the MT system by applying some language specific post-processing techniques. The following sub-sections describe those techniques for each language pair. All the techniques (except section 4.3.1) essentially expand the output given by our SMT system.

Since the methods of expansion yield large numbers of output candidates, a filtering technique is used to be able to distinguish the correct transliterations from the incorrect ones. We build a binary classifier that labels each candidate transliteration as correct or incorrect. We employ two features in training: a language model (LM) log probability for each name from the target side of the training data corpus to ensure that the generated candidate is a fluent target name; the second feature is the string edit distance of each candidate from its nearest name obtained from direct mapping. This second feature is a measure of how much the candidate has changed due to expansion. The filtering classifier is applied to the expanded data. The training data is synthetically generated from expanding the candidates according to the linguistic rules. We label the training data as correct and the expanded data as incorrect. To make sure that incorrect expansions do not overwhelm correct transliterations, we remove some incorrect candidates from the training data for the classifier.

4.1 English-Hindi

4.1.1 Short vs long vowels

Hindi clearly distinguishes between short and long vowels, however English transliterations are not necessarily consistent in faithfully expressing that distinction. For example, the English transliteration of the names **amandip** and **parijat** both have the letter 'i', but in Hindi script it represents a long vowel in the first case and a short vowel in the second. Similarly, the 'a' sounds are short in the first word and long in the second. Accordingly, the SMT output is augmented by expanding short vowels with long vowels and vice-versa.

4.1.2 Initial vs Medial vowels

Like other Indian scripts, vowels in Devanagari are written as diacritic symbols if written after a consonant, and in independent form if not. So, when the SMT system is trained, vowels in English are aligned to both forms and some candidates have incorrect forms of vowels. As a post-processing step, those errors are automatically corrected. This is done by replacing diacritic symbols that occur at the beginning of names with vowel forms and vowels forms that occur after consonants with diacritic symbols.

4.2 English-Persian

4.2.1 Vowel interchange rule

It has been observed from the output of MT system that a common mistake is between long vowels 'A' and 'w', and 'A' and 'y'. To deal with this problem, the output is augmented by adding new candidates that have an 'A' sound replaced with 'w' or 'y' and vice-versa.

4.2.2 Words beginning with A

In many cases where the source word begins with letter 'A', that sound is not transliterated by the SMT system. The transliterated candidate begins with the sound of the consonant following the letter in these cases. This is probably because the sound corresponding to the letter is dropped in cases where it occurs in name medial positions. This is more common with words of Persian origin. Although a good language model takes into account the position of the letter in the name as well, some lower ranked candidates in the output have this error. To deal with this, 'A' is appended in those cases where the source word begins with 'A' and the output candidate does not begin with a vowel.

4.3 Arabic-English

4.3.1 Direct Mapping

A direct mapping of Arabic letters to their equivalent sounds in English is performed, for example an 'm' is transliterated as an 'm'. However some of the letters are tricky since they have no equivalent simple orthographic forms in English such as the Arabic *'ain* or 'E' sound, the Arabic *ghain* or 'g' sound. In these cases we opted for multiple correspondents. In the former 'E' case, we expanded to a possible **′ or A** sounds and for the 'g' sound we expanded to the following possibilities **gh, g, q**. We also noted in the development and training data the existence of some dialectal replacements indicating that the transliterations should also reflect dialectal variants, i.e. the transliteration is not only constrained to the modern standard Arabic (MSA) sound inventory, hence we allowed for dialectal expansions such as for the Arabic letter *thaal* or '∗' was mapped to **th, z, d** and the letter *thaa* or 'v' was expanded to **th, s**. This mapping is devised by a native Arabic speaker. All possible sequences of sounds in English for a given Arabic name are treated as its transliteration candidates.[2] Accordingly, a name such as *mgrby* is translated directly as **maghrebi, magrebi, magreby, maghrabi,** etc.

4.3.2 Vowel Expansion

Arabic similar to Persian is underspecified for short vowels in its orthography hence two names such as *zamar* and *zumur* will be spelled the same way appearing as *zmr* in Arabic. Hence, we expand the names by placing short vowel between any two consecutive consonants. We maintain a vowelless version for every expansion spot. Also we do not epenthesize with a vowel at name boundaries where a name is composite and contains multiple names such as *Abw-MAzn*. We use rules such as: if two consonants are preceded by a long vowel *A, w, y*, then we should expect to expand with one of the 5 vowels of English.

4.3.3 Composite Names and their Internal Boundaries

In case of composite names that have subparts, we applied the following rules:

- If the candidate has a subpart that begins with *bn*, only vowels **i** or **e** is used between the two consonants. **bin** or **ben**, meaning 'son of', is frequent in Arabic names and hence other vowels are not likely to occur between these specific two consonants.
- One common problem in this language pair is to recognize the name may be segmented into parts when written in English such as *Abu-mAzn* may be transliterated in English to **Abu Mazen** or **Abu-Mazen**. To tackle this, if a candidate begins with patterns such as *Abw, AbA, Abn, ibn, bin*, a space or a hyphen is introduced after the first portion of the name.

5 Experimental Results

The official task training data was directly used for training. The official task development data was split into two equal parts, with half the data being used for tuning the system and the other half for initial testing (Dev). We report results of our systems on both the Dev and the official shared task Test data. Details of the data used, their sizes and sources can be found in the Task Organizer's Whitepaper (TOW) (Zhang et al, 2011).

Table 1 contains the results of our system on English-Hindi. The metrics used Accuracy, Fs-core, MRR and MAP are described in detail in TOW. The first set of results is of SMT output containing the top translation candidate for each source name (H-1best SMT[Dev]). H-Nbest SMT[Dev] corresponds to the output containing 10 top ranked transliterations per source language name. H-SMT+exp[Dev] and H-SMT+exp[Test] illustrate the results after application of the two expansion rules described in Section 4.1 on the Dev and Test data respectively. The results clearly indicate that yielding more candidates results in better performance, i.e. returning N-best results is better that the top result (N-best is better than 1-best), improving the overall accuracy, F score, MRR and MAP for the system as a whole. Moreover, applying expansion rules in the form of our devised linguistic rules significantly improves the quality of transliterations for the dev set on nearly all metrics except for MAP, (H-SMT+exp[Dev]) outperforms (n-best H-SMT[Dev]). We note a significant drop in accuracy between the Dev and Test data, however we see an improvement for the MAP metric.[3]

Table 1 shows three sets of results for English-Persian task. The first set is 10-best results from SMT system (P-SMT[Dev]), without any expansion. P-SMT+exp[Dev] and P-SMT+exp[Test] correspond to the output of Dev and Test, respectively, as expanded using rules described in sec-

[2] A full listing of the Transliteration mapping is available upon request.

[3] We do not have access to the Test data key answers for any of the language pairs to perform error analysis.

Condition	Acc.	F Score	MRR	MAP
H-1best SMT[Dev]	0.340	0.850	0.340	0.340
H-Nbest SMT[Dev]	0.631	0.937	0.631	0.393
H-SMT+exp[Dev]	0.718	0.951	0.718	0.316
H-SMT+exp[Test]	0.387	0.860	0.516	0.387
P-SMT[Dev]	0.575	0.920	0.587	0.481
P-SMT+exp[Dev]	0.710	0.953	0.725	0.339
P-SMT+exp[Test]	0.606	0.933	0.697	0.589

Table 1: English-Hindi and English-Persian results

tion 4.2. Clearly, these rules significantly improve the quality of the transliterations on the Dev set for all metrics. We note a similar trend to the English-Hindi results with a significant drop in accuracy, F-score, MRR between the Dev and Test data, however we see an improvement for the MAP metric.

For Arabic-English, Table 2 illustrates the results of the different conditions: 1. the direct mapping as described in section 4.3.1 for Dev; 2. DirectMap with vowel expansion of the Dev (DirectMap+vow-exp[Dev]); conditions 3, 5, and 8. are SMT N-best conditions for Dev data; conditions 4, 6, 9 and 11 are N-Best results for Dev and Test data; finally, conditions 7, 10 and 12 present the results after applying filtering to the output of the SMT expanded system for both Dev and Test data. We use three thresholds for N in the N Best conditions: 10, 40 and 150.

The Direct Map results in the worst performing conditions, however we do note relative improvement from DirectMap to DirectMap+vow-exp across the 4 metrics indicating that vowel expansion is a good move for this language pair. Using SMT for transliteration improves significantly over Direct Mapping as illustrated by the relative improvement of condition 3 (10-best[Dev]) over condition 2 DirectMap+vow-exp[Dev]. Increasing the number of returned N Best results from 10 to 40 and subsequently to 150 shows significant improvement comparing conditions 3, 5, and 8. Further applying vowel expansion shows consistent improvement in performance in conditions 4, 6, and 9. We further applied filtering to the resulting output however this did not yield improvements in the results as illustrated in conditions 7 40-best+vow-exp+filt[Dev] and 10 150-best+vow-exp+filt[Dev], however, filtering helped prune the 100s of outputs generated from the vowel expansion step in smart ways. In fact we note that on the Test data the difference between condition 11

Condition	Acc.	F Score	MRR	MAP
1. DirectMap[Dev]	0.018	0.763	0.045	0.022
2. DirectMap+vow-exp[Dev]	0.065	0.805	0.139	0.065
3. 10-best[Dev]	0.194	0.835	0.330	0.189
4. 10-best+vow-exp[Dev]	0.226	0.847	0.361	0.188
5. 40-best[Dev]	0.363	0.897	0.507	0.286
6. 40-best+vow-exp[Dev]	0.396	0.904	0.535	0.299
7. 40-best+vow-exp+filt[Dev]	0.375	0.898	0.512	0.288
8. 150-best[Dev]	0.559	0.941	0.677	0.426
9. 150-best+vow-exp[Dev]	0.590	0.946	0.702	0.442
10. 150-best+vow-exp+filt[Dev]	0.546	0.936	0.657	0.413
11. 150-best+vow-exp[Test]	0.526	0.928	0.628	0.386
12. 150-best+vow-exp+filt[Test]	0.519	0.927	0.612	0.383

Table 2: Arabic-English - Transliteration Results

(150-best+vow-exp[Test]) and 12 (150-best+vow-exp+filt[Test]) is not that significant, though 11 yields higher results.

6 Discussion

The impact of each approach taken for English-Arabic transliteration can be seen from the example of >**bAbTyn**. When the direct mapping technique is used, one of the best transliterations is **Ababtyn**. When expansions are applied, it becomes **Aba Batyn**. The SMT system produces **Ababatin**, and after expansion, it becomes **Abaa Bateen**, which is in the reference list, although not in the first few ranks. Filtering this list reduced its size from 39 to 5 and removed incorrect names like **Ababwotyn** and **Ababoutyn**.

The English - Hindi system has specific limitations. Words like **Gertrude** and **Canada** are generally not transliterated correctly to Hindi. This can be because of the high number of names of Indian origin in the training data. Hindi names almost always have one to one letter to sound matching. The same holds when they are transliterated to English. So, a foreign origin word that has letters which do not have their most common pronunciation is a challenge for this approach. This may be resolved by trying to filter words that do not have Indian origin and treating them separately.

7 Conclusions and Future Directions

We showed that phrase based SMT systems can be useful for the problem of NE transliteration. But with the application of linguistic rules as a post-processing step, the performance can be significantly improved. For English Persian and English Hindi tasks, direct application of such rules improved the performance of the systems significantly. However, Arabic-English task proved to be a different and a more complex problem, due to the transliteration direction from a highly underspecified orthography (Arabic) to a more phonetically specified one. We showed that this problem can be handled by a vowel expansion technique on the SMT output. Applying a filtering technique using a classifier proved to be an effective method of eliminating incorrect candidates in the expanded output without significantly affecting the performance of the system. In the future, we plan to apply these approaches to larger data sets and more language pairs in various transliteration directions.

References

Ali El-Kahky, Kareem Darwish, Ahmed Saad Aldein, Mohamed Abd El-Wahab, Ahmed Hefny, Waleed Ammar *Improved Transliteration Mining Using Graph Reinforcement.*. Emperical Methods in Natural Language Processing 2011

Philipp Koehn, Hieu Hoang, Alexandra Birch, Chris Callison-Burch, Marcello Federico, Nicola Bertoldi, Brooke Cowan, Wade Shen, Christine Moran, Richard Zens, Chris Dyer, Ondrej Bojar, Alexandra Constantin, Evan Herbst. 2007. *Moses: Open Source Toolkit for Statistical Machine Translation.* Annual Meeting of the Association for Computational Linguistics (ACL), demonstration session, Prague, Czech Republic, June 2007.

Kevin Knight and Jonathan Graehl *Machine Transliteration.* Journal Computational Linguistics archive Volume 24 Issue 4, December 1998

Sara Noeman and Amgad Madkour *Language Independent Transliteration Mining System Using Finite State Automata Framework.*. Named Entity Workshop 2010

Franz Josef Och and Hermann Ney *Improved Statistical Alignment Models.*. Proc. of the 38th Annual Meeting of the Association for Computational Linguistics, pp. 440-447, Hongkong, China, October 2000

Jia Yuxiang, Zhu Danqing and Yu Shiwen *A Noisy Channel Model for Grapheme-based Machine Transliteration.* Named Entiy Workshop 2009, ACL-IJCNLP 2009

Sara Noeman *Language Independent Transliteration System Using Phrase Based SMT Approach on Substrings.* Named Entiy Workshop 2009, ACL-IJCNLP 2009

Balakrishnan Varadarajan and Delip Rao *ϵ extension Hidden Markov Models and Weighted Transducers for Machine Transliteration.*. Named Entity Workshop 2009

Richard Zens, Franz Josef Och, and Hermann Ney *Phrase-Based Statistical Machine Translation.* KI '02 Proceedings of the 25th Annual German Conference on AI: Advances in Artificial Intelligence

Andrew Finch and Eiichiro Sumita *Transliteration by Bidirectional Statistical Machine Translation.* Named Entiy Workshop 2009, ACL-IJCNLP 2009

Andrew Finch and Eiichiro Sumita *Transliteration using a Phrase-based Statistical Machine Translation System to Re-score the Output of a Joint Multigram Model.* Named Entiy Workshop 2010, ACL 2010

Gumwon Hong, Min-Jeong Kim, Do-Gil Lee and Hae-Chang Rim *A Hybrid Approach for English-Korean Name Transliteration.* Named Entiy Workshop 2009, ACL-IJCNLP 2009

Min Zhang, A Kumaran, Haizhou Li NEWS 2011 Shared Task on Machine Transliteration Whitepaper http://translit.i2r.a-star.edu.sg/news2011/news2011whitepaper.pdf

Author Index